TASTE OF
PERSIA

LAHICH, AZERBAIJAN—
Fresh and dried barberries at a village shop.

TASTE OF
PERSIA

A Cook's Travels Through Armenia, Azerbaijan,
Georgia, Iran, and Kurdistan

NAOMI DUGUID

ARTISAN

NEW YORK

Text copyright © 2016 by Naomi Duguid
Location photographs copyright © 2016 by Naomi Duguid
Studio photographs copyright © 2016 by Gentl & Hyers
Photograph on page 282 by Brian John

Library of Congress Cataloging-in-Publication data

Names: Duguid, Naomi, author.
Title: Taste of Persia / by Naomi Duguid.
Description: New York, NY : Artisan, a division of Workman
   Publishing Company, Inc., [2016] | Includes bibliographical
   references and index.
Identifiers: LCCN 2016012875 | ISBN 9781579655488
   (hardback, with dust jacket)
Subjects: LCSH: Cooking, Iranian. | LCGFT: Cookbooks.
Classification: LCC TX725.17 D84 2016 | DDC 641.5955—dc23
LC record available at https://lccn.loc.gov/2016012875

Design by Jan Derevjanik

Artisan books are available at special discounts when purchased in
bulk for premiums and sales promotions as well as for fund-raising or
educational use. Special editions or book excerpts also can be created
to specification. For details, contact the Special Sales Director at the
address below, or send an e-mail to specialmarkets@workman.com.

Published by Artisan
A division of Workman Publishing Co., Inc.
225 Varick Street
New York, NY 10014-4381
artisanbooks.com

Published simultaneously in Canada by Thomas Allen & Son, Limited

Printed in China

First printing, September 2016

10 9 8 7 6 5 4 3 2 1

SHEKI, AZERBAIJAN—*A boy at a corner
fruit and vegetable store.*

HALABJA, KURDISTAN—
Pouring tea at home, for guests.

CONTENTS

INTRODUCTION

ON THE WALL OF MY OFFICE, I HAVE A MAP THAT SHOWS THE PERSIAN EMPIRE under Darius the Great, who died in 486 BC. He ruled an empire first established by Cyrus the Great, the largest the world had ever known. Persia (present-day Iran) lay at the heart of the empire, which stretched as far west as Greece and, to the east, all the way to India.

When I first imagined this book, my idea was to write about the people and food of the Persian culinary region that centers on Iran but includes peoples in the immediate neighborhood: in Armenia, Azerbaijan, Georgia, and Kurdistan. The region extends from the Caucasus Mountains in the north to the southern tip of Iran, and lies between the Black Sea and the Caspian Sea.

The people here speak many different languages and follow many different religions. At the same time, they share a history, and they are all marked by Persian influences that date back to the time of Cyrus and Darius and continue in the modern era. The connections between them are found not in their different places of worship, nor in their many distinctive languages and alphabets, but in the kitchen, in the garden, and at the table.

I want to take you there to engage with the intensities of Georgian dishes; with the creative and subtle culinary traditions of Iran, Armenia, and Azerbaijan; and with the remarkable home cooking of the people of Kurdistan. The food is enticing, and the recipes are very friendly to the home cook. Flavors, textures, and ingredients will be familiar to anyone from a European or North American tradition. And that shouldn't be surprising, for Persian ingredients and culinary wisdom have influenced cuisines from India to Morocco to northern Europe.

Common elements in the cuisines of Persia and her neighbors in the Caucasus and Kurdistan include richly flavored bean dishes, flatbreads of many kinds, generous use of herbs and greens, plenty of cheese and yogurt, walnuts (used in sauces, marinades, and vegetarian pâtés), inventive soups and stews, savory dishes flavored with pomegranate and/or other fruits, and (for all but the Georgians) rice as a beloved staple. Common to all the peoples of the region is a culture of hospitality, of sharing food and drink with both friends and strangers, with generosity.

TABRIZ, IRAN—*A popular local eatery.*

As you read through the recipes and stories, the maps on pages 6–7 and 8 will help familiarize you with place-names and the geographical connections in the region. At the back of the book, there's more detailed information about each country (see A Closer Look, page 341), as well as Travel Notes (page 352), for those who want to explore the food and culture of the region firsthand. The Annotated Bibliography (page 375) provides a list of books and other sources that I've found interesting and inspiring, from cookbooks to novels, movies, and websites. And, finally, if you come across an unfamiliar ingredient, term, or name, the Glossary (page 354) will be of help.

Opposite, clockwise from above left: **NORTH OF YEREVAN, ARMENIA**—*Tsayhlik with her daughters and grandchildren outside their home near Mount Aragats (see Armenian Puff Pastry Cake, page 287);* **MASSOULEH, NORTHERN IRAN**—*a village baker with his tandoor oven (he works with incredible speed making lavash each morning);* **NEAR SHIRAZ, IRAN**—*Khameh girls in the mountains (see Nomad Encounter, page 190);* **TBILISI, GEORGIA**—*a woman selling chicken at Deserteri Market;* **BAKU, AZERBAIJAN**—*a woman carrying a live turkey at the big Taza Market.*

Above: **PERSEPOLIS, IRAN**—*A carved procession of people bears offerings to the emperor in one of the most beautiful parts of the ruins in this ancient Persian capital.*

A NEW ERA

AS IT REJOINS THE COMMUNITY OF NATIONS, IRAN IS AT LAST BECOMING
more open to travelers from the West. Once they go, they will want to keep going
back. There's so much to explore and delight in.

People in Iran are pleased with this opening up. They are familiar with
Western culture through films, the Internet, and social media, but they want
direct contact and a free flow of people and ideas in both directions. Although
many Iranians are not pleased with the rule of the ayatollahs, they're proud of
their country and their heritage: the glorious architecture of Isfahan, the lively
streets of Tehran and Shiraz, their food, their films, their novels, their music, and
much more.

The Caucasus countries are also now much more inviting to travelers, and
they're easier to get to than they have been for a century. After decades of rule
by the USSR, Armenia, Azerbaijan, and Georgia have come out of that gray
period and into full bloom. Travelers are discovering the region's spectacular
landscapes—the snowy Caucasus Mountains, the coasts of the Black Sea and
Caspian Sea, the fertile valleys—and the wine, food, and generous hospitality of
the people. The cities feel very European, from the buildings to the way people
dress. Even in Soviet times, the food markets in Georgia, Armenia, and Azerbaijan
were a break from the harshness of that era, the vendors lively and the fruits and
vegetables glowing with color and ripeness. But now, as each of the Caucasus
countries defines itself independently, there's a pride and confidence, and a
sparkle in the air.

Nearby Kurdistan, the beautiful, hilly part of Iraq that lies along the
Iranian border, is not Arab but Kurdish in language and culture. When I was in
Kurdistan, the people I talked to were confident about the future, hoping that
the underground oil wealth there would bring more prosperity to many people.
But since then, the Kurds have had to repel the advance of ISIL and deal with
thousands of refugees.

We don't know how things will evolve, but in the meantime, I am especially
happy to be able to include stories, photographs, and recipes from Kurdistan in
this book—while wishing for better and easier days to come. I hope that you will come
to feel a connection with the people there too.

Left: *A young Armenian girl at home outside Yerevan.*

Right: *Kurdish men seated by the road on the way to Dohuk, Kurdistan.*

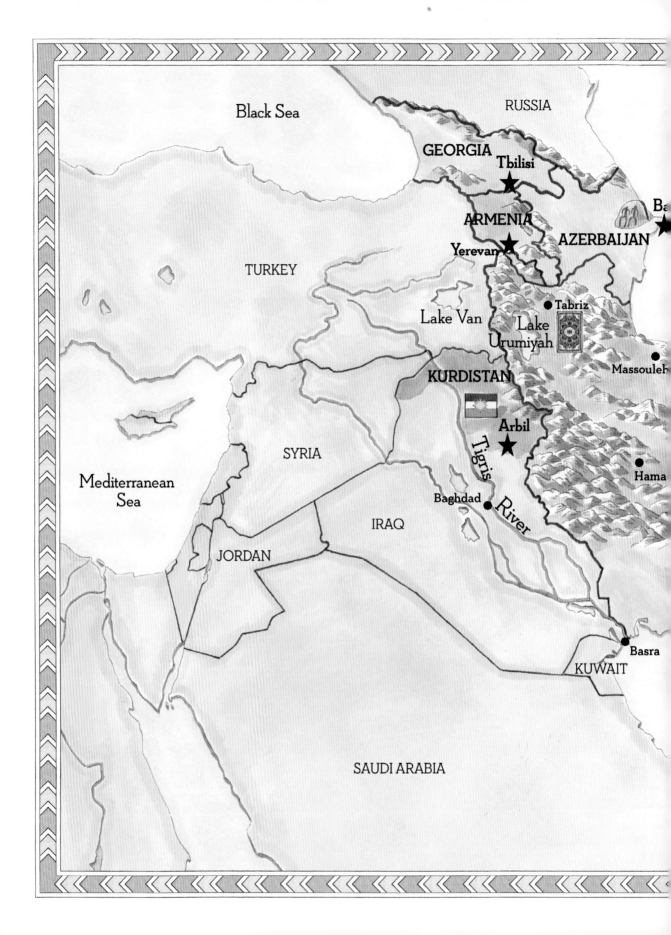

TURKMENISTAN

Caspian
Sea

● Mashad

★ Tehran

● Qom
● Kashan

IRAN

● Isfahan

● Yazd

● Kerman

● Persepolis

Shiraz ●

Bushir ●

● Bandar Abbas

Persian
Gulf

Gulf of Oman

AFGHANISTAN

PAKISTAN

The Caucasus Mountains, tall and snow-covered, and running roughly west to east, separate Russia from Georgia and Azerbaijan, which lie below the mountain wall. To the west is Georgia, with a coast on the Black Sea; to the east is Azerbaijan, with a long coast on the Caspian Sea. Tucked below those two countries is Armenia, a small landlocked nation on a high plateau veined with the occasional river valley.

South of the three Caucasus countries and the Caspian Sea lies the large mass of Iran, and next to it, along its western border, is Kurdistan, an autonomous part of Iraq. Iran's north coast on the Caspian is humid and lush, but the rest of the country has a dry climate, with very hot summers and cold winters.

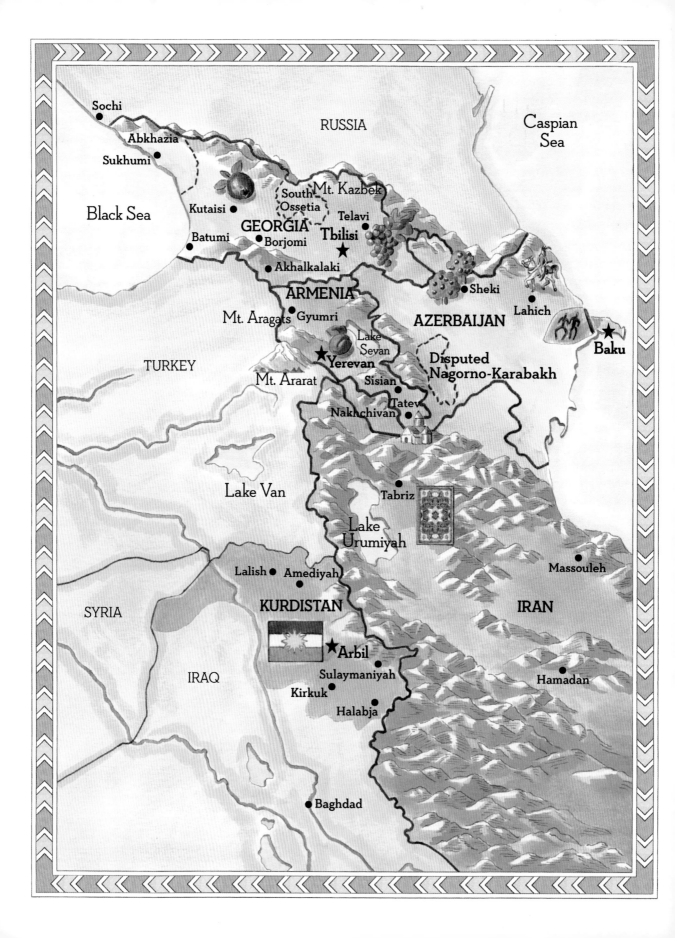

CUISINES WITHOUT BORDERS

PERSIAN FOODWAYS HAVE HAD A HUGE IMPACT ON THE REST OF THE WORLD. The legacy of the Persian Empire includes apricots and bitter oranges, underground waterways and irrigation, ice cream, the *pulao* family of rice dishes, and the use of tart fruits in savory dishes. And winemaking seems to have originated about eight thousand years ago in what is present-day Georgia or Armenia, or perhaps simultaneously in a number of places in the Caucasus.

The mosaic of people in the region reflects history, geography, and culture. When Persian rulers conquered neighboring lands, they brought Persian culture with them, but they also learned from the conquered. They forcibly moved neighboring populations (Georgians, Armenians, Azeris, and others) into Persia. Over the centuries, borders have been redrawn many times, right up to the present day.

Consequently, the current borders of Iran, Kurdistan, and the Caucasus countries enclose many different peoples in a kind of dizzying, overlapping patchwork. In Iran, there are Armenians, people of Georgian ancestry, Kurds, Azeris, and Assyrians, among others. Until the breakup of the USSR in the early 1990s, there were large communities of Armenians in Azerbaijan and of Azeris in Armenia. Georgia was long home to many Armenians, and it still has large Azeri and Armenian populations. Kurdistan's population includes not only Kurds, who are the majority, but also many Assyrians and Yazidis. And there are Kurds and Yazidis living in Georgia and Armenia.

How do people in the region define themselves? They most often identify first as citizens of a particular country (though they may instead start with their native language or ethnicity). Then they mention language and religion. Even when kingdoms and conquerors have vanished into the mists of time, traces of their cultures often remain. Nothing is "pure"—no people or country in the region can claim to be the one origin of a dish or a technique. Too much has happened over the centuries, in the way of mixing cultures and peoples, for any such claim to have credibility.

I'm mentioning this because people in the region have a fierce sense of national pride. In the food sphere, this often translates into "gastro-nationalism"—

assertions that "we" invented the dish that you claim is yours. But the fact that I came upon a particular dish in Armenia or Iran, Georgia, or Azerbaijan does not mean that the dish belongs to the people of that nation, or that its roots lie solely there.

Shared elements in the region's culinary cultures include walnuts, pomegranates, and other tart fruits, all used in many savory dishes as flavorings, and sometimes as a main ingredient. Throughout the region, fruits of many kinds are dried or preserved as syrups, jams, fruit leathers, or juices. Grapes and other fruits are used for making wine and all kinds of liquors, although alcohol is currently illegal in Iran. Today the usual cooking oil all over the region is sunflower oil, though in Iran, local olive oil is now being used by some cooks. Grain in various forms sustains everyone, for rice is at the heart of many meals, especially in Iran and Kurdistan, and bread is always on the table. Dairy products play a big role: yogurt, which is used in soups and drinks; fresh cheeses; and the thick fermented sauce known in Persian as *kashk*. Like another shared tradition, grilling meat on skewers, these are probably a legacy of the nomadic peoples from central Asia who invaded Greater Persia over the centuries.

ISFAHAN, IRAN—*An Iranian couple in the courtyard of Hakim Mosque photographing the lovely tiling on the façade.*

SHIRAZ, IRAN—*Motorcycle trio near the shrine of Shah Chirag (see Mirrors and Patterned Light, page 281).*

COUNTRY BY COUNTRY

Everything I learned while working on this book confirmed the deep interconnectedness of areas within the Persian culinary region. At the same time, each of the cultures here is distinctive and has a very clear view of its own importance. Below are brief sketches of each one; for more detail, see A Closer Look, page 341.

Iran

Iran is known as Persia in many books and writings (the country's name was changed to Iran in 1935), and that is the term I use more often in this book. It's a country of about eighty million people living in a territory about half the size of India. At the moment, the country is a theocracy, ruled by the head of the Twelver sect of Shia Islam, as well as by an elected parliament.

Geographically, Iran is a kind of keystone in West Asia. It's not Arab, not Turkic, not South Asian, not European. It lies between the predominantly Arab and Turkish world of the Middle East and the countries of central Asia and the Indian subcontinent. In the nineteenth and early twentieth centuries, the Russians and British sought to control it because of its strategic location and its oil.

Over its long history, Persia has often been a powerhouse, the center of an empire that conquered not just the Caucasus countries but also huge swaths of central Asia and the Middle East. As a result, it has had a huge cultural and culinary influence not just on its neighbors but also on Europe, North Africa, and India and Pakistan.

The majority population in Iran is Persian and speaks Persian (also called Farsi). There are also peoples of other cultures and ethnicities, including ethnic Azeris, Armenians, Georgians, Kurds, Assyrians, and Arabs. They are minority peoples in a country dominated by the descendants of Darius the Great and Xerxes.

Persians are proud of their cuisine, which is famous for its rice dishes, its subtle and seductive soups known as *ash*, the artful use of pomegranate molasses as a flavoring in dishes such as *fesanjun*, and its varied kebab repertoire. There's much more to discover, a world of home-cooked dishes that have both freshness and depth of flavor, with an inspired use of mint (both fresh and dried), dill, tart barberries, saffron, and the dried limes known in Iran as *limoo omani*, and a lovely balancing of flavors. Among my favorite dishes are Persian *borani*, lightly cooked vegetables dressed with thick yogurt and topped with fried onions (see pages 55 and 62); all of the greens-and-beans-laden soups; and the sophisticated sweets.

Kurdistan

Kurdistan is a small oil-rich region in northeastern Iraq, with an area a little smaller than that of Switzerland. It has a long border with Iran and also borders southeastern Turkey. Although the majority Kurdish population is Sunni Muslim and fairly conservative, modern Kurdistan is determinedly secular and officially tolerant of other religions. The Kurdish languages (three distinct Kurdish languages are spoken in Kurdistan) are all related to Persian, and the people of Kurdistan have close links with Iran. There is active trade (both legal and illegal) across the border, and in the 1970s and '80s, many Kurds took refuge in Iran from Saddam Hussein's attacks.

Iraqi Kurdistan is ridged with a series of hills and valleys that run north to south. Part of Kurdistan lies in the valley of the Tigris River, an area that was at the center of the Assyrian Empire until it was conquered by the Persians about 2,600 years ago. Some Assyrians still live here, in small villages as well as in and around the capital, Arbil. The Yazidis, much persecuted over the centuries, are another distinct minority group in Kurdistan.

The Kurds grow wheat and short-grain rice, as well as fruits, vegetables, and nuts. Flatbreads are part of every meal, and rice is eaten twice a day in most households. Traditional Kurdish rice dishes are more like Mediterranean dishes such as risotto, and very unlike Persian rice. Herbs are served as part of the meal and also used (usually dried) as a seasoning. Like the Persians,

HALABJA, KURDISTAN—*Two Kurdish men wearing traditional clothing chat in the market.*

Kurdish cooks include dried limes, the aromatic limes that they call *limoo basrahi*, in some of their stews. Glasses of liberally sugared tea punctuate the day, both at home and in public places.

Armenia

Like Georgia and Azerbaijan, Armenia was a Soviet republic until the USSR split up in the early 1990s. The newly independent country of Armenia (Hayastan in Armenian) has a long and fascinating history. The early people of Armenia made wine and cultivated wheat and barley, and they left a treasure of early metalwork and other artifacts dating back to prehistoric times. Armenian is an Indo-European language that has had its own alphabet since the fifth century, when the country converted to Christianity from Zoroastrianism.

The smallest of the Caucasus countries, with a population of about three million, Armenia today is a remnant of what was once Greater Armenia, a kingdom whose territory extended across much of eastern and southern Turkey to the Mediterranean. That territory was at times controlled by the Persian Empire and eventually conquered by the Ottomans who ruled Turkey. Tens of thousands of Armenians living under Ottoman rule died during the genocide that began in 1915; the survivors fled the country. The Armenian diaspora includes large

TATEV, ARMENIA—*A young mother and child were part of a family that invited me to join them as they snacked and drank* tutovka.

populations in North America, and there are also Armenians still living in Iran, Syria, and Lebanon.

The tough climate and the intermittently hard times Armenia has suffered have resulted in a remarkably creative cuisine, anchored by the need for frugality and self-sufficiency. The foods of present-day Armenia are quite unlike those of the western Armenians, who until the genocide had lived for centuries in what is now Turkey, and in Syria. Sunflower is the main oil rather than the olive oil of western Armenian cuisine, and is at the heart of everyday dishes based on vegetables, dried beans, and whole grains, subtly flavored with tart fruits and herbs. Because of the fasting traditions of the Armenian church, there's a large repertoire of delectable meatless dishes, such as Cabbage Rolls Stuffed with Beans and Tart Fruit (page 124), a boon for vegetarians.

Azerbaijan

Azerbaijan is an oil-rich country about the size of Austria, with a population of roughly nine and a half million. It's bordered by the steep snowcapped Caucasus Mountains to the north, which define its frontier with Russia. South of the mountains the terrain is mostly fertile low-lying valleys. To the northwest is the Republic of Georgia, while to the east, Azerbaijan has a long coast on the Caspian Sea.

Today more Azeris live in neighboring Iran (where they constitute about 16 percent of the Iranian population) than in Azerbaijan. The whole Azeri-inhabited territory was ruled by Persia for many centuries, but it was divided between the USSR and Iran after a brief moment of independence from 1917 to 1920. Since the breakup of the Soviet Union, the former Soviet Azerbaijan has established itself as an independent country. Though most Azeris are Shia Muslim, Azerbaijan, which is ruled by an authoritarian regime, is determinedly secular. Azeri, a Turkic language that is laced with words of Persian origin, is the mother tongue of most people in Azerbaijan, many of whom also speak (and read) Russian.

As in Georgia, walnuts, pomegranates, grapes, plums, and sour plums are important ingredients. Azeri home cooks, like those in Georgia and Armenia, put up a gorgeous array of fruit juices and *morabas* (jams; see Apricot Moraba, page 318). Fresh cheese is part of most meals. There's also a tradition of filled dumplings and dolmas (stuffed vegetables). And, as you might expect with a Turkic culture, grilled meat, poultry, and fish are much loved (see Turkey Kebabs, page 175).

LAHICH, AZERBAIJAN—*A horseman rides along a rocky streambed at the edge of the village.*

ZAQATALA, AZERBAIJAN—
*Public transport in rural
Azerbaijan is mostly in tired,
though charming, vans. Here,
not far from the Georgian
border, we stopped for a few
more passengers.*

Georgia

A small country about the size of the
Republic of Ireland, Georgia has a
dramatically varied landscape, and a
current population of less than four
million. Like Armenia and Azerbaijan,
Georgia was under Persian rule
intermittently for centuries. But
starting early in the nineteenth
century, Russia fought Persia for the
Caucasus countries, and it finally
took complete control of them in
1828. Georgia had a moment of
independence from 1918 to 1921,
but then was forcibly incorporated
into the USSR. When the Soviet
Union broke up, Georgia regained
its independence.

The early people of Georgia,
like the Armenians and the early
inhabitants of Azerbaijan, cultivated
wheat, other grains, and legumes.
These are still an important part
of Georgian agriculture and
cuisine, along with winemaking,
fruit of all kinds, and shepherds'
cheeses. Georgians are famous for
their cheese-filled breads, called
khachapuri.

Perhaps the most distinctive
element of Georgian cooking is its
use of *utskho suneli,* blue fenugreek.
Together with ground coriander, it is
the basis of the spice blend known
as *kmeli suneli* (see page 28), which
varies according to the cook's taste.
There's more raw garlic in Georgian
cuisine than elsewhere in the region,
and fresh tarragon and coriander
(cilantro) play a big role, along with
tart fruits and walnuts. Among my
favorite Georgian dishes are the
walnut-based vegetable pâtés called
pkhali (see pages 69–71) and the tart
fruit sauces, such as *tkemali* (Sour
Plum Sauce, page 34).

FLAVORS AND CONDIMENTS

IF YOU HAVE A PANTRY SET UP WITH JARS of dried herbs and spices and a few other flavorings, you can transform all kinds of foods into extraordinary dishes. This is what creative cooks in the Persian culinary region have been doing for centuries.

A few simple flavorings such as Mint Oil (page 19) and Saffron Water (page 27) can add a special touch to many dishes, not just those from the Persian repertoire. And there are also several recipes for spice blends and flavored salts here, which are all easy, so you can just put them together when you need them or make them ahead.

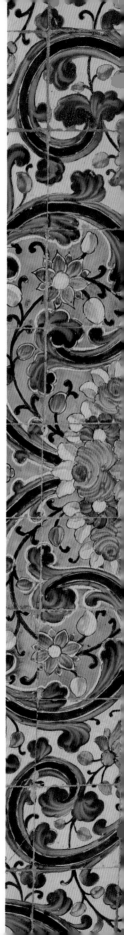

The region is rich in versatile sauces and condiments of all kinds, from Walnut Sauce (page 32) and Sour Plum Sauce (page 34) to Tart-Sweet Apricot and Raisin Relish (page 33). Some are eaten fresh, while a few, notably the red and green Georgian pastes called *ajika* (see pages 40 and 42), can be made in large batches to be stored in your pantry. You'll find other pantry-treasures in the fruits chapter.

Previous pages: SHEKI, AZERBAIJAN—*Plums of many kinds grow in the Caucasus, as do both sweet and tart pomegranates.*

MINT OIL

NANE DAGH

I now use mint oil to brighten all kinds of non-Persian dishes: lentil soups, vegetable soups and stews, and more. You can also drizzle it on salads or sliced cucumbers or chopped tomatoes, or add a swirl of it to lightly salted thick yogurt, to make a sauce for vegetables or grilled meats.

Dried mint is intense, and it keeps its flavor well. In the cuisines of the region, it's not a second-best version of the fresh herb but a precious ingredient in its own right.   **MAKES ABOUT ¼ CUP**

¼ cup sunflower oil, extra-virgin olive oil, or butter-ghee

¼ cup dried mint

Place a small heavy saucepan over medium heat. When it is hot, add the oil or ghee and swirl to coat the pan, then toss in the dried mint, stir, and remove from the heat. Use immediately. Leftovers can be stored in a glass jar in the refrigerator but will lose aroma and flavor over time.

YEREVAN, ARMENIA—
Herbs and greens are plentiful from early spring until late autumn in markets all over the Persian world.

PANTRY BASICS

The dried herbs and spices listed below keep well stored in well-sealed containers in a cool place, and almost all are found in larger grocery stores. The exceptions, marked with an asterisk, are available in Persian, Arab, or Turkish grocery stores, or by mail order. Blue fenugreek is more difficult to get, so all the recipes include an alternative. For more information about any unfamiliar ingredients listed here, see Glossary.

DRIED HERBS

Mint

Dill

Basil

Parsley

Saffron threads

Dried marigold petals

Dried rose petals

Blue fenugreek *

Powdered dried fenugreek leaves*

Summer savory

SPICES

Coriander seeds (whole and ground)

Ground cumin

Ground cassia (cinnamon)

Cardamom (whole seeds and ground)

Turmeric

Ground cloves

Ground sumac

Ground allspice

Nigella seeds*

Black peppercorns

Ground fenugreek

Powdered dried red chiles or cayenne

OTHER USEFUL PANTRY ITEMS

Sunflower oil (the most common cooking oil in the Persian culinary region; you can use a light-tasting extra-virgin olive oil instead)

Pomegranate molasses*

Dried limes*

Rose water

Dried apricots

Sour plums*

Dried barberries*

Tamarind pulp*

Tart fruit leather (homemade—see page 314—or store-bought*)

Verjuice or wine vinegar

Walnuts (store in the refrigerator)

Pistachios (store in the refrigerator)

Sesame seeds (store in the refrigerator)

Dried orange peel*

Kashk (fermented whey) in dried balls*

Small plate, clockwise from top: *Saffron water, a dried red cayenne chile, sumac powder, a branch of rose hips.*

Small blue bowl: *Dried mint leaves.*

Ivory bowl: *Mint oil.*

Large plate, clockwise from top: *Turmeric powder, a spoon of saffron water, and, with it on the white plate, coriander seeds and dried marigold petals; cumin seeds; fenugreek seeds, dried fenugreek leaves and stems, and a bay leaf (in the small bowl); saffron threads; Svanetian Salt (page 31; in the tiny bowl); tamarind pulp; and dried limes.*

HERB PLATE

SABZI KHORDAN

Fresh herbs are a constant at many meals throughout the Persian culinary world. They're put out in generous quantities on a plate, perhaps supplemented by pickled turnip or pickled peppers (especially in wintertime) and a little fresh cheese. The name for this herb plate in Persian is *sabzi khordan*, which literally means "eating greens."

In summer, it's easy to find fresh tarragon, chervil, parsley, watercress, chives, basil, mint, dill, and coriander. But these days large grocery stores are doing a good job of bringing in herbs even in the winter.

A list of the possibilities is below. There may be herbs you don't love—just use one or two of those you do like; you don't have to make it a huge affair. Wash the herbs well, trim off the coarsest stems, and serve as large sprigs. You can also put out radishes, chopped or whole, or pickles of various kinds—whatever you feel will give fresh crunch and flavor to the meal. Persian-style pickles (called *torshi* in Persian) are available in Persian, Turkish, and Arab groceries, and so are whole pickled peppers and pickled garlic. If you have a little fresh cheese or feta, you can serve that too, as another taste option. (Any leftover herbs can be stored in the refrigerator, sealed in ziplock bags.)

In Kurdistan, where people use pieces of supple flatbread as eating utensils, they'll often put a fresh herb sprig or a scallion on the bread before using it to scoop up, say, some bean stew or simmered chicken. The combining of fresh with cooked, of crisp with soft, is a sensual, satisfying way to eat. And it gives diners the freedom to shape each mouthful as they wish.

HERBS AND GREENS

One or more: basil, coriander, mint, summer savory, parsley, scallions (halved lengthwise if large), fenugreek leaves, tarragon, watercress, dill, arugula, chervil, chives, and sorrel

OTHER TASTES AND TEXTURES (OPTIONAL)

Radishes, cherry tomatoes or sliced tomatoes, sliced peeled cucumbers, pickles, fresh cheese, and/or walnuts

Put the ingredients of your choice out on a plate or in a wide shallow bowl to accompany any noontime or evening meal. I like to include fresh herbs in my breakfast too, but that's not traditional.

EAST OF MASHAD, IRAN—*On our way back from our saffron hunt, we stopped to chat with one of the older villagers here. He told us that the villagers were rug weavers, but sanctions had made dyes too expensive, and they had given up weaving.*

SEEKING SAFFRON

I arrived in Mashad, in the far northeast of Iran, in late October. I'd read that the saffron harvest was in late October and November and I was hoping to see saffron crocuses, as the area around Mashad is Iran's primary saffron growing region.

With fingers crossed, I headed out of town on the hunt. I was with Hamid, the man who had arranged my visa. Though he'd grown up in Mashad, he knew nothing about saffron production, and he too was interested to find out more.

Hamid had been told that there were villages near Tus (birthplace and burial place of the revered Persian poet Ferdowsi) that are known for their saffron harvest. We drove past Tus, passing a small elegant stone tower built by the Mongols nearly eight hundred years ago, and out into a spare brown landscape. I was looking for fields of pale purple, or for signs of green leaves, but there were just bare fields edged with tree-lined water channels. We stopped at a baked earth–colored village to ask directions. A group of men and children was busy resealing the flat roof of their house in preparation for the rain and snow of winter.

They shook their heads: We were too early. There would be no flowers for another five or six days. They suggested that we head farther south, where the harvest always starts sooner.

We drove on, taking a road that parallels the Afghan border some fifty miles to the east. The countryside was vast and open, rolling green hills and sheep pastures in all directions, broken up by a few red-brown rocky outcrops. Small villages of stone and brick occasionally appeared, nestled into hillsides far from the road. I could imagine the Mongols sweeping in from the east, and later Tamerlane with his army, bent on conquest and destruction, with no trees or fences to get in their way.

After a while, we came to a scenic village and stopped to ask once again about saffron. "Oh yes, I just picked mine, but if you go over to that red house," said the man we asked, "there should be flowers nearby." There was

no greenery visible, no color at all, at first glance. But when I looked more closely at the bare dirt in the small field, I could see, here and there, a tender beautiful purple bloom, and in the center of each, sticking up taller than the petals, three distinctive deep-orange stigmas.

Aha! The holy grail in all its fragility and loveliness. Seeking out and admiring flowers one by one, rather than finding fields full of them, was an unexpected end to my quest. It also felt very right that the precious saffron should be elusive.

The owner appeared. We explained that we were on the hunt for saffron. He told us that saffron needs cold weather to bloom and that the bulbs will yield a crop for seven years. Harvest is first thing in the morning, but some farmers also come by to pick flowers again in late afternoon, as he was doing.

The flowers sell for the equivalent of five dollars per kilo and buyers employ village women to pluck the stigmas. They accumulate slowly, three by three, as the pluckers work. No wonder saffron is expensive.

Why bother? I used to wonder. The answer is culinary and cultural. Even in small quantities, saffron gives fragrance and flavor to rice and other dishes. And saffron is also a sign of generosity. All the effort and expense involved in saffron production means that adding saffron to a dish makes it special.

I also wonder why and how the passion for saffron first developed. Perhaps it goes back to the reverence for and worship of the sun in Zoroastrian and animist times (see Zoroaster's Legacy, page 36). The golden tint of saffron perhaps became precious because of its association with the divine.

SAFFRON WATER

Once you find a good source of saffron—of saffron threads, as the stigmas are known—start using it. You can use them whole, but you get better color and aroma if you grind them to a powder. Just take a pinch and place it in a small mortar or bowl. Add a few grains of salt or sugar and use a pestle or the back of a spoon to grind the threads to a fine powder.

You can add saffron directly to a broth, but soaking it first in a little hot water is the best way to transform it into an effective flavoring and coloring, especially if you are using it to tint and flavor cooked rice. The proportions are roughly a generous pinch (¼ teaspoon) of saffron threads to ¼ cup hot water.

Pour the water over the threads or powder and stir. Transfer to a clean glass jar and let steep for at least 10 minutes, covered, before using it in a dish. As it sits, the color will deepen to a rich red-orange. Any leftover saffron water will keep in the refrigerator for a week or so, losing a little aroma over time.

GEORGIAN SPICE BLEND

KMELI SUNELI

One of the secrets of the Georgian kitchen is the basic spice blend called *kmeli suneli* in Georgian. I say "the" basic spice blend, but of course it varies among cooks, among regions, and according to the dish it is used for.

These days cooks in Georgia usually buy their *kmeli suneli* at the market, but many adjust the blend they buy, tweaking it to suit different dishes or their own tastes. Several versions of the spice blend are now available, imported from Georgia (see Glossary) and I hope that it will become more accessible in North America. I now most often use a blend from Kalustyan's, in New York, but until recently I would make a batch of the basic powder, without the optional ingredients listed below, so I could have it on hand in a jar. I'd adjust it by adding in black pepper and other flavors if needed for a particular recipe.

Those of us who have no ready access to blue fenugreek (see Glossary) can substitute a mix of ground fenugreek seeds and powdered dried fenugreek leaves as set out below. And if you don't have any dried marigold petals, simply omit them. **MAKES ABOUT ½ CUP (WITHOUT THE OPTIONAL INGREDIENTS)**

3 tablespoons ground blue fenugreek, or
    2 tablespoons powdered dried fenugreek
    leaves plus 1 tablespoon ground fenugreek

2 tablespoons ground coriander

3 tablespoons powdered dried marigold or
    safflower petals (optional)

1 teaspoon powdered dried red chiles

OPTIONAL EXTRAS

2 teaspoons dried dill, or to taste

2 teaspoons dried basil, or to taste

2 teaspoons dried mint

1 teaspoon dried summer savory

1 teaspoon freshly ground black pepper

½ teaspoon ground celery seeds

Combine the fenugreek, coriander, dried flowers, if using, chiles, and optional spices and herbs as you like in a bowl. Store in a widemouthed glass jar.

PERSIAN SPICE BLEND

ADVIEH

Flavorings in Persian dishes are a subtle blend. Each recipe in this book gives specific ingredients, so there's really no need to make up a separate spice blend, but you may want to experiment with this one. It's an aromatic combination that enlivens soups and stews with warm flavors and that will give you an idea of the flavors of the Persian kitchen. Try it in a bean dish, or use it as a rub for a roast.   **MAKES 1 HEAPING TABLESPOON**

1 teaspoon dried rose petals (optional)
1 teaspoon ground cassia (cinnamon)
1 teaspoon ground cardamom

½ teaspoon grated nutmeg
½ teaspoon ground cumin

If using the rose petals, grind them to a powder. Add the other spices and mix together.

Left: **AINKAWA, KURDISTAN**—*A local grocer in this mostly Assyrian town. Ainkawa has grown to become a suburb of Arbil, the capital of Kurdistan.*

Right: **ISFAHAN, IRAN**—*A display of ground spices (turmeric, powdered dried chile, cumin, and coriander) outside a spice shop in the bazaar.*

PERSIAN ANGELICA SALT

GOLPAR NAMAK

In the spice section of Persian grocery stores, you'll find packages labeled *"golpar,"* with the English translation given as angelica. It's not European angelica, but a related spice with an appealing slightly bitter edge. It is used as a seasoning, either on its own or, as here, blended with an equal amount of salt. Sprinkle a pinch over cooked vegetables just before serving, or put some out on the table and invite your guests to help themselves.   **MAKES 2 TABLESPOONS**

1 tablespoon golpar powder   **1 tablespoon sea salt**

Mix together and store in a glass jar.

MASSOULEH, NORTHERN IRAN—
The spice often called angelica in Persian groceries in North America is called golpar in Persian, and is also known as Persian hogweed.

SVANETIAN SALT

PHOTOGRAPH ON PAGE 21

SVANURI MARILI

Svaneti is the highest, wildest, and most mountainous region of Georgia. It's in the northwest, and until recently was cut off by snow for about six months of the year. Svan people have a reputation for toughness and a cuisine that is famous for its intense, distinctive flavors.

The basics of Svanetian salt, apart from salt, are pounded fresh garlic, and a blend of spices that includes dried red chile. The result is an aromatic coarse powder that keeps well in a cool place and is great to sprinkle on cooked and raw vegetables, from fried potatoes to sliced tomatoes to grilled corn, or to put out as a table condiment.

This recipe is adapted from instructions given to me by the Svanetian cousin-in-law of my friend Tamar. Traditionally all the ingredients except the salt would be home-dried herbs and garlic grown in the family garden.   **MAKES ABOUT 4 CUPS**

About 10 fresh, firm garlic cloves
  (to yield ¼ cup coarsely chopped)

1 cup coarse salt

1 cup dried dill

1 cup ground coriander

¼ cup ground fenugreek

½ cup powdered dried fenugreek leaves

½ cup powdered dried marigold petals
  (optional)

2 heaping tablespoons ground caraway

3 tablespoons powdered dried red chiles
  or cayenne

Soak the garlic in cold water for 10 minutes. Peel the garlic cloves, smash with the flat side of a large knife or with a pestle, and set aside.

Place all the ingredients except the garlic in a food processor and process to a fine powder. Add the garlic and process for about a minute, until completely incorporated.

Transfer to two clean 1-pint glass jars and label clearly. Store away from heat and sun as you would any herb or spice.

WALNUT SAUCE

BAZHA

Walnuts have an important place in many dishes from the Caucasus and Persia, sometimes subtle, sometimes in a starring role. In this versatile Georgian sauce, they are the main ingredient, ground in a food processor for ease (traditionally ground in a mortar), along with a little garlic and some balancing spices, and then extended, like a kind of nut mayonnaise, with water and a little vinegar.

If you have *kmeli suneli* (Georgian Spice Blend, page 28), you can use a generous tablespoon of that instead of the coriander, fenugreek, and flower petals.

Serve as a dipping sauce or drizzle over chopped cooked vegetables. It's a great accompaniment to grilled chicken too. Flavors intensify as the sauce rests, so leftovers are a treat; they can be stored in the refrigerator for up to a week. The sauce thickens when chilled, so you may want to whisk in a little hot water to loosen it after you take it out of the fridge.   **MAKES ABOUT 1¾ CUPS**

1 cup walnuts or walnut pieces

1 garlic clove

1 to 1½ teaspoons ground coriander, to taste (see headnote)

2 teaspoons ground blue fenugreek, or 2 teaspoons powdered dried fenugreek leaves plus ½ teaspoon ground fenugreek (see headnote)

1 teaspoon powdered dried marigold or safflower petals (see headnote), or substitute 1 tablespoon Saffron Water (page 27)

½ teaspoon ground fennel seeds or dried dill (optional)

½ to 1 teaspoon cayenne, to taste

1 cup warm water, or as needed

1 tablespoon wine vinegar or cider vinegar, or to taste

1 teaspoon sea salt, or to taste

Use a food processor or a mortar and pestle to grind the walnuts and garlic to a fine, smooth paste. Transfer to a bowl and add the coriander, fenugreek, flower petals, if using (not the saffron water), optional fennel or dill, and cayenne. Add about 2 tablespoons of the warm water and the saffron water, if using, whisking until emulsified. Add the remaining water a little at a time, whisking until the sauce is smooth and quite liquid, like a cream soup. Stir in the vinegar. Add the salt, taste, and adjust the seasoning as you wish.

TART-SWEET APRICOT AND RAISIN RELISH

PHOTOGRAPH ON PAGE 174

This delicious condiment from Azerbaijan is a favorite with me any time I am serving pilaf-style dishes. Tart dried apricots and seedless raisins are transformed by brief cooking with a little butter into a kind of confit or fruit relish with an intense tart-sweet edge. All it takes is a little time.

Serve with Turkey Kebabs (page 175) or other grilled or roasted meat or with rice dishes. Although it was not part of the recipe I learned in Azerbaijan, I add a generous squeeze of lemon juice for an extra hit of tartness. **SERVES 8**

1 cup dried tart apricots, preferably organic and unsulfured, cut into quarters

1 cup dark or golden raisins

2 tablespoons butter

½ cup water

2 tablespoons sugar, or to taste

Pinch of sea salt

Juice of 1 lemon (optional)

Place the apricots and raisins in a bowl, add some water, swirl around to rinse them, and drain. Add water to cover and set aside to soak for 20 minutes, or until plumped.

Melt the butter in a heavy saucepan or skillet over medium heat. Drain the fruit, add to the pan, and cook over low heat, stirring occasionally, for 5 minutes. Add the water, sugar, and salt and bring to a boil, then reduce the heat and cook, partially covered, at a low simmer for 20 minutes. Check occasionally to make sure the mixture is not sticking, and add more water if necessary. Remove from the heat, taste, and add a little lemon juice if you like.

Transfer to a small bowl and serve.

SOUR PLUM SAUCE

TKEMALI

All over the Persian culinary world, tart fruits play an important role in savory dishes. But in Georgia, there's a brasher palate with a strikingly confident use of raw garlic and brilliant exploitation of tart fruits. Nothing exemplifies the Georgian way with flavor better than this knockout sauce.

The main ingredient is a sour plum called *tkemali* (see Glossary). Damson plums are the closest substitute, but they are usually available only for a short period in late summer and early fall. One option is to use unripe plums; another is to add lime or lemon juice, or verjuice. Or substitute other tart fruits, such as sour cherries or cornels (see Glossary). If you have Georgian spice blend, either homemade (see page 28) or store-bought (see Glossary), use 1 tablespoon of the blend instead of the fenugreek, coriander, and chiles. **MAKES ABOUT 4 CUPS**

2 pounds damson or other sour plums or unripe plums, halved, pitted, and coarsely chopped; or substitute other dried fruits (see headnote)

2 garlic cloves, minced (about 2 teaspoons)

1 teaspoon ground blue fenugreek, or 1 teaspoon powdered dried fenugreek leaves plus ½ teaspoon ground fenugreek (see headnote)

1 teaspoon ground coriander (see headnote)

½ teaspoon powdered dried red chiles (see headnote)

½ teaspoon dried summer savory (optional)

½ teaspoon ground celery seeds (optional)

½ teaspoon sea salt, or to taste

1 to 2 tablespoons fresh lime or lemon juice (optional)

Coarsely chopped fresh coriander

Place the plums in a heavy saucepan and add water to cover (about 1 cup). Bring to a boil, lower the heat, cover, and simmer until the plums have broken down into a pulp, about 15 minutes. Stir occasionally to make sure the plums are not sticking, and add a little more water if necessary.

Add the garlic and transfer to a food processor or to a bowl. Add the fenugreek, coriander, chiles, savory, celery seeds, if using, and salt and stir to mix thoroughly, or pulse several times. Taste for tartness—the sauce should be tart. Add the lime or lemon juice if needed.

If not serving immediately, transfer to four 1-cup sterile jars and refrigerate. The sauce will keep for 2 months.

To serve, put the sauce out in a small serving bowl and stir in some chopped fresh coriander (about 3 tablespoons per cup).

POMEGRANATE-CORIANDER SAUCE

PHOTOGRAPH ON PAGE 155

When pomegranates are available, this fresh-tasting uncooked sauce is a lovely way to dress up grilled fish or meat of any kind. For instructions on handling pomegranates, see Pomegranate Techniques, page 333. **MAKES ABOUT 1 CUP**

Seeds from 2 pomegranates
¼ teaspoon sea salt, or to taste

About 2 tablespoons fresh lemon juice
½ cup chopped fresh coriander, or more to taste

Set aside 2 or 3 tablespoons of the pomegranate seeds for garnish. Place the remaining seeds in a large mortar or in a heavy bowl. Add the salt and lemon juice and use a pestle or the back of a wooden spoon to pound and press the seeds for a few minutes. Set aside to steep for 30 minutes or so; the salt will draw the juice out of the seeds.

Mix the pomegranate seeds and liquid with the coriander. Taste for salt and adjust if you wish. Transfer to a serving bowl and sprinkle on the reserved pomegranate seeds.

Pomegranates come in a variety of shades of red—from plum-wine to blush pink—and even in yellow-green. Their seeds are always red, but their flavor varies from sweet in the red fruits to tart in the yellow-tinted (and often smaller) varieties.

ZOROASTER'S LEGACY

Zoroastrianism was the religion of the Persian Empire for about a thousand years, from the time of Darius until the Arab conquest in AD 651. There are still Zoroastrian temples, now maintained as museums, in Baku, the capital of

Azerbaijan, and in Tbilisi, in Georgia. Some Persians who did not convert to Islam after the Arab conquest fled to the coast and then to India, where their descendants are known as Parsis. Others moved to more remote areas, especially to the desert city of Yazd, in central Iran, and to Kerman in the south.

But Zoroastrianism continued to have an impact in the greater Persian region, even on those who converted to other religions, and it still does to this day. Because it centers on the conflict between Good and Evil, and because the symbol of Ahura Mazda, the force of Good, is the sun, the spring equinox, which marks the return of the sun, is the most important festival for Zoroastrians. That celebration is called Nou-Roz (New Day). The spring equinox still marks the New Year in Iran, and Nou-Roz is celebrated by many in all parts of the Persian-influenced world, whether Muslim, Christian, or Zoroastrian.

Because green is the color of new life, food at Nou-Roz always involves herbs and greens (and often fish, another symbol of life). In Persian households, and in Azerbaijan, Georgia, Armenia, and Kurdistan, families sprout plates of wheat and other grains in the spring. The Christian cultures (in Georgia and Armenia) associate the sprouted grains with Easter, another celebration of rebirth, but the practice goes back to Zoroastrianism.

In Armenian households, people make a paste of sprouted wheat through long, slow cooking and serve it at Eastertime. A similar paste called *samanu* is made in Persian households and eaten on the first day of Nou-Roz.

One day long ago, at a small Persian grocery store in Toronto, the owners handed me a small spoon with a little paste on it. "Eat this *samanu*," they said firmly. "It's Nou-Roz today." The paste was smooth, medium brown, slightly sweet, delicious, and unlike anything I'd ever tasted. Now, after immersing myself in Persian culinary traditions, I understand how special that food is.

YAZD, IRAN—*Two boys on their way home from a trip to a bakery to buy bread for the family.*

GEORGIAN AJIKA

Ajika, one of the glories of the Georgian table, is a chile paste that comes in many versions: red and green, chile-hot or milder, thick and dense or else more liquid like salsa. What all *ajikas* share is that they are salty, delicious uncooked condiments made of peppers, herbs, and aromatics. Each region has a different take (*ajikas* from Abkhazia and Samegrelo generally being the hottest), and of course people always prefer the one from their home region.

Red *ajika* is usually served with meat, but you can also mix it with yogurt as a flavoring or dressing for cooked or raw vegetables. Green *ajika* is for serving with beans or vegetables. It can also be used to flavor *bazha* (Walnut Sauce, page 32).

Left: KERMAN, IRAN—*A wall of herbs and greens in the bazaar.*

Right: TBILISI, GEORGIA—*Market vendors sell ajika in whatever containers they can find.* Ajikas *may be thick pourable sauces or dense pastes.*

Opposite: *Green Ajika (page 40) and Red Ajika (page 42).*

GREEN AJIKA

PHOTOGRAPH ON PAGE 39

Although some Georgians have told me that green *ajika* should have no garlic in it, this one does, and it's delicious. (The recipe is Mingrelian, from the Samegrelo region in western Georgia; it was given to me by the mother of a friend.) Smear a little on cooked corn on the cob, or dab some onto sliced cucumbers, or . . . You will find yourself making excuses to use it on all occasions, as I do.

The more finely ground the *ajika* is, the better. Georgians grind the ingredients in a meat grinder, putting them through the grinder over and over until they are smooth, but a food processor does a fine job. The paste is medium-hot, dense, and salty enough that it keeps well. It's meant to be dabbed on as a condiment, not eaten in large dollops. You can also use it, mixed with a little oil, as a flavor paste for grilled chicken, or add a little to a vinaigrette to spice it up.

The recipe calls for dried red chiles that are seeded and soaked overnight to soften them (to shorten the time needed, you can instead simmer them in water for 30 minutes or so). And, once the paste has been ground, it rests for 6 to 10 hours (loosely covered and stirred occasionally). This pause lets some of the moisture evaporate and ensures that flavors are well blended.

If you want to make a larger quantity, I suggest that you make it in two batches and then combine them in a large bowl. **MAKES 3 CUPS**

2 ounces (about 150) dried red cayenne chiles

2 large bunches coriander

1 bunch flat-leaf parsley

1 bunch dill

1 bunch leaf celery (see Glossary)

1 bunch basil

¼ cup coriander seeds

¼ cup dill seeds

4 heads garlic, separated into cloves, peeled, and trimmed of any tough ends

2 medium leeks, white and tender green parts only, chopped and well washed, or 6 or 7 scallions, trimmed

¼ cup sea salt

Remove the seeds from the dried chiles: This is easiest if you work over a bowl, with another alongside for the cleaned chiles. One at a time, break each chile in half and empty the seeds into the first bowl. Break off and discard the stem if it is still there, and place the chile in the second bowl. When all of the chiles have been seeded, add warm water to cover, cover loosely, and set aside to soak and soften overnight. Alternatively, place in a saucepan with 2 inches of water, bring to a simmer, and simmer for 30 minutes, or until very soft.

TELAVI, EASTERN GEORGIA—
Springtime freshness: coriander leaves, scallions, and radishes in front of a stack of tarragon in the Kakheti region of Georgia, famed for its wine.

Remove the coarsest stems from the herbs and set the herbs aside.

Dry-roast the coriander seeds in a small heavy skillet over medium heat, stirring regularly, until aromatic and lightly toasted, 3 to 4 minutes. Set aside. Dry-roast the dill seeds in the same way and set aside.

Drain the chiles and gently squeeze them dry. Place in a food processor and grind to a paste. Add the garlic and process to a paste. Add the leeks or scallions and process to a paste; use a spatula to scrape down the sides of the bowl. Process the herbs, adding them in batches (see Note), until the paste is smooth and thick and everything is finely ground.

Using a coffee or spice grinder or a mortar and pestle, grind the toasted coriander and dill seeds to a powder. Add them to the herb mixture, add the salt, and mix with a wooden spoon until thoroughly blended. Cover with a cotton cloth and let stand for 6 to 10 hours in a cool place; give the *ajika* a stir from time to time.

Transfer to clean dry glass jars and seal. The paste will keep for 3 months in the refrigerator.

NOTE: Grinding the ingredients in the food processor reduces their volume radically, but you may find that from time to time as you add ingredients to the processor, it seems overfull. Just remove some of the paste, process the new ingredients with the rest until blended in, and then add the rest of the paste back.

RED AJIKA

PHOTOGRAPH ON PAGE 39

Georgians make red *ajika* in the late summer or fall, when peppers are perfect and garlic still fresh, and they make large quantities—it's a way of capturing summer and preserving its intensity for use in the winter months. I learned this recipe in Tbilisi from an artist and free spirit named Chuka, and I brought back a huge jar of it in my checked luggage. It soon became my go-to condiment.

A year later, my jar was empty and I was missing it badly. It was time to make some in my kitchen in Toronto. As we'd done in Tbilisi, I made a large batch. It's always worthwhile, because once you have shopped for the ingredients, stripping out seeds and membranes from the peppers goes quickly (especially if you have a friend to help). The food processor does the rest of the work. And a large batch means you have extra to give to friends who love garlic, chile heat, and the taste of Georgia.

The chile paste is salty and intense. It needs to sit out, loosely covered, for 4 or 5 days before it goes into jars. I put it up in small (1- or 2-cup) jars, a good size for giving away.

Use red *ajika* as a spicy condiment with any meal. I love it in the morning with my fried egg, greens, and rice breakfast. And I put it out whenever I am serving meat dishes of any kind, from grilled kebabs to hearty stews. It's an enlivening hit, and a crowd-pleaser. **MAKES A GENEROUS 4 QUARTS**

1 pound garlic, preferably organic

1 pound walnuts or walnut pieces

4 pounds red bell peppers, as ripe as possible

2 pounds fresh red cayenne chiles

¾ cup ground blue fenugreek, or ¾ cup powdered dried fenugreek leaves plus 3 tablespoons ground fenugreek

1 cup ground coriander

1 pound kosher salt

Put the garlic in water to soak for an hour.

Meanwhile, rinse the walnuts, peppers, and chiles and dry thoroughly. Cut the stems off the peppers and chiles. Cut lengthwise in half and remove and discard the seeds and ribs. Cut the peppers and chiles into approximately 1-inch pieces, discarding any imperfect bits, and set aside.

Drain and dry the garlic. Separate the heads into individual cloves and peel them. Set aside.

Check the walnuts and discard any flawed ones.

SHEKI, AZERBAIJAN—*Autumn brings newly harvested walnuts and hazelnuts and freshly dried fruit to the markets of the Persian world.*

To grind the paste, use a food processor and work in batches. Start with some peppers and chiles, tossing in some walnuts and garlic from time to time. Transfer the paste to one or two large bowls as you go. Once all the ingredients are ground, add the fenugreek, coriander, and salt and stir in thoroughly. Cover the bowl(s) with a cotton cloth, and set aside at cool room temperature for 4 to 5 days. Stir several times to make sure the flavors blend.

Transfer the paste to dry sterilized jars and seal tightly. Store in a cool place; the paste will keep for 1 year. Once it has been opened, store in the refrigerator.

SALADS AND VEGETABLES

THE SIMPLE CHOPPED SALADS IN THE Persian culinary sphere are a real pleasure. Made with cucumbers, tomatoes, or onions, or a combination, they're light and refreshing, dressed not with oil but instead with a drizzle of pomegranate syrup or a little vinegar, and sprinkled with herbs, salt, and perhaps sumac.

This chapter opens with a few of these raw salads, and then moves on to the delectable Persian dishes called *borani* (see pages 55 and 62), in which cooked vegetables are dressed with thick yogurt and fried onions.

There's a collection of eggplant dishes from all over the region; not only is eggplant versatile, it is also meaty and satisfying. The nut-rich aromatic Georgian vegetable pâtés called *pkhali* (see pages 69 and 70) are a real pleasure, as is the Armenian walnut and bean pâté (see page 73).

There are two other inviting bean dishes in this chapter, one a classic Georgian *lobio* (see page 88), made from red kidney beans, and the other a Kurdish white bean stew (see page 85). (You'll find more bean and legume dishes in the Soup Paradise chapter.)

Cooks in the Persian culinary world have a repertoire of dishes that combine cooked vegetables with a little egg, a delicious pairing (see Azeri Mushrooms, page 76, and Kurdish-Style Jerusalem Artichokes, page 78). The most sophisticated example of this kind of dish is the Persian *kuku'ye sabzi* on page 80, a kind of frittata that is loaded with greens and herbs.

Previous pages: TBILISI, GEORGIA—*Stacks of vegetables and herbs in Deserteri Market in Georgia's capital.*

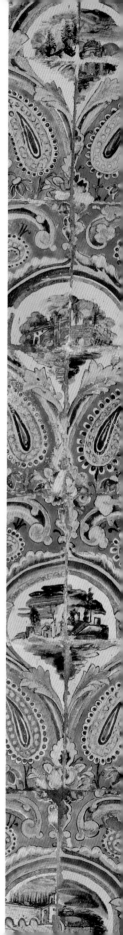

CUCUMBER SALAD WITH SUMAC AND MINT

PHOTOGRAPH ON PAGE 174

In Kurdistan, the families I stayed with in Halabja and Sulaymaniyah would often put out a bowl of small tender-skinned Persian cucumbers when we were sitting around chatting. Alongside the bowl would be several small sharp knives so each person could peel and chop his or her own cucumbers as desired. It seemed so civilized to me, the cucumber refreshing, and the gestures a way of occupying your hands. Most people would peel the cucumber and then cut it lengthwise into long spears. And there was always salt for sprinkling on the cucumber pieces.

The fresh textures of this easy salad, inspired by that custom, are welcome with any meal. **SERVES 4**

About 2 cups ½-inch cubes peeled Persian or English cucumbers (see Note)

½ teaspoon dried mint

1 teaspoon ground sumac

¼ teaspoon sea salt, or to taste

Place the cucumbers in a serving bowl. Add the mint, sumac, and salt and toss. Taste and adjust the flavorings if you wish, toss again, and serve.

NOTE: If your cucumbers are overly mature, with tough seeds, halve them lengthwise and strip out the seeds before chopping.

CUCUMBERS WITH AJIKA

If you have red or green *ajika* (page 42 or 40) on hand, the heat of the chile paste is a great pairing with the cool of the cucumber. Cut the cucumbers into spears or wedges; do not add salt, since the *ajika* is salty. I add a little water and a touch of oil to the *ajika* to make it more liquid, then either pour it onto the cucumbers and toss or put it out in a small bowl as a dip.

CUCUMBER AND TOMATO SALAD WITH POMEGRANATE MOLASSES

PHOTOGRAPH ON PAGE 50

A lively Kurdish restaurant I visited between Arbil, the capital of Kurdistan, and its Assyrian suburb, Ainkawa, like many restaurants in Kurdistan, served families and women on the second floor and men alone on the ground floor. This was one of their salads, long spears of cucumber with a little chopped tomato and plenty of fresh herbs, drizzled with pomegranate molasses. **SERVES 4**

½ pound Persian or English cucumbers, peeled

1 large or 2 small Roma (plum) or other fleshy tomatoes

½ cup chopped fresh herbs: one or more of mint, sorrel, lovage, flat-leaf parsley, and/or leaf celery (see Glossary)

½ teaspoon salt, or to taste

About 2 tablespoons pomegranate molasses

Cut the cucumbers lengthwise in half, cut into 1½-inch lengths, and then cut into spears. Set aside in a shallow bowl.

Bring a small pot of water to a boil. Drop in the tomatoes, then use a large spoon to lift them out, let cool a moment, and peel. Chop the tomatoes into ¼-inch chunks.

Add the tomatoes to the cucumber, then add the herbs and toss to mix. Add the salt and toss. Add the pomegranate molasses and toss. Taste for seasoning and adjust the salt if you wish.

BAKU-STYLE TOMATO SALAD

Attractive chopped salads are very common in Baku eateries, from hole-in-the-wall places to fancier restaurants. This one is a combination of cucumber, onion, and tomato tossed with fresh parsley and basil (usually dark red basil), a sprinkling of salt, and ground sumac. **SERVES 4 TO 6**

½ pound ripe tomatoes, cut into ½-inch chunks

½ pound Persian or English cucumbers, peeled and cut into ½-inch chunks

Scant ½ cup thinly sliced mild onion (1 medium)

Several sprigs of fresh flat-leaf parsley

Several sprigs of fresh purple or green basil

2 tablespoons chopped fresh dill (optional)

About ½ teaspoon sea salt, or to taste

Generous sprinkling of ground sumac

Place the tomatoes, cucumbers, and onion in a bowl. Add the herbs and toss. Sprinkle on the salt and sumac, toss, and serve.

BAKU, AZERBAIJAN—
A quiet square in old Baku has a small produce shop that stays open late.

ONION SALAD
WITH BARBERRIES

This simple dish of seasoned sliced onions, a cross between a salad and a condiment, pairs well with meat or vegetable stews, and with roast meats. It is an Azeri take on onion salad, flavored by and made attractive with a garnish of barberries. The tartness of the berries is a pleasing contrast to the sweetness of the onions. You can use pomegranate seeds instead for a similar effect.

SERVES 4 AS A SALAD/CONDIMENT

2 large onions, thinly sliced

Sea salt

About ¼ cup dried barberries (see Glossary), soaked for 20 minutes in lukewarm water and drained

1 teaspoon dried mint, 2 teaspoons Mint Oil (page 19), or 2 tablespoons finely chopped fresh mint

½ teaspoon ground sumac

Place the onions in a bowl, sprinkle on 2 teaspoons salt, and mix with your hands to distribute the salt. Set aside for 15 minutes.

Pour cold water into the bowl of onions to cover, mix a little with your hand, and drain. Repeat, squeezing the onions gently but firmly to rid them of the salty water.

Place the drained onions in a shallow serving bowl. Add the barberries and toss. Add the dried mint or mint oil or fresh mint and toss. Sprinkle on another ¼ teaspoon salt and toss, then taste and adjust the seasoning if needed. Sprinkle with the sumac and serve.

Clockwise from top: *Cucumber and Tomato Salad with Pomegranate Molasses (page 48), Onion Salad with Barberries, sumac, and mint leaves.*

IRAN TRAVEL

"Your Iran visa has been approved" was the long-awaited e-mail message one August day. At last—I was thrilled. Not so my family and friends, who were worried about my going on my own to take photographs and do research for this book.

The reverse of all that worry by people at home was the reaction of people in Iran. I was made to feel very welcome by everyone I met, English-speaking or no. They were often curious: "What do you think of Iran?" "Were you afraid of Iranians before you came?" I would answer that I had never been afraid of Iranians, but that I had friends who were worried.

When I got there, in October 2013, the newly elected president, Rouhani, was already several months into his charm offensive with the United States and its allies. Iranians I met were pleased that he and President Obama had talked and that there might be a détente. They were tired of sanctions and of their country being treated as a pariah. They were also tired of being ruled by theocrats, the ayatollahs.

In the meantime, they had developed a lot of work-arounds to help them cope with the restrictions imposed on them by those religious leaders. Unlike in Burma, where totalitarian rule left people frightened, in Iran I felt that people refused to be afraid, and instead tried to figure out ways of living their lives as fully and freely as possible.

So they would laugh at my questions about religious observance: "Of course we have respect for mosques and shrines," they'd tell me, "but only ten percent of the population is truly religious, and another ten percent finds it convenient and more practical to act religious." Or they'd say, "In truth, we are not extremists. We are Persians and we have our own calendar, a solar calendar that is not the Islamic calendar. We celebrate the seasons." And they'd tell me that most Iranians try to get by with minimal observance of the rules about avoiding alcohol and about clothing for women and girls.

What I saw confirmed this: People buy liquor and beer from trusted sources, and many women in the more liberal atmosphere of the bigger cities—Tehran, Shiraz, and Isfahan—were wearing head scarves perched way back on their heads, and extremely

MASSOULEH, NORTHERN IRAN—*A tourist destination for Iranians, this hillside village has lush vegetation and a humid climate that's very different from most of Iran.*

Left: **KASHAN, IRAN**—*Two women outside a shop in this town famous for its scented waters distilled from flowers and plants.*

Right: **YAZD, IRAN**—*A Zoroastrian woman (identifiable by her bright clothing and head covering). Yazd is home to a large population of Zoroastrians (see Zoroaster's Legacy, page 36).*

formfitting clothing. People know that there are occasional crackdowns, with the "scarf police," as I thought of them, set up at busy intersections to chastise women for showing too much hair or neck. But most people are relaxed about the rules. Or at least so it seemed to me.

The result was that I felt very at ease in Iran. I walked around with my camera, knowing I was very obviously a foreigner, and felt no sense that people were eyeing me to take advantage. I walked on my own all over, and only at dusk in the rather deserted covered alleys of Yazd, ill-lit and buzzed by the occasional speeding motorcycle, did I ever feel slightly uneasy.

Early on, I traveled by prearranged car between some cities, almost always with a driver who spoke little or no English. Distances were huge, the highways multilane and fast, and there was little incentive to stop. So I began to choose public transit in preference to a car.

I took a long-distance bus south from Yazd to Kerman and an overnight train from Kerman to Mashad. I loved the public transportation, because it was a chance to be thrown into a crowd of strangers, always an interesting experience in another country. Women were very welcoming and generous to me. We shared sunflower seeds and raisins, smiles, and gestural conversations that felt relaxed and intimate.

I want to keep going back.

SPINACH BORANI

BORANI YE ESFENAJ

The Persian dishes called *borani* are a genius combination of cooked vegetable and thick drained yogurt. They are generally topped with fried onions, and often with a scattering of lightly toasted walnuts. People rave whenever I serve them, especially this spinach version.   **SERVES 4 TO 6**

About 1½ cups plain full-fat yogurt

2 pounds spinach

About 2 tablespoons sunflower or extra-virgin olive oil

1 medium onion, thinly sliced

1 teaspoon sea salt, or to taste

1 tablespoon water

OPTIONAL TOPPINGS

About 1 tablespoon Saffron Water (page 27)

2 to 3 tablespoons coarsely chopped lightly toasted walnuts

Drain the yogurt to thicken it: Line a sieve or colander with cheesecloth or a cotton cloth. Moisten the cloth with water. Set the sieve or colander over a bowl and add the yogurt. Set aside, loosely covered, to drain for about 30 minutes.

Meanwhile, trim the tough stems from the spinach. Wash the spinach thoroughly in several changes of water and drain well. Coarsely chop and set aside.

Heat the oil in a wide heavy skillet over medium-high heat. Add the onion, lower the heat to medium, and fry the onion until translucent and touched with color, about 5 minutes. Transfer the onion to a plate and set aside.

Raise the heat under the skillet to medium-high and add the spinach, turning it to expose it to the hot surface. Add about ½ cup water and cook, pressing and turning the spinach, until it is well wilted and deep green, 4 to 5 minutes. Transfer the spinach to a bowl to cool slightly.

Once the spinach is cool enough to handle, squeeze it thoroughly, a handful at a time, to press out excess water.

Transfer the spinach to a bowl, add ½ teaspoon salt, and mix well.

Turn the thickened yogurt out into a bowl; you'll have about 1 cup. Add the remaining ½ teaspoon salt and the water to loosen the yogurt slightly and stir. (Save the whey for another purpose or discard.) Add the yogurt to the spinach

and stir gently to mix them a little, but not into a smooth blend, leaving the mixture with patches of white and dark green. Taste and adjust the seasoning if necessary.

Strew on the fried onions, sprinkle with the saffron water and toasted walnuts if you wish, and serve.

BEET BORANI

You can make *borani* with other vegetables too. One of the most appealing is beet *borani*—the yogurt's slight tartness is a great foil for the sweetness of the beets. Place 6 medium beets (1½ to 2 pounds) in a roasting pan, coat with a little oil, and roast at 400°F until cooked through, about 1 hour, or boil them whole until cooked through. Let cool. Peel the beets and chop into about ½-inch dice. I have a weakness for beets with cumin or fennel, so I suggest tossing a generous pinch of one or the other into the pan as you fry the onion, along with ½ teaspoon salt. Once the onion is softened and touched with color, add it to the chopped beets. To serve, combine the beets with about 1 cup drained yogurt (from 1½ cups full-fat yogurt) seasoned with ½ teaspoon salt, without mixing them completely. Top with about 3 tablespoons coarsely chopped toasted walnuts or, for a splashier look, with coarsely chopped pistachios.

Opposite: *Spinach Borani, topped with saffron water and fried onions.*

Left: DARBAND, TEHRAN, IRAN—*On Saturdays, Darband is an especially popular place with young people. A path leads up past rocky cliffs to Mount Tochal, which towers over Tehran. The first part of the route is where most people hang out, because it is lined with little shops and cafes where friends go to smoke hookahs, sip tea or coffee, eat a little, and relax.*

ARARAT SHEPHERD'S EGGLESS OMELET

HOVIVI

This yogurt, cheese, and herb dish from the Ararat Valley in the far south of Armenia is known as an omelet without eggs. In fact, it's more like a thick vegetable-laden sauce, rich with yogurt and a little cheese, and delectable as a vegetarian main course or as an appetizer.

Shepherds in Armenia, as in many places, set out with their flocks in search of grazing, either for the day or for weeks at a time. They travel light, with some bread and cheese and other staples, and they have access to milk from the flock. But of course there are no chickens in the party, and no eggs available. Hence this improvised dish, which has become fancier over time with the addition of chopped red pepper, tomato, and black pepper. The optional turmeric tints it yellow and makes it look as if there are eggs in it. The original would have been made with only yogurt or fresh cheese, loads of wild herbs, and perhaps some crumbled bread. *Hovivi* has a thick, creamy texture, like a very thick soup. I like to serve it as a first course in small bowls, with flatbread or toast alongside.

SERVES 2 AS A MAIN COURSE, 6 AS AN APPETIZER

1½ cups full-fat sheep's- or cow's-milk yogurt or 1 cup plain thick yogurt (see Glossary)

1 tablespoon all-purpose flour or 2 tablespoons rice flour

½ teaspoon sea salt

2 tablespoons sunflower or vegetable oil

¼ teaspoon turmeric (optional)

1 cup thinly sliced onion

1 small red bell pepper, cored, seeded, and chopped into ½-inch pieces

1 tomato, peeled and chopped

¼ cup crumbled or chopped cheese—a mix of feta and either medium cheddar or aged sheep's-milk cheese

Generous grinding of black pepper

Generous ½ cup chopped fresh sorrel, tarragon, mint, coriander, flat-leaf parsley, and/or dill

Left: **NORTH OF YEREVAN, ARMENIA**—*Most of Armenia is big-sky country whose climate is mild enough for fruit trees. But as the road climbs higher, agriculture is tougher: People grow potatoes and some grain, and perhaps apples, and the rest of the land is used for grazing sheep and goats.*

Right: **NEAR MASSOULEH, NORTHERN IRAN**—*A small rain-soaked herd of sheep and goats on a narrow road between Massouleh and the Caspian coast.*

If using the 1½ cups yogurt, line a sieve or colander with cheesecloth or a cotton cloth. Moisten the cloth with water. Set the sieve or colander over a bowl and add the yogurt. Set aside, loosely covered, to drain for about 30 minutes.

Put the thick yogurt in a bowl and stir in the flour until smooth. Stir in the salt; set aside.

Place a heavy skillet over medium heat and add the oil. When it is hot, add the turmeric, if using, the onion, and red pepper. Stir, cover, and cook for about 5 minutes, until the onion is translucent and the pepper is softened. Add the tomato, stir, and cook for 4 to 5 minutes, until well softened. Stir again, sprinkle on the cheese, and pour in the yogurt mixture. Bring to a low boil and cook, stirring, for 30 seconds. Add the black pepper and herbs, then remove from the heat and let stand for a minute.

Taste and adjust the seasonings if needed. Serve hot in bowls.

GRILLED EGGPLANT

In Iran, as in Thailand, Serbia, and other parts of the world, grilled eggplant is a much-loved everyday food. I had always thought that I needed to grill eggplant over charcoal to get a smoky taste, and that cooking it under a broiler was the only other option. But in Iran, home cooks grill their eggplants directly over a medium-high gas flame on the stove. It's simple, and it gives the desired blackened grilled taste to the eggplants. It's easier and more stable if you place a mesh rack on the gas burner and the eggplants on that.

If you don't have a gas stovetop, either grill the eggplants on a charcoal or gas grill over medium heat until they are softened all over, or put them on a rimmed baking sheet and bake them in a 400°F oven until softened. Remember to prick them all over with a fork before cooking them.

I let the grilled eggplant sit for 10 to 15 minutes in a brown paper bag because it gives the flesh time to steam and cook right through. (This is especially necessary if you are using fatter round Mediterranean eggplants.) Then I scoop the flesh off the skin into a bowl and discard the skin. After that, I can mash it or chop it and use it in a multitude of ways. Yields vary, but in general, 1 round eggplant yields 2 cups cooked flesh.

You'll notice that if you let the cooked eggplant sit for a while in a bowl, liquid accumulates in the bottom. The liquid is full of flavor; stir it back into the flesh before seasoning it.

Grilled Eggplant Options: The repertoire of the Persian culinary world is rich in possibilities for grilled eggplant. Try it topped with Walnut Sauce (page 32) and a scattering of chopped herbs, or with thickened yogurt to make a *borani* (see page 62), or with *kashk* (see page 63). Or instead make it into a Georgian *pkhali*, a walnut-based vegetable pâté (see page 69).

GRILLED EGGPLANT WITH POMEGRANATE SEEDS

ANAR BADEMJAN

This Iranian classic, which I learned from a friend in Shiraz, is a fresh-tasting treat with lovely smoky undertones. A Druse friend from Syria tells me that this dish is the "real" baba ghanouj. That's the name it has in Syria and Lebanon.   **SERVES 4 OR 5 AS A SIDE DISH**

2 cups mashed peeled grilled eggplant (from 1 pound eggplants; see Grilled Eggplant, opposite)

Generous 1 tablespoon dried mint, or to taste

1¼ teaspoons sea salt, or to taste

½ cup finely chopped shallots or sweet onion

2 cups pomegranate seeds (from 1 large fruit; see Pomegranate Techniques, page 333)

Place the eggplant in a bowl, add the dried mint, salt, and shallots or onion, and stir to mix well. Add the pomegranate seeds and fold them in. Let stand for 30 minutes, if you have the time; this gives the flavors a chance to blend.

Just before serving, taste and add a little more dried mint and/or salt if you wish and stir it in thoroughly.

YAZD, IRAN—A motorcycle "packhorse" is parked at the bazaar waiting to be loaded up. Reading license plates is a great way to practice Arabic numbers.

EGGPLANT BORANI

BORANI YE BADEMJAN

Another in the Persian *borani* family (see Spinach Borani, page 55), this combo of smoky eggplant with creamy yogurt and fried onions is a great addition to any meal. I prefer thinner Asian eggplants, which cook more quickly and evenly than the round Mediterranean ones. Use whichever type you prefer.   **SERVES 4 TO 6**

2 cups plain full-fat yogurt

1 pound eggplant (3 medium
    Asian eggplants or 1 to 2 large
    Mediterranean eggplants)

Sunflower or extra-virgin olive oil

2 medium onions, thinly sliced

2 garlic cloves, minced

1 teaspoon sea salt, or to taste

1 tablespoon water

About 2 tablespoons chopped fresh mint
    or tarragon (optional)

Drain the yogurt to thicken it: Line a sieve or colander with cheesecloth or a cotton cloth. Moisten the cloth with water. Set the sieve or colander over a bowl and add the yogurt. Set aside, loosely covered, to drain for about 30 minutes.

Meanwhile, prick the eggplants all over with a fork, ten or twelve times. You can cook them on a gas stovetop, on a gas or charcoal grill, or in the oven.

To use the stovetop, place each eggplant directly on a gas burner turned to medium-high and cook, turning frequently, until very softened and charred, 10 minutes or more, depending on the size of the eggplant. Alternatively, cook them over a medium fire in a gas or charcoal grill, until very soft, turning them frequently. Or preheat the oven to 400°F, place the eggplants on a rimmed baking sheet, and bake in the center of the oven until very softened and sagging, about 15 minutes.

Place the eggplants in a brown paper bag to steam-cook and cool for 10 to 15 minutes. Halve the eggplants, scrape the flesh out of the skin, and discard the skin. Mash or chop the flesh and transfer to a bowl. Set aside.

Heat a scant 2 tablespoons oil in a medium skillet over medium-high heat. Add the onions and cook until translucent and slightly touched with color, about 5 minutes. Remove and set aside. Place the skillet over medium heat and add a little more oil. Add the garlic and cook briefly, until softened.

Stir the garlic into the eggplant, along with ½ teaspoon of the salt. Taste and adjust the seasoning if necessary.

Turn the thickened yogurt out into a bowl; you'll have about 1 cup. Add the remaining ½ teaspoon salt and the water to loosen the yogurt slightly and stir. (Save the whey for another purpose or discard.)

Place the eggplant in a wide shallow serving bowl, add the yogurt, and stir to combine them without blending them completely. Top with the fried onions and a sprinkling of tarragon or mint if you wish. Serve warm or at room temperature.

EGGPLANT WITH KASHK (KASHK-E-BADEMJAN)

A favorite flavoring for grilled eggplant in Iran is *kashk,* a dried-milk product that tastes and smells like pungent cheese. It's available in Persian, Arab, and Turkish grocery stores (for more about *kashk,* see Glossary). Like other fermented foods, *kashk* can be an acquired taste, but I find it delectable. To make *kashk-e-bademjan,* omit the yogurt and garlic and follow the instructions above to the point where you have the eggplant puree in a bowl and the onions sautéed. Dilute ½ cup *kashk* paste (for instructions for reconstituting dried *kashk,* see Glossary) with 1 tablespoon warm water. Stir 1 teaspoon dried mint and 1 teaspoon salt into the eggplant and transfer it to a shallow bowl. Dollop the *kashk* onto the eggplant and stir it in. Sprinkle on the fried onions. Let stand for 5 to 10 minutes to give the flavors time to blend. Invite your guests to scoop up the puree with pieces of flatbread.

EGGPLANT AND TOMATO STEW

BAINJAN SHLEY

I like this Kurdish eggplant and tomato stew for its clean taste and its flexibility: It can be served as a vegetable side—to accompany roast lamb or roast chicken, for example—or as the main dish in a simple meal with Kurdish Black Rice (page 216), a plate of fresh herbs and greens, and cheese. If you wish, you can add a little ground lamb or beef (say ½ pound) when you start to fry the eggplant. Unlike Iranian vegetable dishes, which usually start with a base of cooked onion, Kurdish *shleys* use no onion.

The eggplant, which is peeled in strips and cut into short spears, fries in a little turmeric-and-cumin-flavored oil before it is simmered in a tomato sauce. Serve with a generous heap of fresh greens such as watercress or arugula, and put out some feta or another salty, crumbly cheese. Invite your guests to stir the greens into their stew. They can sprinkle small pieces of cheese onto their bowls of *shley*, or eat the cheese with bread as part of the meal.   **SERVES 4 AS A SIDE DISH, 2 AS A MAIN COURSE**

Left: **NEAR SULAYMANIYAH, KURDISTAN**—*Kurdish women dressed in their finest, at a big festival held out in the country.*

Right: **YAZD, IRAN**—*One of many fruit and vegetable shops in this desert city. Most of the bazaar is roofed to protect against the hot sun of summer and the icy winds of winter.*

1 pound eggplant (3 medium Asian eggplants or 1 large Mediterranean eggplant)

¼ cup sunflower or extra-virgin olive oil

¼ teaspoon turmeric

1 teaspoon ground cumin

2 cups water

1 cup unsalted canned crushed tomatoes or tomato puree

½ teaspoon salt (see Note)

ACCOMPANIMENTS

2 cups chopped watercress, tender arugula, or fresh flat-leaf parsley

About ¼ pound feta or other salty cheese

Trim the eggplant and peel it in strips, leaving about half the skin on. Cut into 1½- to 2-inch lengths, then cut each length into spears about the size of your little finger. Set aside.

Place a wide heavy pot over medium heat. When it is hot, add the oil, and then the turmeric and cumin, and stir for a moment. Toss in the eggplant and turn and stir it to expose all surfaces to the flavored oil. Add 1 cup of the water and the tomatoes or tomato puree, stir, and bring to a vigorous boil. Add the second cup of water and the salt and boil vigorously, uncovered, for 15 minutes, stirring occasionally to make sure that the sauce doesn't burn or stick; lower the heat if necessary.

Cover, turn the heat to very low, and simmer for about 20 minutes, until the flavors have blended.

Serve hot or at room temperature. Put out the greens and cheese, or top each serving with some of each and invite guests to stir them into their stew.

NOTE ON SEASONING: I have kept the salt minimal, because I like to sprinkle salty feta on my *shley*. If you are serving it with cheese on the side, rather than sprinkled on top, increase the salt to ¾ to 1 teaspoon to taste.

OTHER VEGETABLE SHLEYS

You can make this recipe with other vegetables. Substitute 1 pound small young okra, sliced green beans, chopped zucchini, or chopped cauliflower florets for the eggplant. Cooking times will differ (the zucchini will cook in a very short time, and the green beans too if they are young and tender).

SOUTHERN KURDISTAN, NEAR HALABJA—*The beautiful and bare rolling green hills, less than ten miles from the border with Iran, were an escape route for families who fled Saddam Hussein during his war on the Kurds.*

KURDISH WELCOME

Hoshida, who lives in the town of Halabja, in the hills of southern Kurdistan, swept me up into her daily routine as if I were one of her grown children come for a visit. She taught me words in Kurdish as I did kitchen chores alongside her, and she

showed me how to make Kurdish rice and other dishes. I don't know what she thought of me, this visitor from Canada—a friend of her journalist son— busily asking endless questions, taking notes and photographs. Like the rest of her family, she was very tolerant, and I think she found me entertaining. I, in turn, was struck by her calm dignity, her grace, her generous welcome.

In the days that I stayed with her I explored the town; went driving out into the green hills with three of her sons; learned to make *nane-tire* (Kerchief Flatbreads, page 240) from her oldest daughter, Dila; and sat around for hours with various members of her large family—and frequent visitors—on the thickly carpeted floor listening to them speaking Kurdish and picking up a word here and there, while sipping glass after glass of sweet black tea. With no Internet, the pace of life

was different, more deliberate and unhurried, with lots of conversation.

Apart from prostrating herself to pray, Hoshida is constantly getting up and down, for everything in the household takes place on the carpeted floor: eating, sleeping, praying, and sitting around. A sheet of plastic is laid out on the carpet for a dining table and onto it go bowls and plates and stacks of flatbread, as well as the cooked dishes; and at night, sleeping pads and blankets come out of an alcove and are unfolded and laid on the floor. The men sleep in one room and the women and children in another.

When I left Halabja to travel to the city of Sulaymaniyah, there was no chance I could stay in a hotel there; I had to stay with Hoshida's son Yusef and his wife. Everything depends on family and family connection in Kurdistan. Once you belong, the family is committed to you and you have an

HALABJA, KURDISTAN—
*Hoshida, the generous and
loving mother and grandmother
whom I stayed with, sits in her
house talking on the phone to
someone in her large family.*

obligation to them as well, to work within their codes of behavior.

And so when I was in Sulaymaniyah I ran into a problem. I was invited to lunch by a Kurdish couple that Yusef and I had met one day at a bakery. But Yusef told me I couldn't possibly go to their place at noontime, for he'd be at work then. I could only go for the evening meal, when he'd be able to come with me. To explain why, he said, "We don't know them," which meant "they aren't family," and so as the man of the household, he had to accompany me. His protectiveness was a totally new and touching experience for me. But it was also a little confining, a taste of how tradition and modernity must collide every day in Kurdistan.

Another evening in Sulaymaniyah I was taken out to dinner by a close friend and confidant of the family, a successful lawyer named Hillal who is also from Halabja. We ate Italian food (breaking my rule about not eating anything but local dishes when I travel) at a newly opened restaurant. We drank imported red wine, a special pleasure for me after many days with no wine. But Hillal was a little concerned. He told me that Yusef would disapprove of his drinking (and of mine) and that I mustn't tell him.

As it turned out, Yusef never asked me where we'd gone for supper; perhaps he thought it was better not to know.

GRILLED-EGGPLANT PÂTÉ

PKHALI BADEMJAN

Georgian vegetable pâtés—*pkhali*—are delicious. Cooked finely chopped or pureed vegetables are combined with loads of ground walnuts and with spices, minced garlic, and fresh herbs. Among my favorites are the leek pâté on page 70 and this eggplant version. The smoky flavor of the roasted eggplants pairs beautifully with the richness of the walnuts and with the spice blend.

Serve this as a side dish or put out with bread, crackers, or toast as an appetizer. **SERVES 6**

About 1 pound eggplant (3 medium Asian eggplants or 1 large Mediterranean eggplant)

1 cup walnuts or walnut pieces

1 medium garlic clove, minced

1 teaspoon sea salt, or to taste

1½ teaspoons ground blue fenugreek, or 1½ teaspoons powdered dried fenugreek leaves plus ½ teaspoon ground fenugreek (see Note)

1 teaspoon ground coriander (see Note)

½ teaspoon powdered dried red chiles, or to taste (see Note)

¼ cup finely chopped fresh coriander or a mix of coriander and tarragon, plus (optional) a few sprigs for garnish

Prick the eggplants all over with a fork. Grill them over a gas or charcoal flame until they are well charred and softened. Transfer to a brown paper bag, close it tightly, and set aside to steam for 20 minutes.

Halve the eggplants and scrape the flesh out of the skins. Set aside.

Place the walnuts and garlic in a food processor or large mortar and process or pound to a coarse paste. Add the salt, fenugreek, coriander, and chiles and pulse or mix to blend. Add the eggplant and process or pound to a coarse puree. Taste and adjust for seasoning and chile heat. Turn out into a medium bowl and stir in the fresh herbs.

Cover and refrigerate for at least several hours, or overnight, to firm up. (You can serve the *pkhali* immediately, but it will be sauce-like rather than firm.)

Serve the *pkhali* from the bowl or turn out onto a plate and top with herb sprigs if you wish.

NOTE: If you have Georgian spice blend, either homemade (see page 28) or store-bought (see Glossary), use 1 tablespoon of the blend instead of the fenugreek, coriander, and chiles.

GEORGIAN LEEK PÂTÉ

PRASI PKHALI

Leeks are featured in a starring role in this *pkhali*. They are simmered until soft and then combined with ground walnuts and spices. Make this several hours, or up to a day, ahead to give the flavors a chance to blend and the pâté time to firm up. Leftovers are delicious as a spread on bread or scooped up with lettuce leaves.   **SERVES 6 AS AN APPETIZER OR A SIDE DISH**

6 medium leeks, white and tender green parts only, chopped and well washed (about 4 cups)

1½ cups walnuts or walnut pieces

1½ teaspoons minced garlic

1½ teaspoons ground blue fenugreek, or 1½ teaspoons powdered dried fenugreek leaves plus ½ teaspoon ground fenugreek (see Note)

1 teaspoon ground coriander (see Note)

½ teaspoon powdered dried red chiles, or to taste (see Note)

¾ teaspoon sea salt, or to taste

1 tablespoon white wine vinegar or cider vinegar, or to taste

¼ cup finely chopped fresh coriander or a mix of coriander and tarragon

Crackers or bread for serving

Place the leeks in a wide pot, add about 1½ cups water, and bring to a boil. Cover and cook for 10 minutes, then uncover, lower the heat, and simmer until the leeks are very tender, another 10 to 15 minutes. Drain and set aside.

Grind the walnuts and garlic to a coarse paste in a food processor or a large mortar. Add the spices and salt and pulse or stir, then add the leeks and vinegar and process or pound to a coarse paste.

Transfer to a small deep bowl and stir in the chopped herbs. Taste and adjust the seasoning if you wish. Smooth the top, cover, and refrigerate for at least 2 hours, or as long as a day.

To serve, turn the pâté out onto a plate and serve with crackers or bread.

NOTE: If you have Georgian spice blend, either homemade (see page 28) or store-bought (see Glossary), use 1 tablespoon of the blend instead of the fenugreek, coriander, and chiles.

EASTERN GEORGIA—*A small country market not far from the Azerbaijan border. In early spring, local potatoes, cabbage, onions, beets, dried beans, dried fruit and churchkhela (see page 317), dried corn, and other winter staples are on offer, along with citrus, eggplants, and bananas imported from Turkey.*

BEET PKHALI

Start with a generous pound of whole beets and roast or boil them (see page 57). Peel them, chop them coarsely, and grind in a food processor. Combine with a generous 1 cup ground walnuts. Double the amount of garlic and vinegar to balance out the beets' sweetness and stronger flavor. Add the spices as opposite and increase the salt to 1 teaspoon, or to taste.

WALNUT AND BEAN PÂTÉ

LOBAHASHU

This *lobahashu,* a dish from the Lori region of Armenia, which borders on southeastern Georgia, blends finely ground walnuts into cooked mashed kidney beans. The result is a creamy, garlicky pâté tinted pale pink by the beans. If you can, make it a day or even two days before you wish to serve it (and keep it in the refrigerator). The flavors deepen and blend remarkably over time.

I like spreading this on bread or scooping it up with crackers. Guests love it and can't get enough of it. Serve as an appetizer or a snack. I also like to put this out as part of a meal, another hit of flavor available on the table.   **MAKES ABOUT 4 CUPS**

2 cups walnuts or walnut pieces

3 garlic cloves, minced

4 cups cooked kidney beans (see Note)

2 tablespoons sunflower or olive oil

1½ teaspoons sea salt

Generous grinding of black pepper

About ½ cup chopped fresh dill, tarragon, or coriander, or 1½ teaspoons dried mint

Place the walnuts in a wide heavy skillet over medium heat and toast them, stirring them frequently so they don't scorch, until aromatic, about 5 minutes. (The recipe I learned in Armenia did not include this toasting, but it assumed locally grown superb walnuts; the toasting helps bring out the flavor of the nuts.) Let cool for 10 minutes, then transfer them to a food processor and process to a fine texture. Add the garlic and beans and process to a smooth puree. Stop occasionally and scrape down the sides of the bowl to ensure that all the beans are incorporated.

Turn the mixture out into a bowl, add the oil, salt, and pepper, and stir thoroughly. Stir in the herbs.

Serve at room temperature. Refrigerate any leftover pâté in a well-sealed container for up to 5 days (though it is unlikely to last that long).

NOTE: See The Precooked Beans Habit (page 82). And if you want to use canned beans instead of homemade, drain and rinse the beans, place in a pot with about ½ cup water, and bring to a boil. Simmer for 10 minutes or so. Check to see that the beans are tender. Let cool to room temperature, in their liquid, before using.

STREET-FOOD WRAP

In central Tabriz, the largest city in the Azeri region of Iran, I found a street vendor selling boiled potato and hard-boiled egg mashed together, seasoned, and rolled up in a supple flatbread. It's a satisfying combo, one that workingmen stop by for when they have a break.

I stepped up and nodded to the guy. He reached for a flap of flatbread, lifted out a hot potato, slid off its peel, and placed it on the bread, then folded the bread over and pressed down to mash the potato. He opened the bread again, lifted out a hard-boiled egg from a pot, and peeled it with a practiced flip of the wrist, then put the egg onto the potato and flattened it with the side of a knife. Finally, on went some chopped scallions, as well as salt. He folded my bread package and handed it to me with a nod as I handed him his money.

You can extend this idea to include other herbs (tarragon leaves are a good choice, or basil or mint) and sauces: A dab of Green Ajika (page 40) or Walnut Sauce (page 32) gives another layer of flavor.

This is great picnic food for a crowd. Precook your potatoes and eggs. Take along a good stack of supple flatbreads, some fresh herbs and greens, salt and pepper, and a condiment sauce or two. Invite people to make their own wraps, or set up a production line and feed your guests with speed and ease.

TABRIZ, IRAN—*Hard-boiled eggs and boiled potatoes, ready for use (left). A vendor uses a knife to mash egg and potato onto a large flatbread before seasoning it and rolling it into a street-food wrap (right).*

CAUCASUS FRIED POTATOES

In the three Caucasus countries, home cooks have an easy fallback dish that pleases everyone: sliced fried potatoes. Whether it came in with Russian influence or whether it's just a natural solution to what to do with potatoes when there's no oven, it is indeed a pleasure. Once the potatoes are peeled and sliced, they take only fifteen to twenty minutes to cook.

The recipe is easily doubled. **SERVES 4**

1½ to 2 pounds waxy potatoes (6 medium)

About ½ cup sunflower or extra-virgin olive oil

1½ teaspoons sea salt or 1 tablespoon Svanetian Salt (page 31), or to taste

Freshly ground black pepper (optional)

About 2 teaspoons ground sumac (optional)

Peel the potatoes and slice them into ¼-inch-thick slices.

Place a paper towel–lined platter or wide bowl by your stovetop.

Place a large cast-iron or other heavy skillet over medium-high heat and add about ¼ inch of oil. When the oil is hot, carefully slide in the potato slices. It's fine if you have several layers of potatoes in the pan, but more than that and you will find it difficult to get them evenly cooked. If necessary, use two pans. Cook the potatoes until browned and tender. You want them to brown gradually; as they do, use a spatula to turn them and move them around so they cook evenly. (Lower the heat to medium if the slices start to scorch.) Use tongs or your spatula to lift out the slices once they are lightly browned on both sides and tender, and place them on the paper towels.

Once all the potatoes are cooked, blot with another paper towel. Serve hot, sprinkled with the salt and pepper or sumac, or a combination.

AZERI MUSHROOMS

In the mountains of Azerbaijan, about a three-hour drive from Baku, I watched a home cook boil fresh-gathered mushrooms in water, a technique completely new to me. And when we sat down to eat, I was astonished—I'd never tasted mushrooms with such intense flavor. The next day, she made another version, starting the same way but adding whisked egg at the end to make a kind of mushroom scramble. They're both recipes to treasure.

When I got back home, I was keen to experiment. Would ordinarily available mushrooms cooked this way be as delicious as those I'd eaten in Azerbaijan? The answer is a firm yes. Serve either as a vegetable side with meat, or as a vegetarian main dish.   **SERVES 4 AS A SIDE DISH, 2 AS A MAIN COURSE**

½ pound white mushrooms, portobellos, or cremini, cut into bite-size pieces (about 3 cups)

About 1 tablespoon sunflower or extra-virgin olive oil

½ cup water

½ teaspoon sea salt, or to taste

2 tablespoons butter

Generous grinding of black pepper

About 2 tablespoons finely chopped fresh dill or scallions

Place the mushrooms in a wide heavy skillet or shallow pot over medium heat, add the oil, and shake the pan or stir the mushrooms to spread the oil around. Cook for about a minute, then add the water, raise the heat, and bring the water to a boil. Cover tightly and cook at a strong boil for about 5 minutes. Remove the lid, add the salt, and continue cooking at a medium boil to reduce the liquid. When the bottom of the pan is starting to show, add the butter and stir briefly, then cover and cook over very low heat for 5 to 10 minutes, until the mushrooms are very tender.

Taste for seasoning and adjust if needed. Add the pepper and serve hot or warm, topped with the chopped herbs.

NORTH OF YEREVAN, ARMENIA—*A treasure of wild-gathered mushrooms in the village of Melikgyugh, near snow-topped Mount Aragats.*

AZERI MUSHROOMS WITH EGG

This is a great breakfast or, served with soup and bread, light supper dish. Proceed as above until you have added the butter and reduced the heat. Let the mushrooms cook for a minute while you whisk 2 large eggs with ¼ teaspoon salt and the pepper. Raise the heat to medium, pull the mushrooms together into a pile, pour the eggs onto the mushrooms, and turn and stir to coat the mushrooms with egg and expose the egg to the hot pan. As soon as the egg has lightly set, turn the mushrooms out and serve sprinkled with the herbs and with ground sumac if you wish.

KURDISH-STYLE JERUSALEM ARTICHOKES

One of the most delicious foods I tasted while I was in Kurdistan was a simple-seeming combination: young cardoons (*kundeer* in Kurdish) enriched with a few eggs. I've looked long and hard for cardoons in North America. They are sometimes available, but I've never found the young tender ones that the Kurdish home cooks have in springtime. This recipe is the closest I can come to reproducing the enticing flavor and textures of the original.

Jerusalem artichokes, also known as sunchokes, have a flavor reminiscent of artichoke—and cardoons are a kind of wild artichoke relative. I love the way their sweetness and fragrance blend into the eggs. You can dress this up by adding fresh tarragon leaves to the whisked eggs, or by topping the finished dish with tarragon.

In Kurdistan, we ate the cardoon version with lavash and heaps of Kurdish Black Rice (page 216) or Red Rice (page 217). **SERVES 4 FOR BREAKFAST WITH FLATBREADS OR TOAST, 6 AS A SIDE DISH**

1 pound Jerusalem artichokes (sunchokes)

2 tablespoons sunflower or extra-virgin olive oil

½ teaspoon ground cumin

Pinch of turmeric

Pinch of cayenne (optional)

2 tablespoons minced scallions, shallots, or onion

1 teaspoon sea salt

About 1 cup water

3 large eggs

Generous grinding of black pepper

1 tablespoon fresh tarragon leaves, coarsely chopped (optional)

OPTIONAL ACCOMPANIMENTS

Herb Plate (page 23)

Flatbreads

1 lime or lemon, cut into wedges

Scrub the Jerusalem artichokes and trim off any tough or discolored areas. Thinly slice, then cut into ½-inch-wide strips. Set aside.

Place a wide cast-iron or other heavy skillet over medium-high heat. When it is hot, add the oil, cumin, turmeric, and cayenne, if using, then toss in the scallions, shallots, or onion and cook for several minutes, until softened. Add the chopped Jerusalem artichokes and ½ teaspoon of the salt and cook, stirring, for several minutes, until the artichokes are well coated with oil. Add about 1 cup water, or enough to give you a depth of ½ to ¾ inch in the pan, bring to a boil, cover, and cook for 5 minutes.

Meanwhile, whisk the eggs with the remaining ½ teaspoon salt, the pepper, and the tarragon, if using. Set aside.

At this point, the Jerusalem artichokes should be very tender; if they aren't, cover again (add a little water if the pan is dry) and give them another couple of minutes. Once they're done, if there's any remaining water in the pan, cook uncovered for a moment to let it boil off.

Lower the heat, pull the artichokes together into a mound, and pour the eggs over. Turn and stir to coat the artichokes with egg and move them around on the hot surface until the eggs are lightly set, about a minute.

Turn out onto a serving plate or individual plates and serve with any of the optional accompaniments you please. The lime or lemon wedges are not traditional, but I find a squeeze of juice is a great complement to the sweetness of the dish.

ROASTED JERUSALEM ARTICHOKES

If I have the time, I roast the artichokes in a 400°F oven rather than fry them. It makes them even sweeter. Thoroughly scrub them, but do not peel. Toss with a little sunflower or olive oil and spread out on a rimmed baking sheet. It will take 20 to 30 minutes to get them tender. Once they've cooled, chop them, peel and all, into bite-size pieces. You'll need only 1 teaspoon oil for cooking the spices and scallions, then add the artichokes and heat for a moment before mounding them and coating them with egg, as above.

PERSIAN GREENS FRITTATA

KUKU'YE SABZI

When you assemble all the greens and herbs called for in this recipe, it's hard to believe that the eggs will hold them. *Kuku* is best served at room temperature. It can be an appetizer, or an accompaniment to soup for a simple meal, or one of many dishes in a larger spread. It also makes excellent picnic fare.

Many of the quantities for the ingredients below are given as a range, because the format is flexible. For example, if you have plenty of beautiful fresh spinach, use the larger amount for that and less lettuce; or if you have good leeks, then use more leek and less scallion. Make sure the greens are thoroughly washed and that all tough stems are discarded. The walnuts can go into the eggs, but I prefer them scattered on top, so they toast and keep a crisp edge.

You will need a heavy ovenproof skillet that is 10 inches in diameter; I use a cast-iron skillet and then transfer the cut wedges of *kuku* to a platter to serve. **SERVES 6 AS A LIGHT MAIN COURSE, 8 TO 10 AS AN APPETIZER**

1 to 1½ cups finely chopped leeks

1 to 1½ packed cups finely chopped spinach

½ to 1 packed cup finely chopped lettuce

½ to 1 cup finely chopped scallions

½ cup chopped fresh flat-leaf parsley

½ cup chopped fresh coriander leaves and fine stems

¼ cup finely chopped fresh dill

Scant 1 tablespoon all-purpose flour or 2 tablespoons rice flour

2 tablespoons water

8 large or extra-large eggs or 10 medium eggs, preferably farm-fresh

About 2 tablespoons plain full-fat yogurt

1 teaspoon sea salt

Generous grinding of black pepper

About 1 tablespoon sunflower or extra-virgin olive oil

½ to ¾ cup coarsely chopped walnuts

Place a rack in the upper third of the oven and preheat the oven to 325°F.

Place all the chopped greens and herbs in a large bowl and mix together; set aside.

Stir together the flour and water in a small bowl to make a paste; set aside.

Break the eggs into another bowl and whisk. Add the yogurt, the flour and water paste, and the salt and pepper and stir.

Heat a 10-inch cast-iron or other heavy ovenproof skillet over medium heat. Add the oil and tilt to coat the bottom of the pan. Remove from the heat.

TBILISI, GEORGIA—
An herb and vegetable vendor holds a large bunch of flat-leaf parsley. Note the huge bunches of leaf celery, left, and the healthy vigor of the scallions and radishes.

Pour the egg mixture over the greens and stir, then pour the mixture into the hot pan. Sprinkle on the walnuts and bake for 45 minutes, or until the frittata is cooked through and set. Let stand for an hour or more to cool to room temperature before cutting into wedges and serving.

SPRINGTIME NETTLE FRITTATA

In rural Azerbaijan and Armenia, very little goes to waste, and people eat with the seasons. Springtime brings fresh greens—among them, tender nettles. Several people in Azerbaijan told me how wonderful a springtime *kuku* is made with young nettles, which are available in late March. The word for nettle in Azeri is *gigityhan*; people also refer to them by their Russian name, *krapeeva*. Substitute tender young nettle leaves for the spinach in the recipe above. Another early spring green you can use in place of the spinach is dandelion leaves.

But in winter, of course, there are no fresh greens. In all three Caucasus countries, during the summer and fall people gather a form of sorrel or dock, a tall plant, which is called *avalleikch* in Azeri. It's wound into coils or braids and dried so that it can be stored for a long time. Then in winter, the dried greens come into their own: They are soaked and rehydrated, finely chopped, and added to soups, stews, or *kuku*.

THE PRECOOKED BEANS HABIT

Some beans take a long time to cook, and that can take them out of play if you're in a rush. But if you have cooked them ahead they can help you get food on the table very quickly. I like to cook a large pot of beans, unseasoned, and freeze them, with their cooking liquid, in 2-cup batches. I love having a stash of beans in the freezer that I can quickly transform into soups or stews.

Wash about 3 cups dried beans, place them in a tall heavy pot with water to cover by 2 to 3 inches, and bring to a vigorous boil. (A pressure cooker is quicker, if you'd prefer to use that.) Partially cover, lower the heat to maintain a steady boil, and cook until the beans are tender. Navy beans take a generous hour; kidney beans and chickpeas can take 2 hours or more, depending on how dried out they are. Black-eyed peas take about an hour, and split peas and whole mung beans the same. Check the beans every once in a while to make sure the pot isn't running dry, and add more hot water as needed. Once the beans are fully cooked, you'll have about 8 cups soupy beans (about 6 cups beans and 1½ to 2 cups liquid). Leave them unseasoned until you want to use them.

Let the beans cool to room temperature before transferring them, with their cooking liquid, to well-sealed containers. Label and freeze.

Some of the recipes in this book call for plain cooked beans of some kind; you can, of course, start from scratch or substitute rinsed canned beans, but I urge you to get into the precooked beans habit. You'll be pleased with the ease of it all.

KERMAN, IRAN—*A display of nuts and spices at the great Kerman bazaar.*

Kurdish White Beans, shown with Kurdish Black Rice (page 216), supple store-bought lavash, fresh cheese, and Svanetian Salt (page 31).

KURDISH WHITE BEANS

SHLEY FASOULEH

There's a whole category of easy stews called *shley* in Iraqi Kurdistan. Navy beans are the main ingredient in this particular *shley*, but I've also had it made with split peas. Like most *shleys*, this is flavored with a basic *baharat* (spice mix) of turmeric and cumin and cooks in a sauce flavored with a little tomato.

I learned the dish in Iraqi Kurdistan from a woman named Nermi. Nermi includes a dried lime in her *shleys*. It gives a distinctive and pleasingly intense aroma to the beans, but it can be omitted if you wish.

I like to serve this as I had it in Kurdistan, with plenty of bread and a generous bowl of fresh herb sprigs and greens—for example, trimmed scallions, flat-leaf parsley, and arugula or watercress. The other element on the table that goes beautifully with the beans is a salty cheese such as feta. Invite your guests to crumble the cheese onto their *shley*, or to wrap it in a flatbread with some of the fresh greens and eat it as an accompaniment to the beans.   **MAKES 3½ TO 4 CUPS; SERVES 3 OR 4**

2 tablespoons sunflower or extra-virgin olive oil

¼ teaspoon turmeric

1 teaspoon ground cumin

3 cups cooked navy beans, with their liquid (see The Precooked Beans Habit, page 82), or about 2½ cups drained and rinsed canned beans plus ½ cup water

1 to 1½ cups water

½ cup canned crushed tomatoes

1 dried lime (optional)

1 teaspoon sea salt, or to taste

Place a heavy pot over medium heat, add the oil, and toss in the turmeric and cumin. Cook for a moment, until you see the turmeric fizzing a little in the oil. Add the beans, the water, and the tomatoes. If using the dried lime, prick it several times with the tip of a knife (be careful not to cut yourself, since it can ricochet if it's very hard) and add it to the pot. Stir to mix, bring to a boil (press on the dried lime so it takes in liquid and starts to sink, rather than floating on the surface), and boil hard for a few minutes.

Add the salt (only ½ teaspoon if the beans are already seasoned), lower the heat to maintain a strong simmer, partially cover, and cook for 30 minutes. Taste and adjust the seasoning if necessary.

Serve hot or at room temperature.

YAZIDI VILLAGE

The road from Yerevan climbs up out of the
Arax River Valley and then up some more,
leaving behind fertile lands with fruit trees and
settled villages and eventually reaching spare
upland rimmed with snow-topped mountains.

In summertime, it is home to Kurdish
shepherds who graze their herds of
sheep and goats in the high pastures.
In winter it's austere and frigid, with
snow and ice and wind.

On my first trip to Yerevan from
Tbilisi, I passed through this landscape
in a bus and regretted not being able
to stop, because the small villages with
their rare tufts of trees were beautiful
in the slanting light of an October
afternoon. Some days later, I traveled
back up the road again in a car driven
by Armin, a local driver. In the village
of Raya Taza, we stopped to ask about
the shepherds. "They came down from
the mountains last week; it's getting too
cold up there," we were told. And then
we were invited in for tea.

Raya Taza is a Yazidi village. The
people there are the descendants
of Yazidis who lived in Turkey until
1915–16, when they had to flee. The
genocide of the Armenians in that
period was part of an attack on non-
Turkish people, including the Assyrians
(who are Christian) and the Yazidis,
who follow their own distinctive faith
and rituals (for more on the Yazidis,
see Glossary).

The man who had invited us in was
the son of Gozeh, the family matriarch.
She sat in her large stone-walled
kitchen and told us her story. She
had married at fourteen and had had
twelve children. Her husband, Alixan,
had been in a nearby town when the
1988 Gyumri earthquake struck. He
was killed by a falling building, one
of hundreds of victims. Her youngest
daughter, who brought us tea, had
been married at thirteen.

Gozeh smiled with pleasure as she
showed me her treasure: jars and jars of
gleaming fruit stored under the stacked
folded bedding in the main room
(pictured opposite). The other time
she smiled was when I told her that I
had been to Lalish, the village of the
"mother church" of the Yazidis, in Iraqi
Kurdistan. "Ah, Lalish," she said, her
voice lifting.

RAYA TAZA, ARMENIA—*In a Kurdish-Yazidi household, the matriarch, Gozeh, stashes her jars of preserved fruits safely under the shelves that hold the family's sleeping pads and bedding.*

LOBIO WITH POMEGRANATE AND ONION

Kidney beans and other speckled red-and-pink and kidney-shaped beans seem to be a favorite in Georgia. They are especially important on the fasting days of the Georgian church, when meat and dairy are forbidden.

But *lobio* dishes do not need the excuse of religion. They're peasant stews, loaded with flavor, and usually eaten with Georgian corn breads. Special *lobio* restaurants outside Tbilisi, on the way to the ancient cathedral town of Mtskheta, serve customers at all times of year. It was at one of them that I first tasted *lobio* in 1989, on my first trip to Georgia. When I came back to the same place twenty-four years later with friends, a lot had changed. Georgia was an independent country; people felt freer, even if the economy was precarious; and there was a pride in being Georgian that could be openly expressed at last. But some things seemed the same, including the deeply satisfying *lobio* that we ate there.

Serve the beans with bread or Georgian Polenta (page 234) along with fresh herbs. Put out *ajika* (page 40 or 42) if you have it, or Svanetian Salt (page 31) as condiments. **SERVES 4 AS A MAIN COURSE, 6 TO 8 AS A SIDE DISH**

4 cups cooked kidney beans, with their liquid (see The Precooked Beans Habit, page 82), plus 1 cup water, or 4 cups rinsed canned kidney beans plus 1½ cups water

2 bay leaves

¼ cup sunflower or extra-virgin olive oil

1½ cups chopped onions

1 red bell pepper, cored, seeded, and chopped (optional)

5 or 6 garlic cloves, minced

1 tablespoon powdered dried red chiles or 1 teaspoon cayenne

2 tablespoons Georgian Spice Blend (page 28)

2 tablespoons tomato paste

2 tablespoons pomegranate molasses

¼ cup dry red wine (optional; see Note)

2 teaspoons sea salt, or to taste

Fresh flat-leaf parsley, coriander, or tarragon sprigs

Place the cooked beans and water in a pot with the bay leaves and bring to a boil, then reduce the heat to low.

Heat the oil in a wide cast-iron or other heavy skillet. Add the onions and pepper, if using, and cook for 5 minutes. Add the garlic and cook until the onions are translucent. Add the chiles, spice blend, and tomato paste and cook for a few minutes.

TBILISI, GEORGIA—*Shelling pink kidney beans at the market.*

Add 1 cup of the beans and their liquid to the skillet and bring to a boil, then add the contents of the skillet back to the pot of beans. Add the pomegranate molasses, wine, if using, and salt and simmer for 5 to 10 minutes.

Serve garnished with the fresh herbs.

NOTE: I often add a splash of dry red wine to this and other bean dishes, though I have not seen Georgian cooks do it. The acidity and tannins bring out a meatiness in the beans, as does the pomegranate molasses.

SOUP PARADISE

THE LINE BETWEEN SOUPS AND STEWS
is hard to draw in the Persian culinary world,
where soups are often served as a main course,
accompanied by cheese, bread, and generous
plates of fresh herbs. And from the easy yogurt
soups of the Caucasus to the hearty Persian
soups called *ash*, soups here are outstanding.

The yogurt-based soups are delicious,
sometimes loaded with fresh herbs (see Herbed
Yogurt Soup, page 94, one of my favorites),
sometimes thickened with potato and other
vegetables (see Potato and Pumpkin Soup, page
93). There are also soups made with several
kinds of beans or lentils and brightened with
finely chopped greens. The most elaborate

versions of this kind of soup are the thick green Persian *ash* dishes (see Pomegranate Ash with Meatballs, page 107, for example). Kurdish *palpina*, a soup of lentils and purslane (see page 99), is a simpler take on the *ash* idea.

And soup can also be a simple broth bathing a hearty centerpiece, as it is with the Azeri *kofta* (meatball) soups, which are really a main course disguised as a soup. I've included two versions, one from Tabriz, in Iran (see page 100), and the other from the Caucasus foothills in Azerbaijan (see page 102).

Cooks in the region often use tart fruits in soups, most often as a flavoring element to give acidity (see Farmstead Winter Soup, page 110) and occasionally as an appealing main ingredient (as in Dried Apricot Soup with Wheat Berries, page 97).

Previous pages: HALABJA, KURDISTAN—*As in Persian tradition, living spaces in Kurdistan are thickly carpeted with several layers of rugs. Except in the modern houses of wealthier families, everything takes place on the floor, including eating. A sofreh, usually a large plastic sheet on which bowls and plates of food are placed, is set out on the rug. It's an easy, convivial way to eat, and there's no clutter of table and chairs taking up space in the living area.*

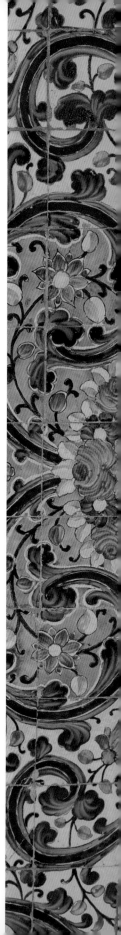

POTATO AND PUMPKIN SOUP

JAJUK

All through the Persian culinary region, yogurt and fresh cheese play an important role in daily meals. Here, in a simple country version of *jajuk*—the Armenian name for yogurt soup—yogurt is stirred into a smooth puree of cooked potato and pumpkin (or winter squash, or zucchini), seasoned with a little dried red chile, and finished with fresh herbs. This makes a great lunch or light supper with filled flatbreads, such as *khachapuri* (page 251) or Half-Moon Hand Pies (page 245), perhaps with a fresh salad on the side. Or serve it before a main course of lamb or turkey kebabs. **SERVES 4 TO 6**

2 cups large cubes unpeeled pumpkin or winter squash, or substitute 3 cups chopped zucchini

2 medium potatoes, peeled and coarsely chopped (2½ to 3 cups)

1 teaspoon sea salt, or to taste

About ¼ teaspoon powdered dried red chiles or cayenne

½ cup finely chopped fresh flat-leaf parsley, dill, or mint, or substitute 2 teaspoons dried mint

1 cup plain full-fat yogurt, or as needed

Place the pumpkin or other squash and the potatoes in a pot, add about an inch of water, cover, and bring to a boil. Lower the heat to maintain a medium boil and cook until the vegetables are very soft, about 25 minutes for pumpkin and winter squash, less for zucchini.

Drain, reserve the liquid, and set aside to cool for 30 minutes.

Remove and discard the skin from the pumpkin or winter squash. Transfer the pumpkin or squash and potatoes to a food processor and process to a smooth slurry. Transfer to a bowl, add the salt, chiles or cayenne, and herbs and stir. Add the yogurt and stir to blend well. The texture will be thick yet pourable; thin it with a little of the cooking liquid or extra yogurt if you wish. Taste and adjust the seasoning if needed. Serve at room temperature.

NOTE: If you are making this in the summer and using zucchini, you might want to serve it chilled: Cover and refrigerate for an hour or so. If any liquid rises to the surface as it chills, just stir it back in before serving.

HERBED YOGURT SOUP

DOVGA PHOTOGRAPH ON PAGE 96

This soup was one of the most surprising dishes I came upon in my travels in the Caucasus. It was so simple and so perfect. I first had it in the old town of Sheki in northwestern Azerbaijan, made by a skilled home cook named Chamala. You'll need to allow forty-five minutes to an hour for it to cook.

You can serve the soup warm or at room temperature. In the heat of summer, it is often served chilled. Leftovers have even better flavor. They always thicken, so just thin the leftover soup with a little water and then adjust the seasoning if necessary. **SERVES 6 TO 8**

1 large or medium egg

½ cup Arborio or other short-grain rice, washed and drained

2 tablespoons all-purpose flour or 3 tablespoons rice flour

4 cups (32 ounces) plain full-fat yogurt

3 cups water

2 teaspoons sea salt, or to taste

4 cups finely chopped fresh herbs, ideally 1 cup each mint, coriander, flat-leaf parsley, and basil or watercress

About 2 teaspoons ground cassia (cinnamon)

Place the egg, rice, and flour in a wide heavy pot and whisk together. Add the yogurt, turn the heat to medium, and whisk until smooth. Add the water and whisk to incorporate it. Place a stainless steel spoon in the bottom of the pot and leave it there during the cooking. (This is a trick I learned from Chamala to prevent the mixture from sticking, and it works.) Bring to a simmer and cook until the rice is tender, about 45 minutes. The soup will have thickened and reduced a little.

Stir in the salt and chopped herbs. Let cook for another couple of minutes, until the herbs have softened a little, and remove from the heat. Taste and adjust the seasoning if necessary.

Transfer to a serving bowl or to individual bowls. Garnish the soup with cassia; Chamala sprinkled a thick line of cassia across the serving bowl of soup, then stirred it in once she had brought it to the table. The cassia pulls all the flavors together in a subtle, surprising way.

SULAYMANIYAH, KURDISTAN—*A dairy shop in the bazaar sells yogurt, milk, and the yogurt drink* ayran *(see the recipe on page 309); dried disks of the fermented whey product* kashk *(see Glossary); fresh cheeses and butter; and eggs.*

ARMENIAN YOGURT SOUP

Armenians make a chilled yogurt soup that is quickly assembled on a hot day: Dilute plain full-fat yogurt with an equal volume of cold water. Season with a little salt, and add some or all of the following: chopped hard-boiled eggs, chopped cucumber, minced scallions, and/or coriander, parsley, and dill leaves. Serve immediately, with plenty of bread. And put out more of all of the flavorings you used, along with black pepper, so guests can dress their soup as they wish.

DRIED APRICOT SOUP WITH WHEAT BERRIES

This warming country soup is from Javakheti in southern Georgia, where the majority population is Armenian. It's made with tart dried apricots, emmer wheat, onion, potato (optional), and herbs. I love the way the flavors of cooked wheat and dried apricot dance together. A dollop of thick yogurt or a sprinkling of crumbled feta intensifies the tart-sweetness of the broth. **SERVES 6**

3 tablespoons sunflower or extra-virgin olive oil

1 cup thinly sliced onions or shallots

1 cup emmer wheat berries, washed well and drained

About 5 cups water or unsalted chicken broth; or 6 to 7 cups if using potatoes

1½ cups chopped tart dried apricots

1½ pounds waxy potatoes (about 4 medium), peeled and chopped into 1-inch cubes (optional)

1 teaspoon dried thyme

1 teaspoon dried mint, or to taste

1 to 2 teaspoons sea salt, to taste

Freshly ground black pepper

About ½ cup chopped mixed fresh herbs, such as tarragon, chervil, mint, basil, and lovage—use at least two

OPTIONAL ACCOMPANIMENTS

1 cup plain thick yogurt (see Glossary) or ½ pound feta or aged goat cheese

Flatbreads or toast

Place a wide heavy pot over medium-high heat. Add the oil, and when it's hot, add the onions or shallots. Lower the heat to medium and cook, stirring occasionally, until the onions are translucent. Add the wheat berries and stir to coat with oil, then add 5 cups water or broth and bring to a boil. Add the dried apricots, lower the heat to maintain a strong simmer, and cook until the emmer is tender and the apricots have softened, about 30 minutes.

If using potatoes, add them along with another 1 to 2 cups water or broth, or as necessary to cover the potatoes. Add the thyme, mint, and 1 teaspoon salt, bring back to a boil, and cook until the potatoes are tender, 10 to 15 minutes. Taste and adjust the seasoning if necessary.

Ladle into bowls, grind on black pepper, and top each serving with a tablespoon or so of the chopped herbs. Serve hot, with one or both of the optional accompaniments if you like.

Herbed Yogurt Soup (left; page 94) and
Dried Apricot Soup with Wheat Berries (right).

ROSE HIP SOUP

In northern Armenia, there's a close cousin of this soup, called *masrabur*, made with rose hip liquid, and it's one of the most hauntingly delicious soups I know. If you can buy organic rose hips at a farmers' market or can gather them in the fall, then do. Boil them in water to cover until tender, then press the liquid through a sieve or food mill and discard the solids. Use the tart bright-tasting liquid as a base for this soup (store any extra in the freezer; see Note). Dilute 3 cups of it with an equal amount of water, bring to a boil in a large saucepan, and add 1 teaspoon salt and ½ cup emmer wheat berries. Boil until the berries are starting to soften. Add 1½ cups chopped dried apricots and 1 cup chopped onion and cook at a low boil until the wheat berries are tender, about 30 minutes. Stir in 2 teaspoons dried mint and another 1 teaspoon salt, then whisk in ½ cup sifted flour (or, more traditionally, small scraps of dried flatbread) and cook for 5 minutes more to thicken. Serve hot or at room temperature, with cheese, fresh herbs, and bread.

NOTE: Rose hip liquid is also used by Armenian cooks to flavor the water for cooking dolmas (stuffed vegetables), especially stuffed cabbage leaves (see page 124).

Left: **TBILISI, GEORGIA**—*Wild-gathered autumn bounty at a market. At top are rose hips, and below, sea buckthorn berries (see Glossary).*

Right: **BAKU, AZERBAIJAN**—*A snack bar by the old city wall in central Baku sells* pide, *the Azeri (and Turkish) word for flatbread topped with ground meat or other flavors, along with fresh-made juices and smoothies.*

PURSLANE SOUP

PALPINA

Springtime in Kurdistan means *palpina,* a thick soup of lentils (*nisik* in Kurdish) and chopped purslane. I love it.

Purslane is a wild green with small, thick, succulent leaves and reddish stems (see Glossary). It's often treated as a weed in North America, but it's a much-valued vegetable from Iran to the Caucasus, as well as in the eastern Mediterranean region, where it's used raw in salads. Some farmers are starting to cultivate it in North America, so it should soon become easier to find.

Though it's not traditional, I like to drizzle a little Mint Oil (page 19) or olive oil over each serving. **SERVES 8**

1 cup brown lentils, rinsed and picked over

½ cup minced onion

½ cup Arborio or other short-grain rice, washed and drained

7 to 8 cups water or unsalted light chicken or vegetable broth, or as needed

3 tablespoons tomato paste

1 teaspoon ground cumin

¼ teaspoon turmeric

2 to 3 teaspoons sea salt, to taste

3½ packed cups finely chopped purslane leaves and stems

Freshly ground black pepper

ACCOMPANIMENTS

Flatbreads

Fresh goat's- or sheep's-milk cheese

A generous Herb Plate (page 23): tarragon, chervil, mint, lovage, and scallion greens (use two or more)

Place the lentils, onion, and rice in a large pot, add 7 cups of water or broth, and bring to a vigorous boil. Skim off any foam, cover, reduce the heat to maintain a low boil, and cook until the lentils are tender, 35 to 45 minutes; add more water or broth if needed.

Stir in the tomato paste, cumin, turmeric, and 2 teaspoons salt, then add the purslane and stir thoroughly. Cook until the purslane is very soft and flavors have blended, about 30 minutes; add more liquid if the soup gets too thick. Taste and adjust the seasoning if needed. Ladle into individual bowls and sprinkle with black pepper. Put out the flatbreads, cheese, and herb plate, and invite your guests to sprinkle a little cheese onto their soup.

TABRIZ MEATBALL SOUP

KOFTA TABRIZI

I'd read about the huge meatballs of Tabriz, so as soon as I arrived there, I hustled out to a local restaurant in search of *kofta tabrizi*. The meatball that came in a light tomato broth was about three inches across. It was tender, studded with rice and tart barberries, and stuffed with more barberries, as well as sour plums and hard-cooked eggs. The tart fruits intensified the rich flavor of the meat. Each mouthful was a complex pleasure. **SERVES 8**

MEATBALLS

3 medium onions, coarsely chopped

2 pounds ground lamb or beef (ideally 25% fat)

1 tablespoon dried mint

½ teaspoon ground cassia (cinnamon)

2 teaspoons sea salt

1 teaspoon freshly ground black pepper

1 cup jasmine or other medium- or short-grain rice, washed and drained

1¼ cups dried barberries (see Glossary), soaked for 30 minutes in cold water and drained

4 hard-boiled eggs, peeled and coarsely chopped

10 dried sour plums or apricots, well washed (if the plums or apricots are very dried out, soak in warm water for 30 minutes and drain)

BROTH

1 medium onion

2 tablespoons sunflower or extra-virgin olive oil

¼ teaspoon turmeric

3 medium tomatoes, peeled and minced

About 4 cups water

2 teaspoons sea salt, or to taste

Generous grinding of black pepper

½ cup chopped fresh flat-leaf parsley (optional)

To make the meatballs, put the onions in a food processor and process, pulsing, to a soft mush. Add the meat, dried mint, cassia, salt, and pepper and process to blend well. Turn out into a bowl, add the rice and 1 cup of the barberries, and mix and knead with your hands, squeezing the mixture through your fingers and blending well. Cover and refrigerate for at least an hour, or overnight.

To shape the meatballs, divide both the meat and the hard-cooked eggs into 10 equal portions. Using wet hands, shape one portion of meat into a firm ball. Hold the ball in one hand and use a spoon to scoop out a portion of one side. Set the scooped meat aside and press your thumb into the center of the ball to make a rounded hollow. Place 1 plum or apricot, 1 teaspoon barberries, and one portion of hard-cooked egg in the hollow. Replace the meat you removed, pressing it into

Left: **SHEKI, AZERBAIJAN**—*Autumn market combo: fresh yogurt, barberries, and ripe pears.*

Right: **LAHICH, AZERBAIJAN**—*A few* kofta *in Jairan's kitchen (see Lahich-Style Kofta Soup, page 102), ready to be cooked. The word* kofta—*sometimes transcribed* kufta—*comes from the Persian word for "pounded," because the meat used for the meatballs is ground or pounded almost to a paste.*

place, and shape the ball again between your wet palms, pressing firmly so it holds together. Place on a lightly oiled plate or small baking sheet. Repeat with the remaining meat and filling. Cover the meatballs and refrigerate. The meatballs can be made up to 2 days ahead.

To make the broth, about an hour or so before serving, grate the onion on a box grater.

Place a wide heavy pot over medium heat and add the oil, then add the turmeric and onion and cook, stirring until the onion is translucent. Add the tomatoes, lower the heat, and simmer for a few minutes. Add the water. The liquid should be about 3 inches deep; add more water if necessary. Bring to a boil and add the salt and pepper.

Slip the meatballs into the boiling soup. Bring back to a boil, then lower the heat to maintain a strong simmer, partially cover, and cook, shaking the pot occasionally to move the meatballs around, for 40 minutes, or until the meatballs are cooked through.

Serve the meatballs bathed in the broth, and sprinkle on the parsley if you wish.

LAHICH-STYLE KOFTA SOUP

KUFTA BOZBASH

I learned this version of Azeri *kofta* from a woman named Jairan, in Lahich. She prefers not to use turmeric, but many people do use it. I like the color it gives. The soup is also colored and flavored by a little tomato, a nice acid balance to the meat. The meatballs are flavored with herbs (dried mint in winter or fresh coriander in warmer months) and stuffed with dried apricots.

   With chickpeas and potatoes giving it body, the soup is heartier than the broth I had with *kofta* in Tabriz, making the dish a filling meal-in-one. Any leftovers are delicious, reheated gently.   **SERVES 8 TO 10**

MEATBALLS

3 medium onions, coarsely chopped

2 pounds ground lamb or beef
   (20 to 25% fat)

1 teaspoon ground ginger

½ teaspoon ground cassia (cinnamon)

2 teaspoons sea salt

1 teaspoon freshly ground black pepper

1 cup jasmine or other medium- or
   short-grain rice, washed and drained

2 teaspoons dried mint or ½ cup minced
   fresh coriander

10 dried apricots, well washed (if the
   apricots are very dried out, soak in warm
   water for 30 minutes and drain)

SOUP

1 medium onion

2 tablespoons sunflower or extra-virgin
   olive oil

¼ teaspoon turmeric

1 large or 2 small Roma (plum) or other
   fleshy tomatoes, peeled and minced

4 cups water

1 cup cooked or canned chickpeas
   (see The Precooked Beans Habit,
   page 82)

10 medium waxy potatoes
   (about 2 pounds), peeled and halved,
   or 4 or 5 larger potatoes, peeled and
   cut into large cubes

2 teaspoons sea salt, or to taste

Generous grinding of black pepper

1 to 2 teaspoons dried mint (optional)

To make the meatballs, put the onions in a food processor and process, pulsing, to a soft mush. Add the meat, ginger, cassia, salt, and pepper and process to blend well. Turn out into a bowl, add the rice and mint or coriander, and mix and knead with your hands, squeezing the mixture through your fingers. You want a very even texture. Cover and refrigerate for at least 1 hour, preferably 6 hours, before using.

   To make the soup, about an hour and a half before serving, grate the onion on a box grater.

Heat the oil in a wide heavy pot over medium heat. Toss in the turmeric and onion, stir in the tomatoes, lower the heat to medium-low, and cook for 2 to 3 minutes. Add the water and bring to a boil, then lower the heat to maintain a steady simmer.

If using chickpeas you cooked, rub them between your palms to loosen their outer skins; discard the skins. If using canned chickpeas, rinse them in several changes of water. Add the chickpeas to the pot and cook for 20 minutes.

Meanwhile, shape the meatballs: Divide the meat mixture into 10 equal portions. Wet your hands, pick up one portion, and shape it into a firm ball. Holding the ball in one hand, make a hole in it with the index finger of your other hand and push an apricot into the hole. Smooth the meat back over the hole to seal it well and shape and firm the ball again. Set aside on a lightly oiled plate (see photo, page 101). Repeat with the remaining meat and apricots.

Add the meatballs, potatoes, salt, and pepper to the broth and bring to a steady low boil. Partially cover the pot and cook for 30 minutes, or until the meatballs are cooked through. Taste the soup and adjust the seasoning if necessary.

Divide the meatballs and soup among individual bowls and sprinkle on the dried mint if you wish. Serve hot.

LAHICH, AZERBAIJAN—
A shepherd on his cell phone in the big Caucasus-foothills landscape outside Lahich (see Feasting in a Garden of Eden, page 172). His flock of sheep and goats drifted along the hillside, while his dog kept a close eye on them.

BETWEEN SHIRAZ AND YAZD IN SOUTHERN IRAN—*Heading off to school, at age fourteen, covered in black from head to toe.*

WOMEN OF IRAN

When I stayed with a family on a farm three hours' drive east of Shiraz, I watched the two daughters, both lively and intelligent, get ready for school in the morning. Niloufer, eleven, wore pants, a long manteau top, and a kind of pink wimple of stretchy knit material that framed her face and covered her hair and neck completely. Over that she put on a looser head covering, a kind of scarf. The older daughter, aged fourteen, was entirely in black, as the school required of girls her age: pants, manteau, and scarf over the hair, and, on top of all that, a black chador to the ground. Her liveliness was drowned in all the black.

As a female visitor in Iran, I had to follow the rules and cover my head, my neck, and my arms and legs. And in any case, I didn't want to give offense. Or that's how I felt at first. But once I realized that most people disliked the rules, though I still complied, I was no longer so worried about offending custom. I was instead aware that I could be chided for having my scarf tied so ineptly that too much hair was exposed.

Even unworried, I found myself after my first few days in Iran taking on the habits of the women there: You reach up and feel the top of your head to check whether your scarf has slipped back. Then you run your fingers along the edge of the scarf, where it meets your face, to check that no hair has strayed forward and that the edges are even. It becomes a tic, endlessly repeated. A time lapse of women on a bus or at a restaurant or in a car—or in a classroom, I suppose, too—would show a pattern of check, adjust, recheck, readjust, going on all over the female landscape.

Extraordinary. And taken for granted by the women of Iran. They have to take it for granted, or it would surely drive them around the bend. In any case, they have more important things to worry about: They are doctors and teachers and filmmakers, mothers and grandmothers, sweepers and cooks, secretaries and managers.

POMEGRANATE ASH WITH MEATBALLS

ASH-E-ANAR

Ash is at the heart of Persian home cooking, a category of slow-cooked sustaining soups that are welcoming, subtle, and rewarding for cooks and eaters alike. The soups are also flexible: You can make substitutions, as long as they stay within the feel of the original.

This *ash* is an inviting blend of legumes and rice, flavored with little lamb meatballs. A crowd-pleaser. Like most *ash* recipes, this one looks long, but please don't be dismayed. Yes, it takes some time to cook, but it's a carefree kind of thing to make: Start it on a weekend afternoon and then set it aside until shortly before you want to serve it. Or make it a day ahead, and reheat it to serve. Just make sure it comes to the table hot. **SERVES 6**

¼ cup sunflower or extra-virgin olive oil

1 onion, sliced

½ teaspoon ground cassia (cinnamon)

½ teaspoon turmeric

¾ cup short-grain rice or broken jasmine or basmati rice (see Note), washed and drained

¾ cup dried split peas, soaked in water for an hour (or as long as 12 hours) and drained

8 to 10 cups water, or as needed

¼ pound scallions, trimmed and finely chopped

2 bunches flat-leaf parsley, leaves and tender stems, finely chopped (about 2 cups)

2 bunches coriander, leaves and stems, finely chopped (about 2 cups)

1 bunch mint, leaves finely chopped (about 1 cup)

1½ tablespoons sea salt, or to taste

4 to 6 tablespoons pomegranate molasses, to taste

MEATBALLS

1 onion, grated

½ pound ground lamb

1 teaspoon sea salt

¼ teaspoon freshly ground black pepper

TOPPINGS

About ¼ cup sunflower or extra-virgin olive oil

2 tablespoons dried mint

1 cup thinly sliced onion

continued

To make the soup, place the oil in a large heavy pot over medium-high heat, toss in the onion, cassia, and turmeric, and cook until the onion is translucent, 4 to 5 minutes. Add the rice, drained split peas, and 8 cups water, raise the heat, and bring to a boil, then lower the heat to maintain a strong simmer and cook for 1 to 1½ hours, or until the split peas are tender.

While the soup is cooking, make the meatball mixture: Mix the onion thoroughly with the lamb. Mix in the salt and pepper. Set aside, covered, in the refrigerator.

Add the scallions, parsley, coriander, and mint to the soup and simmer for 30 minutes. Add another cup or two of water to thin it, as you wish, and bring back to a strong simmer. Add the salt and 4 tablespoons pomegranate molasses and stir. Taste and add a little more pomegranate molasses if you like.

Make the meatballs about 15 minutes before you want to serve: Scoop up about a heaped teaspoon of the meat mixture for each and roll it into a ball between your wet palms, then drop it into the soup. Let the soup continue to simmer while you make the toppings.

Pour 2 tablespoons of the oil into a small skillet and heat over medium-high heat. Toss in the dried mint and immediately remove from the heat; it will fizz up a little. Set aside in a small bowl.

Heat the remaining 2 tablespoons oil in the skillet over high or medium-high heat, add the sliced onion, and fry until starting to brown and crisp, about 6 minutes. Set aside on a plate.

Ladle the hot soup into individual bowls, making sure to serve several meatballs in each, and top with a drizzle of mint oil, and with a sprinkling of fried onions if you wish.

NOTE: Short-grain rice or broken rice will break down more easily than long-grain rice as it cooks, and the starch from the rice helps thicken the soup.

SHEKI, AZERBAIJAN—*A market vendor stacking her fresh beans.*

FARMSTEAD WINTER SOUP

ASH-E-ABGOUREH

I spent a couple of days at a small farm run by Afsar and her husband, Abbas, in a fertile valley northeast of Shiraz. Afsar's storage room was loaded with treasures: jars of verjuice and pomegranate molasses, as well as distilled flower essences, fruit jams, raisins, dried mint and other herbs, and more.

Verjuice, from the French *verjus,* is the tart-tasting juice from unripe grapes. The vines are pruned partway through the growing season to ensure better grapes on the bunches that remain. The unripe grapes on the prunings don't go to waste—they are pressed for their juice. It's a common practice, not just in wine-producing countries such as France, but also in Iran. If you don't have verjuice, you can substitute wine vinegar or lemon juice to give the distinctive tart accent that characterizes this satisfying soup.

You can use precooked beans (see The Precooked Beans Habit, page 82) or drained and rinsed canned beans, or you can start from scratch.

Although Afsar made her *ash* without meat, you can include a little ground meat as a topping (*gheimeh* in Persian) if you wish, as set out below. She didn't use any fresh greens either, to show me the way she makes it in winter. If you do have fresh greens such as spinach or kale, finely chop about 4 cups and add them once the beans are cooked. **SERVES 4 TO 6**

SOUP

½ cup dried whole mung beans or black-eyed peas, or about 1½ cups cooked beans, with their cooking liquid, or 2 cups canned

1 cup dried split peas, or 2½ to 3 cups cooked split peas, with some of their cooking liquid, or 3 cups canned

8 cups water, or as needed; or about 3 cups if starting with cooked or canned beans

½ cup short-grain or broken rice, washed and drained

¼ cup butter-ghee or sunflower oil

½ cup minced onion

3 tablespoons dried mint

2 teaspoons sea salt, or to taste

2 to 3 tablespoons verjuice, or substitute white wine vinegar or fresh lemon juice

Generous grinding of black pepper

OPTIONAL MEAT TOPPING

2 tablespoons sunflower or vegetable oil

1 cup minced onion

¼ pound (½ packed cup) ground lamb or beef

2 tablespoons split peas, washed and drained

About 1½ cups water

½ teaspoon sea salt

Generous grinding of black pepper

About 1 tablespoon tomato paste

If you're starting with dried beans and peas, rinse them and place in a large pot with 8 cups water, or enough to cover by 2 inches or so. Bring to a boil, add the rice, partially cover, and cook at a strong boil until the beans are softened, 1 to 1½ hours; check occasionally to make sure the pan is not running dry and top up with another cup or two of water if needed.

Meanwhile, if you want to include the meat topping, heat the oil in a medium skillet over medium-high heat, toss in the onion, and cook until translucent, about 4 minutes. Add the meat and split peas and cook, stirring, until all the meat has changed color. Add enough water to cover by ½ inch and simmer, partially covered, for 15 minutes, or until the split peas have softened; if the pan starts to run dry, add a little more water. Add the salt, pepper, and 1 tablespoon tomato paste and stir in, then cook over low heat for another 10 minutes or so. Taste and add a little more tomato paste if you wish. The mixture should be fairly dry. Transfer to a small bowl. The topping is served at room temperature.

If using precooked or canned beans, place in a pot with about 3 cups water and the rice and bring to a boil. Simmer, partly covered, for 15 minutes.

To prepare the flavorings, heat a heavy wide skillet over medium-high heat, add 1 tablespoon of the ghee or oil, toss in the onion, and cook, stirring, until it is just translucent, about 4 minutes. Add the onion to the beans and stir.

Put the skillet back on the heat, add the remaining 3 tablespoons ghee or oil, and toss in the dried mint. Stir briefly and add to the beans, along with the salt. Stir in 2 tablespoons verjuice or vinegar or lemon juice; taste and add more tartness if you wish. (The soup and topping can be prepared ahead to this point and set aside until just before you wish to serve. Refrigerate if the wait will be longer than 2 hours.)

Bring the soup back to a boil (add extra water to thin it if needed), then lower the heat and simmer for a few minutes. Taste and adjust the seasoning and tartness if you wish. Stir in the black pepper.

To serve, ladle the soup into individual bowls and sprinkle on some topping, if using.

NEW YEAR'S BEAN SOUP

ASH-E-RESHTEH

Cooks all over Iran make *ash-e-reshteh,* a slow-simmered dish of beans, greens, and fresh noodles—*reshteh*—topped with mint oil and other flavors. It's one of the dishes everyone eats at Nou-Roz (see Zoroaster's Legacy, page 36).

I include instructions for making the noodles, but you can substitute dried pasta. Traditionally the noodles are cooked with the beans, but I find it easier to cook them separately in boiling water until nearly done, then add them to the soup. **SERVES 6**

NOODLES (or substitute ½ pound dried linguine)

2½ cups all-purpose flour, plus extra for surfaces

1 teaspoon sea salt, plus extra for boiling

About 1 cup water

SOUP

1 cup mixed dried beans and lentils, such as ½ cup navy beans or black-eyed peas, ¼ cup fava beans, and ¼ cup lentils

6 cups water, or as needed

½ pound spinach, finely chopped (4 packed cups)

1 cup packed chopped fresh flat-leaf parsley

½ cup finely chopped fresh scallion greens or Chinese chives

1 tablespoon sea salt, or to taste

½ teaspoon freshly ground black pepper

1 tablespoon Mint Oil (page 19)

TOPPINGS

¼ cup sunflower or extra-virgin olive oil

¼ teaspoon turmeric

1 cup sliced onion

About ½ cup *kashk* (see Note and Glossary) or thick sour cream (optional)

2 tablespoons Mint Oil (page 19)

About ½ cup plain thick yogurt (see Glossary; optional)

2 tablespoons Saffron Water (page 27; optional)

If making fresh noodles, place the flour and salt in a bowl, add 1 cup water, and stir until a dough forms. Alternatively, place the flour and salt in a food processor, add the water, and pulse until a dough forms. Turn the dough out onto a well-floured surface and knead until smooth and elastic, incorporating flour as necessary so that it is firm and no longer sticky, 3 to 4 minutes. Set aside, covered with plastic wrap, to rest for at least an hour.

Rinse the beans and lentils in several changes of water and put them in a heavy pot with the water. Bring to a vigorous boil, then lower the heat to maintain a medium boil and cook, partially covered, for 1 hour, or until nearly tender.

Meanwhile, if making fresh noodles, cut the dough into quarters. Place one piece on a floured surface, flatten it with lightly floured hands, and use a rolling pin to roll it out to a thin (less than ¼-inch-thick) rectangle or oval. Dust both sides of the dough with flour, cut it into long strips less than ¼ inch wide, and hang over the back of a chair. Repeat with the remaining dough.

(If using dried *kashk*, soak it now; see Note.)

Add the spinach, herbs, salt, and pepper to the beans and stir. Add more water if necessary; you want a very soupy texture. Bring back to a boil, then reduce the heat to very low and simmer for 15 minutes.

Make the onion topping: Heat the oil in a large heavy skillet over medium-high heat. Toss in the turmeric and the sliced onion and cook over medium heat, stirring occasionally, until the onion is translucent and starting to crisp at the edges. Lift out of the oil with a slotted spoon and set aside.

About 20 minutes before serving, bring a large pot of water to a rolling boil. Add 2 tablespoons salt, bring back to a boil, and toss in the fresh noodles or dried pasta. Cook until just barely cooked through, about 4 minutes for fresh noodles or about 12 minutes for dried. Drain the noodles, add to the pot of beans and greens, folding them in gently, and remove from the heat.

Add the tablespoon of mint oil to the pot of beans. Serve the soup hot in large deep bowls. Stir about 1 tablespoon *kashk* or sour cream into each serving, if using, top with some of the reserved fried onions, and drizzle on about a teaspoon of mint oil. If using the yogurt and saffron water, dollop about 1 tablespoon yogurt onto each serving and top with a drizzle of saffron water. Serve immediately.

NOTE ON KASHK: If using disks or balls of dried *kashk*, measure out about ¼ cup of them and soak in ½ cup lukewarm water for 30 minutes or so. Once they have softened completely, whiz the mixture briefly in a blender. If using *kashk* paste, put ⅓ cup paste in a small bowl, add 2 tablespoons water, and whisk or stir until smooth.

STUFFED VEGETABLES AND DUMPLINGS

STUFFED VEGETABLES AND LEAVES ARE A tradition in the Caucasus and Kurdistan. They're usually known in the West by the Turkish and Arabic name *dolma*. In restaurants and for feasts, the filling is often meat-based, whereas home cooks are more likely to use herbs and aromatics held together with rice or ground nuts or legumes.

The other thing to know about dolmas is that people disagree about where the idea originated. It's one of the footballs that gets kicked around when there are culinary nationalists arguing about whose heritage is richer or older or better. Whatever their origins, dolmas are a good way to feed a crowd.

The easiest vegetables to stuff, of course, are those that make good containers: bell peppers, for example, with their tops cut off and seeds and membranes stripped out. In Armenia, a larger vegetable container—pumpkin—is stuffed with rice, nuts, and dried fruit (see page 120). The cabbage, workhorse of the garden and the larder, comes into its own: its leaves make ideal wrappers for meat fillings, and for vegetarian ones too, especially in winter, when other vegetables are not easily available. See Cabbage Dolmas, page 122, and Cabbage Rolls Stuffed with Beans and Tart Fruit, page 124.

It's a short step from using vegetables as containers to using dough to enclose flavorful fillings of meat or vegetables or cheese. Dumplings may be large, like the succulent topknot-shaped dumplings the Georgians call *khinkali* (see page 130), or small, like Azeri *jirs* (see page 133). They're always welcome, and such a pleasure to eat.

Previous pages: **SHEKI, AZERBAIJAN**—*Homemade jirs, or tiny pleated dumplings, shaped in Matanet's kitchen, where I learned to make them (see Mini Dumplings, page 133).*

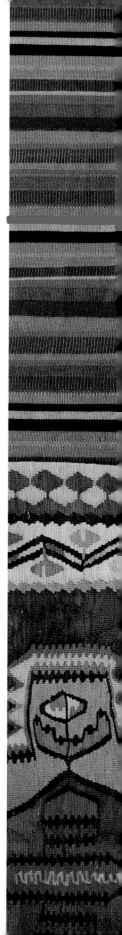

FRIED EGGPLANT ROLL-UPS

BADRIGIANI

These succulent roll-ups are one of the treasures of the Georgian table. Strips of fried eggplant are coated with spiced walnut paste and rolled up. They're best if made an hour or more ahead of time and slightly chilled, so that the filling firms up and the flavors have time to blend.

Badrigiani make a great appetizer, though in Georgia they are usually served as part of a wide selection of dishes at a meal. **SERVES 6 TO 8**

5 narrow Asian eggplants, about 12 inches long; or 10 Asian eggplants, about 8 inches long; or 2 pounds Mediterranean eggplant

Sea salt

About 3 tablespoons sunflower or extra-virgin olive oil

FILLING

¾ cup walnuts or walnut pieces

2 garlic cloves, minced

1 teaspoon ground coriander (see Note)

1 teaspoon ground blue fenugreek, or ¾ teaspoon powdered dried fenugreek plus ½ teaspoon ground fenugreek leaves (see Note)

½ teaspoon sea salt

Scant ¼ teaspoon powdered dried red chiles (optional; see Note)

½ cup minced fresh coriander

½ cup minced fresh mint

3 scallions, trimmed and finely chopped

1 tablespoon white wine vinegar or fresh lemon juice

Trim the stems off the eggplants and discard. Slice the eggplants lengthwise into ¼-inch-thick strips; if the eggplants are very long or very wide, cut the slices in half crosswise or lengthwise to yield strips 4 to 6 inches long and 1½ to 2 inches wide. Lay the slices on a parchment-lined baking sheet and sprinkle on salt generously. Set another baking sheet on top and weight it down with a heavy cast-iron pan (or set up an equivalent arrangement) and set the eggplant aside for an hour or so to drain and compress.

Meanwhile, make the filling: Combine the walnuts, garlic, ground spices, salt, and chiles in a food processor or a mortar and process or pound to blend thoroughly. Transfer to a bowl and stir in the herbs, scallions, and vinegar or lemon juice.

Rinse the eggplant strips thoroughly in a colander and squeeze dry. Place a wide heavy skillet over medium-high heat, add 2 tablespoons oil, and heat until

hot. Slide some eggplant strips into the oil, without crowding, lower the heat to medium, and fry, turning once, until cooked through, about 10 minutes. Lift out onto a paper towel–lined plate or baking sheet and set aside until cool enough to handle. Repeat with the remaining eggplant, adding more oil as necessary and heating it until hot before adding more eggplant.

Spread some filling on each eggplant strip, roll up, and set seam side down on a platter. Serve at room temperature.

NOTE: If you have Georgian spice blend, either homemade (see page 28) or store-bought (see Glossary), use 1 tablespoon of the blend instead of the coriander, fenugreek, and chiles.

PEPPERS WITH WALNUT PASTE

I've also eaten red bell peppers with walnut paste in Georgia. It's a very successful combo. The peppers are blanched in boiling water for several minutes to soften them slightly, cut into boat-shaped sections, stripped of membranes and seeds, and topped with the paste.

Opposite, clockwise from top: *Georgian Topknot Dumplings (page 130), Fried Eggplant Roll-Ups, Red Ajika (page 42), and Garlic-Vinegar Dipping Sauce (page 132).*

Right: *Strips of eggplant that have been fried in preparation for making Fried Eggplant Roll-Ups. With them are walnuts in a bowl.*

THANKSGIVING-PUMPKIN RICE

KHAPAMA

Until recently, in Armenian villages at harvesttime, a huge pumpkin would be filled with flavored rice and put like a large pot in the waning heat of the community oven. The whole village would share in the feast.

This is a home-style version of that warming comfort food. A small pumpkin is filled with a mixture of rice, walnuts, dried apricots, and dried sour plums (for which I usually substitute dried barberries). Be sure not to fill the pumpkin more than halfway, because the rice needs space to expand.

I discovered when I made this at home for the first time that pumpkin is a great insulator: When I checked on it after an hour in the oven, the rice-cooking water inside the pumpkin was barely lukewarm. Now I start with warm water. You need to allow about two hours for the rice to cook. The pumpkin rice can be served hot or at room temperature. Grill some Turkey Kebabs (page 175) or other kebabs, and start with Herbed Yogurt Soup (page 94) with its fresh greenness or a *borani* of some kind (see pages 55 and 62). **SERVES 8**

One 9- to 11-inch-wide pie/soup pumpkin

1½ to 2 cups (depending on the size of the pumpkin) Arborio or other short-grain rice

2 tablespoons butter

About ½ cup coarsely chopped walnuts

About ½ cup coarsely chopped dried apricots

6 dried sour plums, coarsely chopped, or 2 to 3 tablespoons dried barberries (see Glossary), soaked for 10 minutes in warm water and drained

About 2½ cups warm water

1½ teaspoons sea salt

Place a rack in the center of the oven and preheat the oven to 400°F.

Wash and dry the pumpkin. Leave the stem on; it's a useful handle. Cut out a lid, about 4 inches across, taking care to hold your knife at an angle; you want the sides of the opening slanted so the lid won't fall in as the pumpkin cooks. Clean the seeds and membranes from the lid and set the lid aside. Use a strong spoon to scrape the membranes and seeds out of the pumpkin. (Set the seeds aside for another purpose or discard.) Place the pumpkin on a rimmed baking sheet or in a roasting pan.

TBILISI, GEORGIA—*Market women with their produce in October. Pumpkins are used as a vegetable throughout the Caucasus countries and in Iran and Kurdistan.*

Wash the rice in several changes of water and set aside in a bowl.

Melt the butter in a large heavy skillet over medium heat. Add the walnuts and dried fruit and cook, stirring frequently, for about 5 minutes, until the fruit is well softened. Add to the rice and mix together.

Spoon the filling into the pumpkin; it should be barely half-filled. Add enough warm water to cover the rice by half an inch or so, then add the salt. Place the lid on the pumpkin and transfer the pumpkin to the oven. Bake until the rice is tender and the outside of the pumpkin is slightly soft to the touch, about 2 hours. Remove from the oven and let stand for 20 minutes to 1 hour to allow the filling to firm up.

To serve, place the pumpkin on a platter; it's fun to serve this at the table. Remove the lid and use a long-handled spoon to scoop out the rice, along with tender pumpkin flesh.

CABBAGE DOLMAS

This wintertime classic exists in various forms all through the Caucasus countries, perhaps because of the Russian influence there. The filling is spiced ground meat: beef or lamb in Azerbaijan, beef or pork in Armenia and Georgia, mixed with rice and spices. There are also meatless versions for fasting times: see Cabbage Rolls Stuffed with Beans and Tart Fruit, page 124. **SERVES 8**

FILLING

2 medium onions (½ pound), coarsely chopped

2 medium Roma (plum) tomatoes, peeled and chopped

2 pounds ground lamb or beef (at least 25% fat)

1 teaspoon ground ginger

2 teaspoons sea salt

1 teaspoon freshly ground black pepper

1 cup jasmine or other medium- or short-grain rice, washed and drained

½ cup minced fresh coriander

One 3-pound green cabbage

Sea salt

ACCOMPANIMENT

Plain full-fat yogurt or Pomegranate-Coriander Sauce (page 35)

SHEKI, AZERBAIJAN—
Peeling the outside (less-perfect) leaves off a beautiful firm cabbage, in Chamala's kitchen. Next we cut the cabbage in half and steamed it until just tender, so its leaves were supple and easy to roll around the filling.

Make the filling at least 3 hours and as long as a day before you want to serve the rolls: Put the onions in a food processor and pulse until reduced to a soft mush (be patient, they will eventually turn to mush). Add the tomatoes and process until smooth. Add the meat, ginger, salt, and pepper and process to blend well.

Turn the mixture out into a large bowl. Add the rice and coriander, and mix and knead with your hands, squeezing the mixture through your fingers; you want a very smooth texture.

Cover and refrigerate for at least an hour to firm up and blend the flavors before using.

At least 2 hours before you wish to serve the dolmas, wash the cabbage and cut it lengthwise in half. Place in a large heavy pot. Add about 2 inches of salted water, cover, and bring to a boil. Reduce the heat and cook until the cabbage is just tender, about 30 minutes. Drain and set aside to cool.

Cut out the core of the cabbage and separate the leaves. Use a few of the less-than-perfect leaves to line the bottom and lower sides of a wide heavy pot. Pick up one cabbage leaf and trim away the thickest part of the central rib, so the leaf has flexibility. If the leaf is very large (the size varies), cut it in half lengthwise, and just use a half leaf. Lay the leaf on one hand and put 1 heaping tablespoon to 2 tablespoons filling on it (whatever fits comfortably), about an inch from the stem end. Fold over the stem end, fold over the sides, and roll up; patch any gaps with pieces from another leaf if necessary. As you shape them, place the dolmas seam side down in the pot: Arrange them around the sides of the pot first, then fill in the center. Once you have one layer, build a second layer on top.

Add water to just cover. Cover the dolmas with more leaves and put a plate on top to weigh them down. Put the lid on the pot and bring the water to a boil over medium heat. Cook for 30 minutes. Lift the lid and check that the pot has not run dry; add a little water if needed. Cover and cook for another 20 minutes or so. Let cool to lukewarm or to room temperature in the pot before serving. The rolls will firm up as they cool.

Stack the dolmas on a platter, or serve each guest 2 or 3 rolls in a soup bowl or on a plate. Serve with yogurt or Pomegranate-Coriander Sauce.

CABBAGE ROLLS STUFFED WITH BEANS AND TART FRUIT

BASUTS DOLMA

For the "fasting days" of the Armenian Church, on which no meat or dairy is eaten, Armenian cooks have come up with different versions of many classic dishes. They're handy for vegetarians as well as for believers.

But these cabbage rolls give no hint of deprivation. They are astonishing: moist, richly flavored, and deeply satisfying. As for the meat-filled cabbage rolls on page 122, the cabbage is steam-cooked until softened (in earlier times, brined cabbage would have been used, especially in the early spring, at the Lenten fasting period). The filling is cooked beans, lentils, and some bulgur, flavored with dried fruit and with plenty of onions cooked in generous quantities of oil (a combination known as *so karats*). **SERVES 8**

One 3-pound green or white cabbage

½ cup coarse bulgur

1 cup hot water

1 cup sunflower or olive oil

1 cup thinly sliced onion

1½ cups mixed cooked or canned beans and legumes, with a little cooking liquid (see The Precooked Beans Habit, page 82), preferably roughly equal parts chickpeas, lentils, and kidney beans

About 2 tablespoons tomato paste

½ cup chopped dried apricots, sour plums, or sour Fruit Leather (page 314)

Generous grinding of black pepper

1 tablespoon dried mint

1 teaspoon dried thyme or oregano

1 cup chopped mixed fresh herbs, such as coriander, flat-leaf parsley, summer savory, tarragon, and watercress

2 teaspoons sea salt, or to taste

½ cup rose hip liquid (see page 98) or ¼ cup tart cranberry juice (optional)

Wash the cabbage and cut it lengthwise in half. Place in a large heavy pot, add about 2 inches of salted water, cover, and bring to a boil. Lower the heat and cook until the cabbage is just tender, about 30 minutes. Lift out of the liquid and set aside to cool.

Meanwhile, place the bulgur in a bowl, add the hot water, and set aside to soak for 30 minutes.

Heat the oil in a large pot over medium heat. Add the onion and cook until very softened and translucent, 5 to 7 minutes. Add the beans, bulgur, and tomato paste and stir. If the mixture seems dry, add a little water to moisten it. Add the dried fruit, pepper, and dried herbs and cook, stirring, for a few minutes, until

Left: **SHEKI, AZERBAIJAN**—*Pouring water into a pan of shaped cabbage rolls, in Chamala's kitchen.*

Right: **BAKU, AZERBAIJAN**—*A cabbage seller in Taza Market.*

blended and soft. Remove from the heat and stir in the fresh herbs and salt. Taste and adjust the seasoning; set aside. (You will have about 4 cups filling.)

Carefully core the cabbage and separate the leaves. Use a few of the less-than-perfect leaves to line the bottom and lower sides of a wide heavy pot. Use the rest to make dolmas, trimming the central rib of the leaf when necessary to make it supple, cutting very large leaves lengthwise in half, and using about 2 tablespoons of the bean filling for each roll. Lay the leaf on one hand; place the filling about an inch from the stem end, fold over the stem end, fold over the sides, and roll up. As you shape them, place the dolmas seam side down in the pot: Arrange them around the sides of the pot first, then fill in the center. Once you have one layer, build a second layer on top. Cover the stacked dolmas with more cabbage leaves.

Add water, preferably flavored with the rose hip liquid or cranberry juice, to just cover the dolmas. Top with a plate to weigh them down. Cover the pot and bring to a steady boil. Cook for 45 minutes. Remove from the heat and let cool completely in the liquid, or chill in the refrigerator, to firm up the filling.

Serve at room temperature or chilled.

NOTE: I was told that the cooking liquid may instead be flavored with ground cannabis seeds, which are apparently widely available in the region. I did see large cannabis plants growing in rural Iran.

STUFFED VEGETABLES

DOLMASY · DOLMA · TOLMA · YAPRACH SALAT

Stuffed vegetables (*dolmasy* in Azeri, *dolma* in Armenian, *tolma* in Georgian, *yaprach salat* in Kurdish) make great appetizers and also are very good additions to a feast. Make them up to 3 hours ahead.

The filling makes 3½ to 4 cups; multiply it for larger batches. Make it at least two hours and up to a day ahead of when you wish to serve the dolmas. If you are using tomatoes as one of your container vegetables, add 2 tablespoons of the reserved tomato pulp to the meat mixture and omit the tomato paste.

FILLING

1 pound ground lamb or chicken

1 cup minced onion

1½ teaspoons ground cumin

1 tablespoon tomato paste (see headnote)

Pinch of turmeric

1 teaspoon sea salt

1 teaspoon sunflower or extra-virgin olive oil

1 cup cooked short- or medium-grain rice

½ cup chopped fresh mint, basil, tarragon, or flat-leaf parsley

VEGETABLES

4 or 5 bell peppers or 10 large tomatoes, or about 20 small eggplants or 25 small zucchini, or a combination

Salt, if using eggplants

To make the filling, place the lamb or chicken, onion, cumin, tomato paste (or tomato pulp), turmeric, and salt in a food processor and process to a smooth paste.

Place a heavy skillet over medium heat. Add the oil and the meat mixture and cook, stirring frequently, until the meat has changed color, 5 to 10 minutes. Stir in the rice and fresh herbs. Remove from the heat and set the mixture aside until you are ready to use it (in a sealed container in the refrigerator if the wait will be longer than an hour).

Meanwhile, prepare your vegetables:

For bell peppers: Cut off the tops and save to use as lids. Strip out and discard the seeds and membranes. Drop the peppers into boiling water for just 30 seconds to blanch them; drain.

For tomatoes: Choose firm large tomatoes. Cut off the tops and set aside to use as lids. Scoop out the flesh and stir 2 tablespoons of it into the meat filling.

For eggplants: Choose small ones. Cut off the stems and make a slit down one side of each one, cutting deeply but not all the way through the eggplant.

If using Mediterranean eggplants, rub salt inside the slits and set aside for 30 minutes, then rinse well. Drop the eggplants into a pot of boiling water and blanch for about 3 minutes. Drain.

For zucchini: Choose firm small zucchini that are 4 to 6 inches long. Cut a slit in one side of each one.

Allow about 1 cup filling per pepper, ¼ to ½ cup filling per tomato, about 2 tablespoons filling per small eggplant, or 1 to 2 tablespoons per small zucchini.

Fill the vegetables to the top with the filling. Place the "lids" on the peppers and tomatoes. Place the vegetables in a deep skillet or a wide heavy pot. If you're making a lot, you'll need two pots. Stand the tomatoes and peppers upright and place the zucchini and eggplants on their sides, slit side up. The vegetables should fit in snugly so they support each other and stay upright. Add hot water to the pan until it is ¼ inch deep if cooking zucchini, and almost ½ inch deep for other vegetables. Cover tightly and bring to a boil, then reduce the heat and simmer for 15 minutes for tomatoes and zucchini, 30 to 40 minutes for eggplants and peppers, until tender.

I like to serve these at room temperature when the textures have firmed up, so the vegetables are easier to eat, but you can also serve them hot.

SHEKI, AZERBAIJAN—*The market in September is full of the bounty of the rich farmland and gardens in the area.*

MAR ODISU, NEAR AMEDIYAH, KURDISTAN—*Amediyah is a hilltop town that dates back to Assyrian times. Nearby, a sign in Aramaic indicates the way to Mar Odisu, a small Assyrian church and the remnants of a monastery. This woman was sitting in the church when I got there.*

ASSYRIAN ENCOUNTERS

In the tiny international lounge at Tabriz airport in northwestern Iran, I fell into conversation with a middle-aged man who spoke fluent English. He was Iranian-born, from the Urumiyah area. He'd been back for a family visit and was now

returning to Los Angeles, where he lived with his family. I asked whether he and his wife spoke Persian with their children at home. "No," he said. "We are Assyrians; we speak Aramaic with them."

I told him that I had a lot of questions for him about Assyrians, if he didn't mind? "I'm happy to talk about this," he said. And so I learned that there are still substantial populations of Assyrians in northwestern Iran, especially near Urumiyah, as well as in Iraqi Kurdistan.

Assyrians are a tenacious people. They have been without a country or kingdom of their own for about 2,600 years, and yet they have kept their written and spoken language, Aramaic. Like Armenians and Georgians, they embraced Christianity early in the Christian era.

In the British Museum, there are extraordinary carved sandstone blocks that were excavated at Nineveh, the

Assyrian capital, the ruins of which lie near the east bank of the Tigris River in present-day northern Iraq. They date from the era when the Assyrian Empire under Ashurbanipal stretched from North Africa to central Iran and the Caucasus. They commemorate lion hunts and battles, including one in which the Assyrians defeated the Elamites (the ancestors of present-day Persians). A century after that battle, the Elamites defeated the Assyrians (in 605 BC); the Assyrians never regained an empire.

Six months after that encounter in Tabriz, I was in northern Kurdistan, near the village of Amediyah, visiting an old Assyrian church called Mar Odisu. It was like a chapel, built of whitewashed stone and very spare. An older Assyrian woman who was tending some flowers told me it had been destroyed twice, once long ago by the Mongols, and once by Saddam Hussein. Each time the community had rebuilt it.

TOPKNOT DUMPLINGS

KHINKALI

PHOTOGRAPH ON PAGE 118

Khinkali are Georgian classics, found in small eateries and devoured by the bowlful, hot and steaming. The dough is a simple combination of flour, salt, and water that needs to rest before it is rolled out and cut into wrappers. Because the dumplings are boiled in water, it's very important that the wrappers be well sealed—that is the origin of the twisted topknot: The dough is pleated together around the filling and twisted firmly to seal it (the process is easier than it sounds).

To eat *khinkali,* you pick one up by the topknot handle, nibble a hole in the dumpling, and suck out all the juices before eating the rest. Then you set the dough handle aside rather than eat it. You want to leave room for the next dumpling, say the Georgians.

These *khinkali* are meat-filled. The filling is delicious, so if you have any left over, make it into a small meat patty and fry or grill it for a little snack. Vegetarian *khinkali,* eaten at fasting times such as Lent, are filled with mushrooms; see the variation that follows.

Tkemali sauce, made from sour plums, is a classic accompaniment, as is a garlic-vinegar sauce, but other dipping sauces also work well, from tomatillo salsa to soy sauce–based Asian sauces to Georgian *ajika* (see page 38). The dumplings are substantial. If you are serving them as an appetizer or as part of a meal, serve 2 or 3 per person. For a light lunch, allow 5 or 6 per person, with a side salad of some kind. **SERVES 8 AS AN APPETIZER, 4 AS A MAIN COURSE; MAKES 20 TO 24 DUMPLINGS**

DOUGH

About 3 cups all-purpose flour, plus extra for surfaces

1 teaspoon sea salt

1 cup water

FILLING

1 pound ground lamb, beef, veal, or pork, or a mixture

½ cup chopped scallion greens

½ teaspoon ground cumin

½ cup chopped fresh coriander

1 teaspoon sea salt

Generous grinding of black pepper

Sea salt

Sour Plum Sauce (page 34), Garlic-Vinegar Dipping Sauce (recipe follows), or another sauce (see headnote)

To make the dough, place the flour and salt in a bowl, add the water, and mix well. Turn the dough out onto a lightly floured surface and knead for a couple of minutes, until smooth. Alternatively, place the flour and salt in a food processor and, with the processor running, add the water through the feed tube. Process just until the dough comes together, then turn out onto a lightly floured surface and knead briefly. If the dough is still sticky, add more flour to your work surface and knead it in. Seal the dough in a plastic bag and set aside for at least 30 minutes, or up to 6 hours.

To make the filling, mix all ingredients in a bowl and knead well to blend them together, then cover and set aside (refrigerate if the wait will be longer than an hour).

Half an hour before you want to serve the dumplings, bring a large pot of water to a boil over high heat and add 2 tablespoons salt. Cover and keep at a simmer while you prepare the dumplings.

Flour your work surface and turn the dough out. Cut it into 4 pieces. Flatten and stretch one piece of dough, or use a rolling pin to roll it out; you want a thin oval about 10 inches long. Use the rim of a jar or bowl that is about 4 inches in diameter as a guide and cut out circles with a knife, cutting them close together. Pull the scraps together, roll out again, and cut out another circle or two.

Fill the first circles: Place a generous tablespoon of filling in the center of one circle. Pull up a bit of the edge and then another bit next to it, pleating the second one over the first, and continue around the circle until you have created a pillow with a gathered top. Pinch the top ½ inch below the top edges of the dough and twist to seal the topknot well. Set aside on a well-floured surface. Repeat to fill the remaining rolled-out circles of dough. (If your kitchen is very dry, cover the shaped dumplings loosely with plastic wrap or a slightly damp cloth.) Then stretch or roll out a second piece of dough and make more dumplings.

Once the first two batches are shaped, bring the pot of water back to a vigorous boil and toss in the dumplings. They will sink to the bottom and rise again after 5 to 7 minutes; once they have floated up, boil for another minute. Meanwhile, roll out the other pieces of dough and shape the rest of the dumplings.

Lift the cooked dumplings out of the pot with a slotted spoon and serve immediately in individual bowls or on a serving plate. Serve the sauce of your choice on the side. Cook and serve the remaining dumplings.

MUSHROOM KHINKALI

Mushrooms make a wonderful substitute for meat in many dishes, and they come into their own in the fasting (meatless) recipes of the Armenians and Georgians. To make topknot dumplings with a mushroom filling, sauté 2 or 3 minced garlic cloves in 2 tablespoons sunflower or olive oil in a large heavy skillet until softened. Add 1 pound chopped mushrooms (about 4 cups) and 1 teaspoon sea salt and cook until the mushrooms start to soften. Turn out into a bowl to cool.

Stir ½ cup minced scallions, ¼ cup chopped fresh coriander, ¼ teaspoon ground cumin and a generous grinding of black pepper into the mushrooms. Shape and cook the dumplings as above. Total cooking time for each batch of dumplings will be 5 to 6 minutes. Serve with lightly salted thick yogurt or the garlic-vinegar sauce, or with red or green *ajika* (pages 42 and 40).

GARLIC-VINEGAR DIPPING SAUCE
Photograph on page 118

A last-minute quick-hit kind of sauce, this is especially good when the garlic is very fresh. Do *not* make it with tired, overstrong winter garlic! Serve with dumplings or with roast lamb.   **MAKES ABOUT ½ CUP**

10 medium crisp, fresh garlic cloves
    (to yield about 3 tablespoons
    garlic paste)
Pinch of sea salt
About 3 tablespoons red wine vinegar or
    cider vinegar

2 tablespoons water
Pinch of sugar
A little finely chopped fresh coriander
    (optional)

Mash the garlic to a paste with the salt in a mortar or a small food processor, or finely mince and mash with a spoon. Place in a small bowl, add the vinegar, water, and sugar, and stir to blend. Taste and adjust the seasoning if necessary. Stir in the coriander if you wish.

MINI DUMPLINGS

JIRS

PHOTOGRAPH ON PAGE 114

Jirs are distant cousins of Georgian Topknot Dumplings (page 130) and of the boiled dumplings of central Asia that spread to Russia and eastern Europe (think of pierogi, for example). All are a way of creating a filling meal from very little meat.

I learned these in the town of Sheki, in Azerbaijan. My teacher, Matanet, serves *jirs* in the light broth she creates by cooking them in boiling water tinted very elegantly with saffron threads. Other cooks drain the dumplings and simply serve them topped with a dollop of yogurt. Both options are given below.

You may balk at the busywork of shaping small dumplings, but if you have a friend to work with, the shaping goes quickly and is a pleasure. (If you don't want to shape dumplings, the filling here can instead be shaped into small sliders, then fried or grilled and served as an appetizer.)

A note on names: Matanet called these little dumplings *jirs*. But several Azeri sources call small dumplings *dushbarai* and use the word *jirs* for larger dumplings. The instructions below are for dumplings that are larger than the *jirs* I made and ate in Sheki; at 2 inches in diameter, they are easier to shape.   **SERVES 6; MAKES ABOUT 80 SMALL DUMPLINGS**

DUMPLINGS

1 large egg

½ cup plain full-fat yogurt

1 teaspoon sea salt

1½ cups all-purpose flour, plus extra for surfaces

¼ pound ground lamb or beef

1 medium onion, coarsely chopped

2 tablespoons tomato paste

¾ teaspoon ground cassia (cinnamon)

¼ cup packed minced fresh coriander, dill, or tarragon

1 teaspoon dried mint

BROTH

Generous pinch (¼ teaspoon) of saffron threads

¼ cup hot water

5 cups water

1 teaspoon sea salt

ACCOMPANIMENTS

2 tablespoons chopped fresh coriander or 1 teaspoon dried mint

Garlic-Vinegar Dipping Sauce (opposite)

Ground sumac

Sea salt and freshly ground black pepper

continued

To make the dumplings, mix together the egg and yogurt in a medium bowl. Add ½ teaspoon of the salt and stir. Add 1 cup of the flour and stir to blend it in well. Add another ¼ to ½ cup flour and stir. Turn the dough out onto a well-floured surface and knead until very smooth and not at all sticky. Set aside, covered with plastic, to rest for half an hour.

Meanwhile, put the meat, onion, tomato paste, cassia, herbs, and the remaining ½ teaspoon salt in a food processor and process to a paste. Set aside, covered, in the refrigerator for 30 minutes.

For the broth, put the saffron threads in a small bowl, add the hot water, stir, and set aside to steep.

Line a baking sheet with parchment paper or wax paper.

Cut the dough in half and set one piece aside, covered, to prevent it from drying out. On a well-floured surface, roll out the other piece until very thin. Just keep at it, rolling from the center outward and rotating the dough slightly after each stroke, until it is a round or an oval about 15 inches across or more. Use a glass or a round cookie cutter, dipped in flour, to cut out 2-inch rounds. Pull together the remnants, roll them out thinly, and cut out more rounds.

Place about ½ teaspoon filling in a line down the center of one round. Press the filling to compact it and make sure the edges of the dough are bare. Using your lightly floured thumb and forefinger, pinch the dough together at one end of the line of filling. Then, pinching over a tiny pleat, first from one side and then the other, work your way along the two edges, sealing them together (see photo, page 114). Place the dumpling on the baking sheet and fill and shape the remaining rounds. Repeat the rolling out, cutting, and shaping with the remaining dough and filling.

Pour 5 cups water into a wide pot and bring to a rigorous boil. Add the salt and the saffron liquid. Carefully transfer all the dumplings to the water and stir gently to prevent them from sticking together. Cook at a medium boil for about 12 minutes, until the dough is very tender.

To serve, ladle the dumplings and broth into individual soup bowls. Sprinkle with the coriander or dried mint. Put out a dish of the sauce. Set a small bowl of ground sumac on the table, as well as salt and pepper. Serve with flatbreads.

DUMPLINGS WITH YOGURT

If you prefer to serve the dumplings without their broth, omit the saffron. Serve them in individual shallow bowls or plates, sprinkle on chopped fresh herbs or a little sumac, and offer a bowl of thick yogurt seasoned with salt and a little minced garlic as a side sauce.

SWEET FANTASY JIRS

Matanet told me about a "fantasia" version of *jirs*, filled with a mix of chopped dates and walnuts. They're sweet morsels, and unusual. To make them, chop ½ cup soft pitted dates. Add to ½ cup finely ground walnuts and stir and blend the two together. Add ½ teaspoon ground cardamom and/or ½ teaspoon ground ginger. Fill each dough round with about ½ teaspoon filling, as above. You can make the dumplings ahead and set them aside for up to 4 hours, loosely covered with a cotton cloth.

When ready to proceed, bring a large pot of water (unsalted) to a rolling boil and add the dumplings. Stir gently and cook for 6 to 7 minutes until the dough is very tender. Use a slotted spoon to transfer the dumplings to a platter. Drizzle on a little melted butter and toss gently to coat. If you wish, lightly dust them with cinnamon sugar (2 teaspoons sugar combined with ½ teaspoon cassia or cinnamon). Serve warm with tea or coffee.

Left: **NEAR SHAMAKHI, AZERBAIJAN**—*Many shepherds in Armenia and Azerbaijan work from horseback, keeping their flocks fed by finding new pasture for the animals. This guy had real style.*

Right: **SOUTHERN IRAN**—*Detail of a nomad tent (see Nomad Encounter, page 190).*

FISH

THOUGH IRAN HAS A LONG SOUTHERN coast on the Gulf of Oman and the Indian Ocean, and a Caspian seacoast too, most Iranians who don't live on the coast eat very little fish. This probably reflects earlier times, when transporting fresh fish to the cities of the interior was difficult if not impossible. But almost all Iranians *do* eat fish at Nou-Roz, the New Year that falls at the spring equinox (see Zoroaster's Legacy, page 36).

Perhaps my favorite recipe in this chapter is one I learned in Shiraz from a woman who is from the southern Iranian port city of Bushir, on the Persian Gulf. Whole fish is stuffed with a tamarind-tart dressing, and then fried (see page 144). What could be better? Another whole-fish recipe here comes from Azerbaijan, where

it's called *baliq levangi* (see page 151). The fish is stuffed with aromatics and then baked loosely sealed in foil so that no moisture or flavor is lost.

Long ago, in 1989, at a restaurant in Tbilisi, I ate sturgeon for the very first time. It came with a seductive pomegranate-walnut sauce, and I was blown away by both the fish and the sauce. But all varieties of sturgeon in both the Caspian and the Black Sea are now endangered and rare. Luckily, North American farmed sturgeon is becoming available, and so it is possible to use it, or salmon or any other rich fish, for another recipe from Azerbaijan, a simple fish kebab (see page 156). The fillets are marinated in lemon juice, threaded on skewers, and then quickly grilled and served with a pomegranate-coriander sauce. I like to serve the simple grilled fillets on page 157 with Pomegranate-Walnut Sauce to remind me of that long-ago first taste of sturgeon.

This chapter also includes a Georgian fried trout (see page 147), its cavity perfumed with lemon slices, and a lightly spiced fish version of the walnut-sauce-dressed Georgian dish called *kuchmachi* (see page 149).

Previous pages: **TELAVI, EASTERN GEORGIA**—*An abundant jumble of fresh fish at the town market.*

PERSIAN-STYLE FRIED FISH FILLETS

At the New Year celebrations of Nou-Roz in Persian households, fried fish is served with Herbed Persian Rice (page 214). Here fish fillets are seasoned with herbs and spices and then quickly pan-seared. Serve them as a main with a vegetable side such as Spinach Borani (page 55) and with rice. Or cut into smaller pieces and serve as an appetizer, with some sliced cucumber or leafy greens on the side.

I like freshwater fish, so I use fillets of yellow bass, whitefish, trout, or pickerel. And I prefer skin-on fillets, which cook more evenly and hold together better. If your fillets are large, slice them crosswise into serving-size pieces.

Serve hot or at room temperature, with lemon wedges alongside.   **SERVES 4 AS A MAIN COURSE, 6 AS AN APPETIZER**

About 1½ pounds fish fillets, preferably skin on

¼ cup all-purpose flour

2 tablespoons powdered dried fenugreek leaves

½ teaspoon cayenne (optional)

¼ teaspoon turmeric

1 teaspoon sea salt

Grinding of black pepper

About 2 tablespoons sunflower or extra-virgin olive oil

1 or 2 lemons, cut into wedges

Rinse the fillets and pat dry. Combine the flour, fenugreek, cayenne, if using, turmeric, salt, and black pepper in a wide shallow bowl and mix together.

Place a wide cast-iron or other heavy skillet over medium-high heat. Add enough oil to just cover the surface of the pan and heat until hot. Place one fillet in the flour mixture and turn it over so that both sides are lightly coated, then carefully lay the fillet in the hot oil, skin side down. Continue to flour the fillets and place them in the oil without crowding; heat and oil a second skillet if necessary, or fry in two batches. After a couple of minutes, use a wide spatula to turn the fillets over; allow each about a minute on the second side. Then turn them back over so they are skin side down and fry until just barely cooked through, another minute or so, depending on the thickness.

Use a slotted spoon or spatula to transfer the fillets to a platter or to individual plates. Serve the lemon wedges alongside.

CASPIAN INTERLUDE

I met two young brothers in a tea shop in the hillside village of Massouleh in northern Iran. They were showing a visiting friend the sights and planned to take her to visit their mother, who lived in a nearby town. There was plenty of

room in the car; did I want to come along? When we got to the house, Farahnoz told her sons that we should do a quick jaunt to the seashore. It was a gray and windy day, but never mind, she said, let's show them the Caspian.

We reached a sandy low-lying stretch of shore that looked a little forlorn in the overcast dull light, with a sagging, closed-for-the-season snack bar and some rough-looking boats pulled up on shore. There were no holidaymakers in sight, just a lone fisherman, who told us how poor the catches were these days, and how hard it was to make a living. We were miles

away from the energy and optimism of Tehran, with its crowded freeways, lively bazaars, and high-rise downtown.

We walked along the shore, the waves rippling quietly beside us. Farahnoz took off her shoes and waded barefoot into the sea. There was no one else nearby, so she was free to be barefoot, free to do as she pleased. Her scarf slipping in the wind, she laughed with delight.

And then it was time to go, time for us women to cover our hair, put on our shoes, and return to the public world of constrained behavior.

CASPIAN SHORE, RASHT AREA, IRAN—*Farahnoz delighted in walking barefoot by the Caspian Sea.*

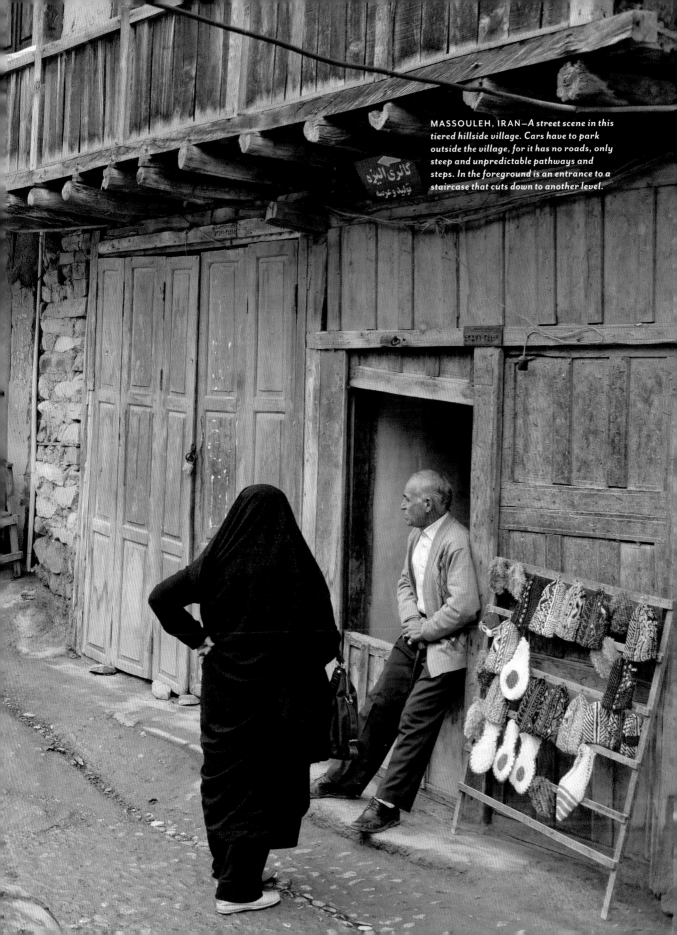

MASSOULEH, IRAN—*A street scene in this tiered hillside village. Cars have to park outside the village, for it has no roads, only steep and unpredictable pathways and steps. In the foreground is an entrance to a staircase that cuts down to another level.*

گالری الیزه
تولید و عرضه

FRIED STUFFED FISH, BUSHIR-STYLE

The aromatic stuffing makes this a knockout dish for a special occasion. I learned the recipe from a woman who had moved to Shiraz from the port city of Bushir some years earlier. She'd invited me to lunch, knowing that I wanted to learn more about Persian regional cooking.

There's a delicious tart flavor in the stuffing, as there is in a lot of Persian dishes. Here it comes from tamarind, an ingredient characteristic of the food of the southern coastal areas of Iran. (Inland and farther north, pomegranate molasses, verjuice, or sour plums give tartness.) The fish is coated in turmeric and rice flour, a reminder that in southern Iran we're on the trade routes with the Indian subcontinent, where turmeric is always part of fish cookery.

My hostess fried her stuffed fish rather than baking it, because stovetop cooking is much more common than oven-baking in Iran. Like her, I prefer to fry (there's just more flavor with frying!), but directions for baking the fish are also given below. It is easier to make this with two smaller fish rather than one large one. You will need toothpicks, fine skewers, or a needle and thread for pinning or sewing the fish cavities closed.

Serve the fish hot or warm, with Herbed Persian Rice (page 214) and a fresh salad, as well as a generous Herb Plate (page 23). **SERVES 4 TO 6**

1 heaping tablespoon tamarind pulp (1 ounce)

¼ cup hot water

Two 1-pound whole fish (red snapper, for example), cleaned and scaled

1½ teaspoons sea salt

½ teaspoon plus a pinch of turmeric

3 tablespoons rice flour

2 tablespoons sunflower or extra-virgin olive oil, plus about ¼ cup oil for shallow-frying the fish

1 cup minced onion

1 tablespoon minced garlic

2 tablespoons powdered dried fenugreek leaves

½ teaspoon cayenne (optional)

¼ cup chopped fresh coriander, plus ¼ cup coriander sprigs

OPTIONAL ACCOMPANIMENT

Tender lettuce leaves or arugula

Cut the tamarind pulp into small pieces and place in a small bowl. Add the hot water. Mix and press the pulp with a fork or spoon so it starts to soften and give off flavor. Set aside to soak for 10 minutes.

LAHICH, AZERBAIJAN—*Houses here are built almost entirely of stone, and so are the lanes. Most transport is on foot or horseback, but occasionally a car bumps uncomfortably along.*

Rinse the fish and pat dry. Trim off the fins and discard. Rub inside and out with 1 teaspoon of the salt. Mix together the ½ teaspoon turmeric and the rice flour and put on a wide plate. Dredge the fish in the mixture, turning to coat, and rub some in the cavities too. Set aside on a clean plate.

Press the tamarind pulp and liquid through a sieve into a bowl, using the back of a spoon to extract as much flavor as possible from the pulp. Discard the solids and set the liquid aside.

Heat a heavy wide skillet over medium-high heat. Add the 2 tablespoons oil, and when it is hot, toss in the pinch of turmeric and then the onion. Lower the heat to medium and cook, stirring, until the onion is softened and translucent, 4 to 5 minutes. Lower the heat to medium-low, add the garlic, and cook for about 30 seconds. Add the fenugreek, cayenne, if using, and the remaining ½ teaspoon salt and stir to incorporate. Add the tamarind liquid and cook, stirring, for about a minute. Remove from the heat and set aside to cool for 5 minutes.

Stir the chopped coriander into the onion mixture. Spoon it into the cavities of the fish. Use a needle and thread to sew the cavities closed, or pin the cavities closed with toothpicks or fine skewers.

Place a large plate or long platter by your stovetop. Line it with tender greens if you like.

Place two large skillets over low heat. Add oil to a depth of a scant ¼ inch, raise the heat to medium-high, and wait until the oil is hot. Carefully slide the fish into the oil (it's okay if the tails hang over the edge) and fry for 5 minutes or so, until crisped and firm on the first side. Use tongs and a wide spatula to carefully turn the fish over. Fry until browned and a little blistered on the second side. Transfer the fish to the plate or platter. Serve hot or at room temperature, sprinkled with the coriander sprigs.

ROASTED STUFFED FISH

Proceed as for the main recipe, but omit the turmeric–rice flour coating. Once you have soaked the tamarind, mix ¼ teaspoon turmeric with the salt and rub the mixture over the fish, inside and out. Prepare the stuffing as above and set aside to cool.

Place a rack in the center of the oven and preheat the oven to 400°F.

Place two large sheets of aluminum foil (double the length of the fish) on a rimmed baking sheet. Place one fish on each sheet.

Spoon the stuffing into the cavities of the fish. Cover each fish loosely with the foil, creating a tent for it to steam in, rather than wrapping it tightly, and crimp the edges to seal.

Place the baking sheet in the oven and bake for 30 minutes. Remove the pan from the oven and open the foil, being careful not to burn yourself with the steam. The fish should yield to the touch; if they are still firm, reseal their foil tents, return to the oven, and cook for another 10 minutes before testing again.

FRIED TROUT
WITH LEMON SLICES

If you have access to trout or to other freshwater fish, such as pickerel, make this fresh-tasting Georgian version of fried fish. Cornmeal gives it a crisp coating, and slices of lemon and sprigs of coriander or tarragon in the cavity of the fish perfume it as it cooks. Serve with boiled new potatoes and a tomato salad or vegetable dish. **SERVES 2 TO 4**

1 whole medium-small trout or other
   freshwater fish (1 to 1½ pounds),
   cleaned and scaled

2 to 3 tablespoons sunflower or
   extra-virgin olive oil

1 teaspoon sea salt

1 lemon, thinly sliced

4 or 5 fresh coriander or tarragon sprigs

About 2 tablespoons cornmeal

ACCOMPANIMENT

Svanetian Salt (page 31) or Green Ajika
   (page 40)

Rinse the fish. Rub the cavity with a little of the oil and ½ teaspoon of the salt. Tuck the slices of lemon inside the cavity and add the herb sprigs.

Place the cornmeal in a wide shallow bowl. Add the remaining ½ teaspoon salt and mix together. Dredge the fish in the cornmeal, turning to coat on all sides.

Place a large heavy skillet over medium-high heat. It should be wide enough to hold the fish comfortably; if the head and tail ride up the sides or even hang over the edge, don't worry, but you want the body of the fish to lie flat in the pan. Add enough oil to cover the bottom of the pan completely, and when it is hot, carefully slide the fish into the oil. Fry for 5 minutes or until well browned and a little crisp on the first side. Using one or two wide spatulas, carefully turn the fish over and fry for another 5 minutes, or until just cooked through (the flesh inside the cavity should be opaque rather than shiny).

Serve with Svanetian salt or *ajika* as a condiment.

SPICY FISH SALAD

FISH KUCHMACHI

Kuchmachi is a Georgian dish that's most often made of simmered chicken or beef or lamb, a kind of meat salad dressed with a savory rich walnut sauce (see Chicken Giblets in Spiced Walnut Dressing, page 206) and served at room temperature. This version is made with poached fish.

I first tasted a version of fish *kuchmachi* at a Palm Sunday fasting feast in Akhalkalaki hosted by the Bishop of Javakheti. The guests, most of whom were keeping the Lenten fast (no animal products except for a few days when fish is permitted), were happy to be able to eat fish on this special day. Outside, the landscape was spare and beautiful, with snowcapped peaks on the horizon. Not far away lay the borders with Turkey and Armenia.

Serve this on a hot day as a main course with an assortment of salads, or serve it as one course in a winter feast, preceded by a clear soup and followed by roast meat or roast vegetables. **SERVES 6**

2 or 3 bay leaves

5 medium garlic cloves, or to taste

About 3 pounds whole white-fleshed fish (1 large or 2 smaller fish), cleaned and scaled, or 2 pounds fish fillets (see Note on Fish)

2 cups walnuts or walnut pieces

2 tablespoons white wine vinegar

1 teaspoon ground coriander (see Note)

1 teaspoon ground blue fenugreek, or 1 teaspoon powdered dried fenugreek leaves plus ½ teaspoon ground fenugreek (see Note)

1 teaspoon powdered dried marigold petals (optional; see Glossary)

½ teaspoon powdered dried red chiles (see Note)

½ teaspoon dried summer savory or thyme

1 teaspoon sea salt, or to taste

About 1 cup pomegranate seeds (optional)

1 small red onion or 2 shallots, minced (about ½ cup)

½ cup coarsely chopped fresh coriander or dill

Pour ½ inch of water into a wide heavy skillet. Add the bay leaves and 3 of the garlic cloves and bring to just below a boil over medium heat. Slide in the fish, cover, reduce the heat, and poach until the fish is barely cooked through, 5 to 10 minutes, depending on thickness, turning it after 4 minutes. Remove the fish from the water and set aside on a plate to cool. Reserve the cooking broth.

continued

If using whole fish, pull the flesh off the bones and discard the bones and skin. Separate the flesh (from whole fish or fillets) into bite-size pieces, using your fingers or a knife. Set aside in a bowl.

Grind the walnuts to a fine powder in a food processor or in a large mortar. Mash the remaining 2 garlic cloves to a paste. Place the walnuts and garlic in a bowl, add the vinegar and about ¼ cup of the reserved cooking broth, and whisk until smooth. Add the coriander, fenugreek, marigold petals, chiles (or substitute Georgian spice blend; see Note), summer savory, and salt and whisk again. The sauce should be pourable; if necessary, add a little more fish broth.

Pour the sauce over the fish and toss gently to coat it with dressing. If you have the pomegranate seeds, add them, reserving a few for garnish, and mix gently. Let the salad stand for 10 minutes, or as long as an hour, before serving to give the flavors time to blend.

Just before serving, add the minced onion or shallots and the fresh herbs and toss gently to mix well. Taste and adjust the seasoning if necessary. Transfer to a platter or wide shallow bowl and sprinkle on the reserved pomegranate seeds, if using.

NOTE ON FISH: Fish you might use include black sea bass, striped bass, or snapper.

NOTE: If you have Georgian spice blend, either homemade (see page 28) or store-bought (see Glossary), use 1 tablespoon of the blend instead of the coriander, fenugreek, and chiles.

TBILISI, GEORGIA—
A dried-fruit seller with garlands of dried apple and dried apricot, boxes of fresh walnuts and hazelnuts, and lots of churchkhela *(nuts coated with dried fruit; see page 317).*

ROASTED FISH WITH WALNUT PASTE

BALIQ LEVANGI

This Azeri version of baked stuffed fish is filled with a rich paste, called *levangi*, of ground walnuts, minced onion, and tart dried fruit.

Serve with rice, Onion Salad with Barberries (page 51), and a vegetable dish such as Beet Pkhali (page 71). **SERVES 6**

About 2 tablespoons sunflower or
   extra-virgin olive oil

1 cup chopped onion

1½ cups walnuts or walnut pieces

¼ cup chopped sour fruit leather, homemade
   (see page 314) or store-bought, or sour
   plums or dried apricots, soaked in water
   for 15 minutes and drained

About 1½ teaspoons sea salt

1 tablespoon fresh lemon juice

Two 1½-pound whole fish, cleaned
   and scaled

Place a rack in the center of the oven and preheat the oven to 400°F.

Place a heavy skillet over medium-high heat. Add about 1 tablespoon of the oil and then the chopped onion, lower the heat to medium, and cook, stirring occasionally, until the onion is softened, about 5 minutes. Remove from the heat.

Grind the walnuts finely in a food processor. Add the onion, dried fruit, and ½ teaspoon salt and pulse to blend to a paste. Add the lemon juice and pulse again. Transfer to a bowl and set aside.

Place two large sheets of aluminum foil (double the length of the fish) on a rimmed baking sheet. Wash and dry the fish. Place one fish on each sheet of foil. Rub a little oil over each fish and in the cavities. Rub about ½ teaspoon salt in each cavity, then stuff with the paste. Cover the fish very loosely with the foil, creating a tent for it to steam in, and crimp the edges to seal.

Place the baking sheet in the oven and bake for 30 minutes. Remove the pan from the oven and open the foil, being careful not to burn yourself with the steam. The fish should yield to the touch; if they are still firm, reseal their foil tents, return to the oven, and cook for another 10 minutes before testing again. Serve hot or at room temperature.

BAKU, AZERBAIJAN—*A view of the city from the south, with the busy harbor in the foreground, and a huge Azeri flag.*

ANOTHER CASPIAN VIEW

Less than a year after I was first at the shore of the Caspian Sea in Iran (see Caspian Interlude, page 140), I saw it again, this time when I was in the bustling city of Baku, capital of Azerbaijan. What a difference context makes. Baku gleams

with affluence, at least in the central city. The tidy cobbled streets of the restored old city have a sheen to them, and so does the high fashion in the shop windows along the Bulevar, the main shopping street, which overlooks the shore. Flashy European cars race along the streets at terrifying speeds. New buildings break the horizon with their self-consciously architected shapes: the Flame Towers high on a hill, the rolled-carpet cylinder of the Rug Museum. And the grand buildings from an earlier era have been restored and given back their elegance.

It's only when you go farther afield, to the lively, earthy Taza food market, for example (see photo, page 125), that you see how large the gap is between Caspian oil affluence and the life of most working-class Azeris. And once I left the city, I felt I was in an entirely different world, back in Soviet times in some ways, for not much seems to

have changed since then in the Azeri countryside and villages. The public transport between towns is old run-down vans or rackety buses. Some people had cars, but many were still herding flocks of sheep and goats on foot or on horseback, and generally using horses to get around. There was a self-sufficiency in people's way of life. And there was a warmth in my encounters that was worlds away from the moneyed glossy surfaces of Baku.

Below: *The Caspian at dawn, seen from a rooftop in the old city.*

Overleaf: *Baku Fish Kebabs (page 156) with Pomegranate-Coriander Sauce (page 35).*

BAKU FISH KEBABS

BALIQ SHASHLIK

PHOTOGRAPH ON PAGES 154–155

Although sturgeon from the Caspian Sea is the classic and most highly regarded fish in Azerbaijan, you can use any firm, rich fish for these kebabs. The chunks of fish marinate briefly in a blend of lemon juice, salt, and dill before being threaded onto skewers and grilled. They make a great summer meal. **SERVES 4 TO 6**

2 pounds skin-on fish fillets: sturgeon or other rich fish, such as salmon or Alaskan black cod

About ¼ cup fresh lemon juice (from 2 lemons)

About 2 tablespoons minced fresh dill

1 teaspoon sea salt

1 tablespoon sunflower or extra-virgin olive oil

2 medium red onions, thinly sliced

2 medium tomatoes, sliced (optional)

¼ cup minced scallions (optional)

1 tablespoon ground sumac, or to taste

ACCOMPANIMENTS

1 cup Pomegranate-Coriander Sauce (page 35) or wedges of lemon

Herb Plate (page 23)

Cut the fillets crosswise into pieces about 1½ inches wide. Place in a bowl. Add the lemon juice, dill, and ½ teaspoon of the salt and mix gently to coat the fish. Add the oil and mix again. Set aside to marinate for 30 minutes to an hour.

Preheat a charcoal or gas grill to medium hot and place a rack about 5 inches above the coals or flame.

Thread the fillets onto skewers. It's easiest to use two skewers in parallel to hold the fish: Pierce 2 or 3 pieces of fish with one skewer, not through the center, but close to one end; then pierce the other end of the pieces with a second skewer, so the arrangement looks like a ladder with fish rungs. Make sure the skin side of all the pieces is facing the same way. Set aside on a tray and repeat with the remaining fish.

Place the skewers skin side down on the rack over the coals or flame and grill for 10 minutes. Turn over and grill until the fish is just cooked, another 4 minutes or so.

Cover a platter with the sliced onions and the sliced tomatoes, if using. Slide the fish off the skewers onto the platter. Sprinkle the remaining ½ teaspoon salt, the scallions, if using, and sumac over the fish, and serve with the accompaniments.

SIMPLEST GRILLED FISH

Thanks to advice from friends, I now grill fish fillets skin side down only. The other side steam-cooks a little once the grill lid is closed. Here it picks up delicate flavor from fresh tarragon. Serve the fish with Georgian-style pomegranate sauce and, if you like, green *ajika*. **SERVES 6**

Sunflower or extra-virgin olive oil for brushing

About 2½ pounds skin-on sturgeon or trout or other fish fillets

About 1½ teaspoons sea salt

Leaves from about 10 sprigs fresh tarragon, coarsely chopped, or substitute chopped fresh mint

ACCOMPANIMENTS

Pomegranate-Walnut Sauce (recipe follows)

Green Ajika (page 40; optional)

A plate of fresh herb sprigs: chervil, dill, and flat-leaf parsley are all good options

Preheat a charcoal or gas grill to moderate heat.

Brush a little oil on the fillets and rub on the salt. Place skin side down on the grill and top with the herbs, pressing them gently onto the fish. Close the lid and cook until just done, 15 to 20 minutes; the flesh on the top surface will be opaque rather than shiny and the fish will yield to the pressure of a finger, rather than feeling firm and resistant.

Transfer the fish to a platter or individual plates. Put out a small bowl of the sauce, as well as the *ajika* if you wish, and the herbs.

POMEGRANATE-WALNUT SAUCE

Place ½ cup pomegranate molasses in a small saucepan, add ½ cup water, stir to mix, and bring to a boil. Lower the heat and simmer for 5 minutes. Meanwhile, place 1 cup walnut pieces and a garlic clove in a food processor or a mortar and process or pound to a paste. Blend the walnut paste into the pomegranate liquid and add ½ teaspoon salt. Taste and adjust the seasoning if necessary. Remove from the heat and stir in some torn fresh coriander leaves.

GRILLED MEAT AND POULTRY

ON MY FIRST TRIP TO GEORGIA, IN 1989, I traveled by car from Tbilisi to Borjomi, about a five-hour drive in those days. I was with a young Georgian woman named Nino and her father. We passed a number of roadside grills, and eventually we stopped at one for a bite of lunch.

The meat we ate had been cut into small pieces, not like the larger chunks of today's more prosperous times (see Marinated Pork Kebabs, page 170, and Wine-Country Beef Kebabs, page 171). It came to us on skewers hot from the grill, with bread (see Boomerang Breads, page 255) and simple pickles alongside.

In the West, we are apt to use the Turkish words *kebab* or *shashlik* for meat cooked on skewers over coals. The Persian culinary region has many different words. In Armenia, a skewer of grilled meat is *khorovats*, meaning grilled; in Georgian, it's *mtsvadi*; in Azeri, *shishlik*; and in Kurdish, *shishe*. In Iran, *shashlik* refers to large pieces of meat, *kebab* to smaller ones. And here, as elsewhere, tending the fire and grilling the meat is usually a man's job.

The cooking method seems to have arrived with nomads from the north and the east: Kurds, Seljuks, Mongols, Ottomans, and other peoples who came even earlier and whose identity is unknown. It's practical, requiring no pot of water, just hot coals and skewers. But like any cooking, it does take some practice.

At its simplest, grilling starts with chunks of meat and calls for very little else, apart from a sprinkling of salt and perhaps sumac. An alternative when the meat is tough is to grind it, spice it, and then wrap it onto skewers (see Persian Café Kebabs, opposite). Or instead tough meat may be marinated, which tenderizes and also adds flavor (see Pomegranate-Marinated Kebabs, page 165).

A favorite kebab in Azerbaijan is made with pieces of turkey that are first marinated in vinegar with onion (see page 175). The marinade and the grill transform the turkey into something special. You can use the same approach with chicken.

Previous pages: **NEAR LAHICH, AZERBAIJAN**—*Kebabs of lamb and potatoes grill over a wood fire. This was part of the feast when I picnicked for a second time with the guys from the apple orchard (see Feasting in a Garden of Eden, page 172).*

PERSIAN CAFÉ KEBABS WITH GRILLED TOMATOES

KOOBIDEH KEBAB

This basic kebab is served at little café-eateries all over Iran. It's always the least expensive kebab on the menu, and the most tender, since it uses ground meat rather than chunks. The meat is flavored with grated onion, salt, and pepper. Fancier versions of *koobideh kebab* may also include dried mint or a little tomato. It's sprinkled with sumac as it grills and served with grilled tomato on the side. Make sure your ground meat is not extra-lean: Fat helps the meat cook evenly.

The most important ingredient is a set of flat metal skewers. Wide ones work better than narrow ones, but I've found that even narrow flat skewers work fine if the meat is chilled so that it holds together on the skewer.

If you don't have skewers, you can use this recipe to make patties, panfried or grilled over gas or charcoal. Instructions for these are given on page 162.

Serve with supple flatbreads and grilled tomatoes, along with wedges of raw onion if you wish. Leftovers make great sandwiches.   **SERVES 4 AS A MAIN COURSE, 6 TO 8 AS AN APPETIZER**

1½ **pounds ground lamb, goat, or beef (about 25% fat)**

About 1 cup grated onions (2 medium onions)

1½ **teaspoons sea salt**

½ **teaspoon freshly ground black pepper, or to taste**

About 1 tablespoon ground sumac

Grilled Tomatoes (recipe follows)

Flatbreads for serving

2 lemons, cut into wedges (optional)

Wedges of raw onion (optional)

Put the meat in a food processor, along with the onions, salt, and pepper. Pulse for about a minute; if the meat rides up the sides of the bowl, use a spatula to push it back down. (If you are doubling the recipe, or if your processor is small, divide the meat and onions into two batches to process and then combine them.) Turn the meat out into a bowl and knead it for half a minute. It should be paste-like.

Cover the bowl of meat and refrigerate it for at least 30 minutes. This makes it easier to shape, and it will adhere to the skewers better too.

Preheat a charcoal or gas grill. Put the ground sumac near your grill, as well as a plate or platter to hold the cooked skewers.

continued

To make the kebabs, scoop up about ¼ cup of the chilled meat mixture in one hand, pick up a skewer with your other hand, and press the skewer against the mound of meat in your palm to embed it. Smooth and squeeze the meat along and around the skewer so that you have a long, skinny kebab. Set aside. Shape the remaining skewers the same way. You will have about 12 kebabs.

Place the skewers about 4 inches above the coals or flame and cook, turning several times, until lightly tinged with color or until done the way you like them; sprinkle with the sumac partway through cooking. (As the meat cooks, it will shrink a little, which may mean that it no longer grips the skewer, and if you're using narrow flat skewers, it will tend to slide around. If that happens, use tongs to help roll the kebabs over.) Remove from the heat. You can serve the kebabs on the skewers or slide them off onto a serving platter. Put out the lemon wedges and onion wedges, if using, and tomatoes, and serve hot.

PERSIAN MEAT PATTIES

To shape the meat mixture into patties, scoop up a scant ¼ cup of the meat, shape it into a ball without squeezing it tightly, then press down lightly to flatten it a little. Repeat with the remaining meat. You'll have about 15 patties.

Grill the patties or grease a heavy skillet with a little oil and cook them over medium-high heat. Turn the patties after about 3 minutes and cook until the second side gets touched with brown, or to your desired doneness. Lower the heat if necessary. Sprinkle on sumac shortly before they are done.

GRILLED TOMATOES

Plan on serving a skewer of grilled tomatoes—say 3 smallish tomatoes—per person. Use Roma or other fleshy tomatoes; you want the tomatoes to be firm enough that they won't become soft and mushy when grilled.

Thread the tomatoes on skewers and grill, turning them frequently, until softened, a little shrunken, and touched with black here and there. Sprinkle with salt and serve hot or at room temperature, heaped on a platter.

TEHRAN, IRAN—*An old covered bazaar in the center of the city is busy with customers shopping on their way home from work in the late afternoon.*

POMEGRANATE-MARINATED KEBABS

TORSHE KEBAB

The combination of walnuts and pomegranate molasses is classic in Georgia, and also in northern Iran. This Persian marinade serves two purposes spectacularly. First, it makes the meat extremely tender. Second, it gives it an extraordinary flavor. And there's a bonus, because the remaining marinade can be cooked up and used as a sauce for the rice.

Although my first choice for these is lamb, I often make some with beef also to accommodate those in my family who prefer it. Serve with rice and a plate of herbs, as well as a chopped salad if you wish (see pages 47–49). **SERVES 6 GENEROUSLY**

MARINADE

1 cup walnuts or walnut pieces

½ cup pomegranate molasses

1 teaspoon sea salt

2 garlic cloves, mashed or minced

2 tablespoons sunflower or extra-virgin olive oil

½ cup minced fresh flat-leaf parsley (optional)

2 pounds boneless lamb or goat shoulder, or boneless beef top round or hanger steak, cut into approximately 1-inch cubes

Sugar (optional)

Fresh tarragon leaves (optional)

ACCOMPANIMENTS

Herb Plate (page 23): scallions and sprigs of fresh mint, tarragon, or basil

Basic Persian Rice (page 211) or another plain rice (see Note)

To make the marinade, place the walnuts in a food processor and pulse to chop them to smaller than raisin size. Add the remaining ingredients and pulse to blend. Transfer to a large bowl. (Alternatively, very finely chop the walnuts and pound to a coarse powder in a large mortar. Transfer to a large bowl, add the remaining ingredients, and stir to blend thoroughly.)

Add the meat to the bowl and stir, turning to make sure all surfaces are coated with marinade. Cover and set aside to marinate for at least 1 hour or as long as overnight; refrigerate if the marinating time is more than 2 hours.

Bring the meat to room temperature before grilling.

continued

Pomegranate-Marinated Kebabs, with Herbed Persian Rice
(page 214), a side of thick yogurt, and some pickles.

Preheat a charcoal or gas grill.

Brush off most of the marinade that is clinging to the meat and reserve the marinade. Thread the meat onto metal skewers so that the pieces are barely touching each other, not crowded together; this helps the meat cook evenly. Place the skewers 4 to 5 inches from the coals or flame and grill, turning occasionally, for 7 to 12 minutes, depending on the heat of your fire and the desired degree of doneness.

Alternatively, you can broil the meat: Preheat the broiler with a rack about 5 inches below it. Line a baking sheet with parchment or lightly oil it. Place the pieces of meat on the sheet and cook for 8 to 10 minutes, turning the meat at the halfway point and checking it for doneness after 7 minutes.

While the meat is grilling, or once it comes off the grill, pour the marinade into a small saucepan, add about ½ cup water, and bring to a boil over medium heat. Cook for a few minutes, stirring occasionally. Taste it and season with salt if you wish; if it is too tart for your taste, stir in a teaspoon of sugar or more to taste. You might want to stir in some tarragon leaves once it comes off the heat. Pour into a small serving bowl.

If you grilled the kebabs, you can either remove the meat from the skewers or simply serve it on the skewers. Put out the platter of herbs, the rice, and the sauce for the rice.

NOTE ON RICE: The classic combination of rice and kebab in Iran is called *chelo-kebab*, but in fact any rice, plain or flavored, is a great partner for these kebabs.

TABRIZ, IRAN—*Kebabs grilling street-side: The lamb kebabs in the foreground are a mix of meat and, to keep them moist, small pieces of fat. The aroma drifted down the street attracting customers, including me.*

LIVER KEBABS FROM YAZD

VIVER KEBAB

The desert city of Yazd is a mesmerizing place, with a labyrinth of lanes and bazaars, many of them roofed for coolness from the sun. In the markets are stalls selling mountains of fresh herbs, vivid green in the shade, and little eateries offering drinks and sandwiches. But there are also small, almost seedy cafés that have a simple menu for people who find themselves far from the comfort of a home-cooked meal. They offer a variety of kebabs, served with flatbreads, rice, chunks of onion, and grilled tomatoes.

My favorite meal at a little place I went to several times for lunch was the liver kebab: small pieces of liver lightly grilled and perfectly matched by grilled tomatoes and a plate of fresh herbs. This is a great way to convert friends to the pleasures of eating liver. **SERVES 3 OR 4**

1 pound liver: young beef, calf, or sheep

About 1 teaspoon sea salt

About 1 tablespoon sunflower or extra-virgin olive oil

ACCOMPANIMENTS

Grilled Tomatoes (page 162)

1 medium onion or 2 shallots, thinly sliced

Herb Plate (page 23)

Rice, such as Basic Persian Rice (page 211) or Barberry Rice (page 215), and/or flatbreads

Wash the liver and trim off and discard any tough bits. Cut into 1-inch pieces and put in a bowl. Sprinkle on ½ teaspoon of the salt and set aside for an hour.

Preheat a charcoal or gas grill. Thread the pieces of liver onto skewers, allowing 5 or 6 per skewer and not crowding them. Brush the kebabs with oil and place 5 inches over the coals or flame. Grill for about 2 minutes on each side, until browned on the outside but still pink inside; sprinkle on the remaining ½ teaspoon salt as they cook.

Remove from the heat and serve with the grilled tomatoes, sliced onion or shallots, herb plate, and rice and/or a stack of flatbreads.

SHIRAZ, IRAN—*Inside the dome of Hafez's tomb.*

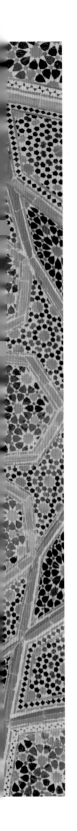

FOUNTAINS AND GARDENS, PICNICS AND POETRY

The arts of Persia, from poetry to painting, celebrate beauty and historic events, and they also celebrate pleasure. Writing and painting are often intertwined, for the manuscripts of works by the great poets of the past have been copied and

recopied by hand (rather as the Bible was in medieval Europe, by monks) and, like illuminated scriptures, those copies were decorated with paintings.

What we see in those paintings, finely detailed and in miniature, is often a world of courtiers and ease. Poets recite to their rulers, people sit talking and picnicking on carpets. All this is strongly echoed today, as Persians still have a special love for gardens, flowing water, picnicking, poetry, and music. Other paintings show daily life in all its busyness and give us glimpses of earlier times that still resonate: A baker works at his oven while his customers wait to buy bread; a street-side cook tends a brazier on which skewers of meat are grilling; gardeners tend plants and trees; lovers sit together at a picnic. It's striking how often food and pleasure feature in the paintings.

The works of many of the great Persian poets of long ago (Hafez, Saadi, and Omar Khayyam, among others) celebrate wine, women, and song, and beauty of all kinds. The eleventh-century poet Ferdowsi is revered for his epic *Shahnameh*, which recounts the history of Persia from earliest times. The great poem helped revive the Persian language, which had been in retreat following the Arab conquest in AD 651.

All this poetry is still alive and well in Iran. The poets' tombs are places to visit not out of duty, but for a treat. They are set in cool green gardens, with fountains, trees, flowers, and inviting places to sit. The day I visited Hafez's tomb in Shiraz, couples and families and singles were there, strolling, chatting, and enjoying the day. An older man sat down near me and began to read aloud. Soon a small group had gathered. Even without understanding Persian, I could see the pleasure that everyone was taking in the poetry.

MARINATED PORK KEBABS

BASTURMA

Georgians have a meat-grilling tradition with roots in shepherd life, but it also probably owes something to the raiding and conquering peoples who swept across the country over the centuries. Because so much of the population of the Persian culinary region does not eat pork for religious reasons, this is the only recipe in the book that features pork. The meat is marinated in vinegar and pomegranate juice; use wine if pomegranate juice is not available, or substitute pomegranate molasses diluted with water, as suggested below. Note that the pork marinates for at least 12 hours, and up to 24 hours.   **SERVES 6**

2 pounds boneless pork loin or shoulder roast, cut into 1-inch pieces

2 medium onions, thinly sliced

¼ cup red wine vinegar or apple cider vinegar

¼ cup pomegranate juice or red wine, or 2 tablespoons pomegranate molasses mixed with 2 tablespoons water

About 2 teaspoons sea salt

OPTIONAL ACCOMPANIMENTS

Boomerang Breads (page 255) or flatbreads

Cucumber Salad with Sumac and Mint (page 47)

Herb Plate (page 23)

Red Ajika (page 42)

Place the pork and onions in a nonreactive bowl. Mix together the liquid ingredients, add 1 teaspoon of the salt, and pour over the pork, stirring to make sure all surfaces are exposed to the marinade. Cover and refrigerate for 12 to 24 hours. Bring the meat back to room temperature before grilling. Prepare a medium fire in a charcoal or gas grill; you don't want a quick surge of heat, but instead a lower temperature so the meat has time to cook through.

Slide the meat onto metal skewers, not packing it tightly. Grill the meat about 5 inches from the coals or flame for 10 to 15 minutes, turning the skewers frequently to prevent burning, until the meat is cooked through or to your desired doneness. Keep an eye on them—if you have flare-ups from fat dripping into the flames, the meat will char and blacken. Sprinkle on the remaining 1 teaspoon salt as the meat cooks.

Slide the pork off the skewers and onto a platter. If you wish, serve with breads, the cucumber salad or another salad, and the herb plate, along with red *ajika*.

WINE-COUNTRY BEEF KEBABS

MTSVADI

Picture a snowcapped wall of mountains about fifteen miles in the distance, visible through the green-leafed fruit trees by a farmhouse. And imagine a fire made of grapevine clippings, the flames hot at first, then dying down to graying embers. That's what it was like the day I visited Irakli Nikolashvili's uncle's place. He and Irakli have an organic vineyard in eastern Georgia, across the Alazani River Valley from the town of Telavi. Their wine is delicious, especially their Saperavi.

The food we had at lunch was as good as the wine. Irakli's aunt made *khachapuri*, and she and her husband grilled large kebabs of tender baby beef. They did nothing to interfere with the taste of the meat: Other than a little salt, their wonderful flavor came from the meat itself, and from the fire of vineyard trimmings.

As with any simple recipe, the quality of the ingredients is important. Look for baby beef, or ethical veal, with its fat on, preferably grass-fed. Make a fire from hardwood or charcoal if you can. Wait until the flames have died down, so the heat is even. Serve with red wine and a salad of leafy greens or some chopped cucumber or tomatoes. **SERVES 8**

2½ to 3 pounds boneless baby beef (flank steak or sirloin) or ethical veal, cut into 1-inch chunks, at room temperature
About 1 tablespoon sea salt

OPTIONAL ACCOMPANIMENTS
Red *Ajika* (page 42)
Cheese-Filled Quick Breads (page 251)

Preheat a charcoal or gas grill.

Thread the meat onto metal skewers, leaving a little space between the pieces. Sprinkle with salt. Grill the meat about 5 inches from the coals or flame, turning the skewers frequently, until done as you like it.

Slide the meat onto a serving platter and serve with the red *ajika* and cheese-filled breads if you wish.

FEASTING IN A GARDEN OF EDEN

Tucked away in the Caucasus foothills above Lahich, in Azerbaijan, is a lovely Garden of Eden. I walked up there one morning in late September. The barberry and sea buckthorn bushes by the grassy track were laden with colorful berries, and

sheep grazed on the hillside. Around a curve in the path, I suddenly came upon several hundred, maybe more, mature apple trees loaded with fruit, apples in every shade from pale green-yellow through pink- and orange-tinged to deep, almost wine red. I sampled apples until my mouth was raw.

A horseman came by, his horse carrying large wooden panniers. We exchanged a quick *"Salaam aleikum,"* and he cantered off. Sometime later, I heard a laboring engine, a strange modern sound in that peaceful orchard, and around the corner came an old Lada.

Several men emerged from the car. One of them, lean and bony, in his seventies, with a high-cheekboned face and a smile, came over and shook my hand as he said, *"Salaam."* He invited me to join them for a drink of *tutovka,* mulberry "vodka." "No, thank you," I said. But then he mentioned *shashlik.* Ah, well then, I thought. . . .

We gathered dried bits of twigs and wood, and Ajdar, for that was the thin man's name, made a fire. As it burned down, he threaded pieces of lamb onto long, wide metal skewers, arranged two rocks on either side of the fire, and placed the skewers across the embers. He also buried some potatoes to cook in the coals.

As he felt the embers get too hot, Ajdar would sprinkle water on them, and sometimes onto the meat, to cool things down a little. The other men laid cardboard on the ground as a table and placed glasses and napkins on it. They opened the bottle of *tutovka* as well as jars of pickled tomatoes and homemade yogurt, then sliced one of the flat loaves of bread they'd brought.

Soon Ajdar brought over the first skewer and slid the meat onto a plate. Then came the others, making a heap of beautifully grilled lamb that had been flavored only with salt. As we started eating, a man came walking

NEAR LAHICH, AZERBAIJAN—*The rugged foothills of the Caucasus Mountains are veined with streams and rivers that run in steep-sided valleys. Winters can be harsh, but fruit trees such as this apple tree can thrive in sheltered areas.*

down the hillside. It was the horseman who'd ridden past earlier. He too was included in the feast.

This readiness to share food and drink with a stranger is part of the culture in rural Azerbaijan, as it is in Georgia and Armenia. In North America and Europe, people seem to be less open, but in the Caucasus, a place where people have suffered a lot from war and change, there's a hospitable generosity.

TURKEY KEBABS

SHISLIK HINDUSKA

Until I went to Azerbaijan, I had never eaten, or even seen, turkey kebabs. They're a big thing in Azerbaijan. Now that I've made them at home for friends, we all agree that it's our favorite way to eat turkey.

Use boneless leg or breast meat, whichever you prefer, or a mixture. You might take the opportunity to put some eggplants on to grill.   **SERVES 8**

3 pounds boneless turkey (see headnote), cut into 1½-inch chunks

2 medium onions, grated

¼ cup verjuice, cider vinegar, rice vinegar, or white wine vinegar

About 1 tablespoon ground sumac

About ¼ cup sunflower or extra-virgin olive oil

About 2 teaspoons sea salt

ACCOMPANIMENTS

Cucumber Salad with Sumac and Mint (page 47)

Herb Plate (page 23)

Pomegranate-Coriander Sauce (page 35) or Green or Red Ajika (page 40 or 42)

Basic Persian Rice (page 211)

At least 3 hours before you want to grill, rinse the turkey pieces, pat dry, and put in a large bowl. Add the grated onion, verjuice or vinegar, and 1 teaspoon of the sumac and stir and turn to expose all surfaces of the meat to the marinade. Cover and refrigerate to marinate for at least 2 hours, and as long as 5 hours; bring back to room temperature before grilling.

Preheat a charcoal or gas grill; you want moderate heat.

Slide the turkey pieces onto skewers, leaving a small space between each piece (discard the marinade). Brush lightly with oil and sprinkle on a little salt. Place the skewers on the grill and cook, turning them frequently, until the meat is touched with color and cooked through, about 15 minutes. Partway through cooking, sprinkle on about 2 more teaspoons sumac and 2 teaspoons salt.

When the meat is cooked, remove from the grill and slide off the skewers, heaping it on a platter. Serve with the salad, herb plate, sauce of your choice, and rice.

Clockwise from top: *Cucumber Salad with Sumac and Mint (page 47), Turkey Kebabs, a bowl of sumac powder, and Tart-Sweet Apricot and Raisin Relish (page 33).*

ROAST CHICKEN
WITH PERSIAN FLAVORS

This roast chicken is stuffed with a walnut-rich mixture of onion and tart fruit and bathed in lemony saffron butter or oil. It roasts for an hour wrapped in foil (which keeps it very moist) and then another hour or so with the foil open, so that it gets good color. You can make the stuffing up to a day ahead if that's more convenient. A stuffed bird takes longer to cook; put the chicken in the oven a full 2½ hours before you want to serve it.   **SERVES 6 TO 8**

STUFFING

2 tablespoons sunflower oil, butter-ghee, or extra-virgin olive oil

1½ cups chopped onions

½ cup walnuts or walnut pieces, coarsely chopped

¼ cup dried barberries (see Glossary), soaked in warm water for 10 minutes and drained

¼ cup coarsely chopped dried sour cherries, or sour plums, or fresh or frozen cranberries

¼ cup pomegranate molasses

One 3- to 4-pound chicken, at room temperature

About 1 teaspoon sea salt

2 tablespoons butter, melted, or sunflower or olive oil

About 2 tablespoons fresh lemon juice

1 tablespoon Saffron Water (page 27)

To make the stuffing, heat the oil or ghee in a large heavy skillet over medium-high heat. Add the onions and cook until nicely golden. Toss in the walnuts, lower the heat to medium, and cook, stirring, for a few minutes. Add the barberries and other fruit and the pomegranate molasses, reduce the heat to low, and cook for 5 minutes, stirring occasionally. Set aside to cool. (The stuffing can be covered and refrigerated overnight; bring to room temperature before using.)

Preheat the oven to 400°F.

Rub the chicken all over, inside and out, with the salt. Combine the melted butter or oil, lemon juice, and saffron water in a small bowl; set aside.

Figure out an arrangement for wrapping the chicken completely in aluminum foil: I use two long wide pieces, one laid at a right angle across the other in an X. Place the cross of foil on your roasting pan, and then the bird in the center of the foil. Stuff the chicken with the stuffing and use a large needle and thread to stitch the cavity closed, or pin it closed with one or two small skewers. Stir the

Left: **TBILISI, GEORGIA**—*A street stand selling sunflower seeds and sunflower oil, the standard cooking oil in the region.*

Right: **YEREVAN, ARMENIA**—*Plums at the market.*

saffron-lemon liquid and pour it over the bird. Fold up the ends of the foil and seal the foil: Pull up the inner sheet of foil, align the ends, and fold them over and over to seal the foil firmly around the bird. Repeat with the second piece of foil. (If you feel that there's not enough overlap of foil and that the packaging might leak, add a third length of foil on the diagonal and fold it up around the bird in the same way.)

Place in the oven and roast for 1 hour. Open and fold back the foil to expose the breast of the chicken. Baste the bird with the liquid that has pooled in the foil. Place the chicken back in the oven to roast for another 45 minutes; baste it once more halfway through. Test for doneness by trying to wiggle one of the legs: If the joint is still tight, the bird needs another 15 minutes or so. Remove from the oven and let rest for 20 minutes or more.

Transfer the bird to a rimmed carving board or platter. Pour the juices from the foil into the roasting pan and heat gently; set aside in a bowl.

If you stitched the cavity closed, cut through the stitching; if you used skewers, remove them. Use a spoon to scoop the stuffing into a small bowl. Carve the bird at the table or in the kitchen and arrange the meat on a platter. Drizzle the sliced chicken with the warm pan juices.

STOVETOP MEAT AND POULTRY

THE MANY MEAT AND POULTRY DISHES IN the Persian culinary world that are cooked on the stovetop (rather than being grilled or roasted) are an expression of home cooking at its best. Some, like Georgian *chakapuli* (page 185), are vibrant combinations of meat and tart fruit, loaded with herbs and greens. Others, for example the wonderful Persian stews called *khoresht* (pages 181 and 186), are slow-cooked and deeply flavored, ideal for eating with plenty of rice to soak up the gravy. Azeri *piti* (see page 188), called *abgusht* or *dizi* in Iran, is a much-loved blend of lamb and vegetables that's a soup and a meat course in one. In Persian *fesanjun* (see page 204), chicken cooks in a thick walnut sauce that is tart with pomegranate molasses. There are two easy recipes here for less-favored cuts: a tongue salad from Yerevan (see page 198) that is a satisfying blend of crunch and tenderness, and a richly sauced chicken giblet dish from Georgia (see page 206). Two unusual and easy recipes from Kurdistan call for poaching: Spiced Beef Shank (page 195) and Fried Chicken in Broth (page 200).

The recipes that call for lamb, both here and in the grilling chapter, are mostly from the Muslim-majority regions: Iran and Kurdistan, as well as Azerbaijan. There are very few Georgian or Armenian recipes that call for lamb; beef, especially baby beef, is favored.

Previous pages: EAST OF SHIRAZ, IRAN—*Thin unleavened flatbread called* nane-tire *accompanies every meal for the Kurds and for the nomads living in the mountains of southern Iran (see page 190). It's used to scoop up pieces of meat, sop up gravy, and thicken stews.*

TART LAMB STEW WITH FRIED POTATOES

KHORESHT-E-GHEIMEH

In this Persian dish, the tartness comes from dried limes, known as *limoo omani* in Iran and as *limoo basrahi* in Iraq (see Glossary). The limes add an oddly delicious form of citrus aroma and taste that is one of the distinguishing elements of Persian and Persian-influenced cuisine.

Dried limes are sold in Persian and Arab grocery stores (look for dull-brown rounds), and they keep for a long time in a plastic bag. This recipe calls for both whole dried limes and dried lime powder. You can grate whole limes to get the powder or buy it.

If you're starting with precooked black-eyed peas, cooking time is less than an hour. **SERVES 4 TO 6**

½ cup dried black-eyed peas, rinsed, or 1½ cups cooked or rinsed canned black-eyed peas (see The Precooked Beans Habit, page 82)

4 to 6 cups water

¼ cup plus 2 tablespoons sunflower or extra-virgin olive oil, or rendered lamb fat

2 medium onions, thinly sliced

1 teaspoon turmeric

½ teaspoon freshly ground black pepper, or to taste

About 1 pound boneless lamb shoulder or leg, cut into 1-inch pieces

2 tablespoons tomato paste

1 tablespoon powdered dried lime (see headnote)

2 whole dried limes (see headnote)

2½ teaspoons sea salt, or to taste

3 to 4 medium waxy potatoes, peeled and chopped into ½-inch cubes (about 3 cups)

Juice of 1 lemon

ACCOMPANIMENTS

Herb Plate (page 23)

Sliced tomatoes or cucumbers or a green salad

Basic Persian Rice (page 211)

If using dried black-eyed peas, place them in a large heavy pot, add about 3 cups of the water, and bring to a boil. Cook at a strong boil, half covered, for about an hour, until the peas are tender.

Meanwhile, heat 2 tablespoons of the oil or fat in a large skillet over medium heat. Add the onions and cook until translucent and starting to brown. Add the turmeric and pepper, then toss in the lamb and stir to expose all sides to the hot oil. Once the meat is touched with color all over, add the tomato paste and turn and stir the meat.

If you are using cooked or canned black-eyed peas, place them in a large heavy pot, add a generous cup of water, and bring to a gentle simmer.

Add the meat and onions to the black-eyed peas. Pour a little hot water into the skillet, swirl it around, and add to the pot, to make sure no flavor is lost. Add water to cover, stir in the dried lime powder, and bring to a boil. Lower the heat to maintain a strong simmer and cook, partially covered, for about 20 minutes.

Prick the dried limes 4 or 5 times each with the tip of a knife (be careful not to cut yourself, since they can ricochet if they're very hard) and add to the stew. Stir in 2 teaspoons of the salt and simmer for 10 minutes. Set aside.

Meanwhile, heat the remaining ¼ cup oil in a large heavy skillet over medium-high heat. Add the potatoes and the remaining ½ teaspoon salt and cook, stirring frequently, until the potatoes are crisp and golden all over, about 10 minutes. Drain.

Just before serving, reheat the stew and stir in the lemon juice. Taste for seasoning and adjust it if you wish. Divide the stew among individual wide bowls or plates and top with the fried potatoes. Serve with the herb plate, sliced tomatoes (or cucumbers or salad), and rice.

Left: MASSOULEH, IRAN— *Legumes are widely used in Persian cooking, especially in the delectable soup-stews called ash (see recipes on pages 107, 110, and 112). Here, from left to right, are white beans, lentils, black-eyed peas, and split peas.*

Opposite: SULAYMANIYAH, KURDISTAN—*The streets in the bazaar area downtown are crowded with shoppers in the evening, most of them men picking up meat, vegetables, and breads to take home. The vegetable for sale here is a cousin of rhubarb and available for only a short time in spring.*

EASTER STEW WITH TARRAGON

CHAKAPULI

Chakapuli is a vibrant, easy stew, green with tarragon and the tartness of sour plums (*tkemali* in Georgian), for which tomatillos are an ideal substitute. Like most meat dishes from Georgia, it is usually made with meat from young cattle. At Eastertime, though, there's a special version of *chakapuli* made with lamb.

Serve as a main course with one of the Persian rices on pages 211–215, or with boiled potatoes. Include a vegetable dish or two, such as Georgian Leek Pâté (page 70) and Azeri Mushrooms (page 76).   **SERVES 6**

2 to 3 tablespoons sunflower or extra-virgin olive oil

1 cup chopped onion or shallots

¼ teaspoon turmeric

About 2 pounds boneless lamb shoulder or leg or baby beef rump roast or shoulder (see headnote), cut into bite-size pieces

4 to 5 cups water

About 12 sour plums, or substitute tomatillos, husked and rinsed

½ cup chopped scallions (including the green tops)

1 cup fresh tarragon leaves

¼ cup chopped fresh coriander

2 tablespoons minced lovage (optional)

1 tablespoon powdered dried fenugreek leaves

2 garlic cloves, minced or mashed, or ½ cup chopped fresh garlic chives

1 dried red chile or fresh green cayenne chile, broken or halved, or 1 teaspoon cayenne

1 teaspoon sea salt, or to taste

About ¼ cup dry white or red wine

Place a wide heavy pot over medium-high heat. Add the oil, and when it is hot, add the onion or shallots and sauté until softened. Add the turmeric and stir. Add the meat and cook, stirring occasionally, until it has all changed color, about 5 minutes. Add water to cover, raise the heat, and bring to a boil. Lower the heat and simmer, partially covered, for 30 minutes if using lamb (1 hour if using beef).

Add the plums or tomatillos, bring to a strong simmer, and cook for 20 minutes. (The dish can be made ahead to this point, covered, and set aside until 30 minutes before you want to serve it. If holding it for longer than an hour, refrigerate it after it cools; bring to a simmer before proceeding.)

Toss in the scallions, tarragon, coriander, lovage, if using, fenugreek, garlic, chile or cayenne, and salt and stir well. Simmer for about 10 minutes, covered. Add the wine. Simmer for another 10 minutes, uncovered.

Taste for seasoning and adjust if necessary just before serving.

KERMAN-BAZAAR LAMB STEW

KHORESHT GORMEH-SABZI

I am still haunted by the *gormeh-sabzi* I had at a little eatery near the entrance to Kerman's bazaar. Its gravy had a deep meaty flavor with a subtle edge of tamarind tartness. This is my homage to that stew.

Like most stews, this tastes best if made ahead (refrigerate if the wait is longer than an hour), then reheated when you want to serve it. Hold back on the final seasoning until the last moment: You may want to add a squeeze of lemon at that point. Or instead serve lemon wedges alongside.   **SERVES 4**

½ cup dried black-eyed peas, rinsed

About 8 cups water, plus 2 to 3 tablespoons

5 to 6 tablespoons sunflower or vegetable oil or rendered lamb fat

1 large bunch coriander, trimmed and finely chopped (2 packed cups)

1 to 2 bunches flat-leaf parsley, trimmed of coarse stems and finely chopped (2 packed cups)

½ cup chopped fresh dill or 2 tablespoons dried dill

½ cup chopped fresh fenugreek or 2 tablespoons dried fenugreek leaves

1 large or 2 medium leeks, white and pale green parts only, chopped and washed well (2 to 3 cups)

¼ teaspoon turmeric

1 large or 2 medium onions or 2 large shallots, thinly sliced

About 1 pound boneless lamb shoulder, cut into 1-inch pieces

2 tablespoons powdered dried lime, or about 2 tablespoons fresh lemon juice

2 teaspoons sea salt, or to taste

1 tablespoon tamarind pulp

4 dried limes

1 or 2 lemons, cut in half

ACCOMPANIMENTS

Basic Persian Rice (page 211)

Herb Plate (page 23)

Place the black-eyed peas in a pot, add about 3 cups water, and bring to a strong boil. Partially cover, lower the heat slightly, and boil for 30 minutes or so while you prepare the herbs and meat. Check occasionally to make sure that the pot isn't too dry; add more water if necessary.

Place a wide heavy pot over medium-high heat. Add about 3 tablespoons of the oil or fat, then toss in all the herbs and the leeks and cook, stirring frequently, for a minute or two. Reduce the heat to medium-low and cook, stirring occasionally, until the herbs and leeks are very wilted and their color has darkened, 15 to 20 minutes; add a little extra oil if they start to stick. Transfer to a bowl and set aside; place the pot back over medium-high heat.

KERMAN, IRAN—
The tall, graceful vaulted roof of the Kerman bazaar dwarfs this group of schoolgirls on an outing.

Add 1 to 2 tablespoons oil or fat to the pot, then add the turmeric and stir. Toss in the onions or shallots and cook until well softened. Raise the heat, add the meat, and cook, stirring and turning it, until all surfaces have changed color, about 5 minutes. Add the cooked herb mixture, the softened black-eyed peas with their cooking liquid, and the dried lime powder or lemon juice and stir well. Add hot water to cover generously, about 3 cups, and bring to a boil. Add 1 teaspoon of the salt, lower the heat to maintain a strong simmer, and cook, covered, for an hour or so.

Meanwhile, cut the tamarind pulp into pieces and place in a bowl with 2 to 3 tablespoons hot water. Use a fork to mash it to help it dissolve in the water. Set aside to soak for 15 minutes or so, then mash it a little more. Place a sieve over a bowl, pour in the tamarind mixture, and use the back of a spoon to press it through the mesh. Discard the tamarind debris and set the tamarind liquid aside.

At this point, the meat and black-eyed peas should be very tender. Prick the dried limes several times with the tip of a knife (be careful not to cut yourself, since they can ricochet if they're very hard) and add them to the stew, along with the remaining 1 teaspoon salt. Cover and simmer for about 50 minutes, checking occasionally to make sure that the stew is not sticking to the bottom of the pot—add water if needed—and that the dried limes are immersed in the liquid; press down on them if need be.

Add the tamarind liquid. There should be plenty of thin dark gravy; if the stew has thickened, add more water. Cover and simmer for about 10 minutes longer.

Taste for salt and for tartness; adjust as necessary, with salt and squeezes of lemon juice. Serve with the rice and herb plate.

HEARTY LAMB STEW WITH CHICKPEAS AND POTATOES

ABGUSHT · DIZI · PITI

Called *abgusht* in Persian (*ab* means water or liquid, and *gusht* means meat), but known casually as *dizi* in Iran and *piti* in Azerbaijan, this stew of lamb and chickpeas comes in many versions. It's a peasant dish, often served at workingmen's cafés and at market stalls as a hearty affordable meal-in-a-bowl.

The name *dizi* comes from the word for the deep, straight-sided iron bowl used for serving the stew in Iran. Traditionally the stew was cooked in an earthenware pot. In Azerbaijan, *piti* comes in an earthenware pot, and in both Azerbaijan and Iran the basics are the same: a brothy lamb stew with chickpeas, chunks of potato, and a little tomato, served very hot. The traditional tools for eating it are a spoon, a pestle, flatbread, and an empty bowl.

The first time you are served *dizi*, whether by a home cook or in a café, you have to figure out how to eat it. The broth and solids are served together but are eaten separately. Start by tearing up some flatbread into the empty bowl and pouring the broth over it to make your "first course." After you have spooned up the broth and soaked bread, it's time for part two: Mash the meat, chickpeas, and potato to a coarse paste with the pestle (or the back of a large spoon), then scoop up the paste with more flatbread, taking the odd bite of fresh herbs or sliced onion from time to time as a refresher.

For the cook, the most important ingredient is time, a long, slow boil and simmer to get the meat and chickpeas tender and the flavors blended. Many cooks in Iran use a pressure cooker to speed up the cooking of the chickpeas. I prefer to put the stew on well ahead and let it cook slowly, without worrying about it. I make it with lamb shanks or even bone-in lamb chops; the marrow in the bones adds extra richness. You can start with boneless lamb, but in that case, be sure to include some chunks of lamb fat.

This recipe makes a large amount; when serving fewer people, I still make the whole batch, just to have the leftovers. As with most stews, it is even better the next day. **SERVES 8**

3 pounds bone-in lamb (chops, or shank cut into short lengths) or 2¼ pounds boneless lamb shoulder or leg

A few chunks of lamb fat (optional; see headnote)

2 medium onions, chopped

1 cup chickpeas, soaked for at least 3 hours, or overnight, in water to cover and drained

½ cup dried navy beans or other white beans

1 dried lime (optional)

1 cassia (cinnamon) stick

½ teaspoon turmeric

2 teaspoons sea salt, or to taste

About 1½ pounds waxy potatoes, peeled and cut into 1½-inch chunks

2 medium tomatoes, coarsely chopped, or ½ cup canned crushed tomatoes

6 dried sour plums (optional; see Note)

1 tablespoon dried mint (optional)

ACCOMPANIMENTS (SEE NOTE)

Lavash or other flatbreads

2 thinly sliced onions (optional)

Ground sumac (optional)

Herb Plate (page 23; optional)

Place the lamb, lamb fat, if using, onions, chickpeas, and beans in a large heavy pot, add water to cover, and bring to a vigorous boil. If using the dried lime, prick it several times with the tip of a knife (be careful not to cut yourself, since it can ricochet if it's very hard), and toss it in. Add the cassia, turmeric, and salt. Lower the heat to maintain a medium boil, partially cover, and cook for 2½ hours, or until the chickpeas and beans are tender. If the water level drops during the long cooking, add more.

Add the potatoes, tomatoes, and sour plums, if using, and cook until the potatoes are tender, about 20 minutes. Taste for seasoning and adjust as needed.

Serve in large bowls, topped with a sprinkling of dried mint if you wish. Put out the flatbreads and whatever other accompaniments you choose. Give each guest a large extra spoon and an extra bowl, and explain how the dish is eaten.

NOTE ON CHOICES AND DIFFERENCES: In Azerbaijan, I had several versions of *piti* that included sour plums, which is why they are an option here. The sliced onions and sumac are served with Azeri *piti* but not usually with Iranian *dizi*. Instead, in Iran, the stew is served with a simple plate of scallions and fresh herbs.

NOMAD ENCOUNTER

In Iran and Azerbaijan, butchers' shops routinely display clean, gleaming-white sheeps' heads and shanks in tidy rows. They're the essential ingredients for making *kaleh poche*, which means "head and shank" in Persian. It's a frugal dish and a favorite of home cooks. It originated as a way of making use of the bits left over when a sheep was slaughtered, and that's how I first encountered it in Iran, on the day after Eid e-Ghorban, the Feast of the Sacrifice.

Elsewhere in the Muslim world, the Feast of the Sacrifice is a time when sheep or cattle are butchered and the meat shared at family feasts. Persians had told me that in Iran the feast is celebrated by only a few, families of those who have made the pilgrimage to Mecca (the *haj*).

Up in the mountains, about three hours' drive from Shiraz, lives a group of nomads known as Khamseh. They have a mixed heritage, partly Arab, and among themselves, they speak a form of Arabic, rather than Persian. They keep herds of sheep and goats, and a few of the wealthier families keep a camel.

Every fall in late October before the cold weather sets in (there is heavy snow in the mountains in the winter months), the Khamseh families set off on foot—with their herds and their donkeys, which are loaded with household goods—on a twenty-day journey south through the mountains to their winter pastures above the port city of Bandar Abbas. There they set up their dark wool tents. Winter is the time for dyeing the wool that the women have spun in the summer months, and for weaving their lovely rugs. After Nou-Roz (the Iranian New Year, at the spring equinox), they pack up and head back north to their summer pastures.

When I stayed near the mountains, my host, Abbas, took me up to visit the nomads. His second wife, Leila, came with us; it was her family we were going to visit. When we arrived, her mother, Heshmat, was hard at work cleaning the head and legs of a sheep, which were about to be transformed into *kaleh poche*. The family patriarch, Hajji Hossein, had made the pilgrimage to Mecca some years earlier. As a result, the whole family and their neighbors had celebrated Eid the day before; the head and legs were all that remained after the feast.

EAST OF SHIRAZ, IRAN—
I arrived at this nomad encampment in the mountains when the matriarch of a large family was preparing kaleh poche, *a stew of sheep's head and shanks. Here she is cleaning the sheep's head carefully, before adding it to the pot.*

I photographed Heshmat as she worked out in the sunshine and clear air. Once she had the head and shanks thoroughly cleaned and cracked open, they all went into a large pot of boiling water with salt, turmeric, chopped onion, a little tomato, and wild-gathered aromatics.

Nearby was the family tent, woven of black-brown wool and hung over a light frame to make an airy shelter from the sun. But the family also has a one-roomed brick house with a door and a thickly carpeted floor. It was there that we ate. We sat around the *sofreh*, a sheet of plastic placed over the carpet, onto which went piles of thin unleavened *saj*-baked breads like those in Kurdistan, which both the nomads and Kurds call *nane-tire* (see page 240). Hajji Hossein was served first by his wife. As the guest, I was next; then she served her sons, and finally her daughters. The bones had been transformed into a rich broth that was served in individual bowls. We ate by dipping pieces of bread into our soup, and we also used it to pick up morsels of meat from a shared platter. Each mouthful was a pleasure. Leila had brought a chicken dish and rice to contribute to the meal, but I stuck with the *kaleh poche*.

EAST OF SHIRAZ, IRAN—*A family at a nomad encampment in its large, airy tent. The tent frame of light poles that are lashed together holds wool fabric woven from the family's sheep. The two girls taught me a game resembling jacks, played with small stones.*

KURDISH STEW WITH DRIED FRUIT AND SPLIT PEAS

SHLEY GOSHT E NARIM

This easy stew is traditionally made with water, but if you have vegetable or meat broth, use that instead for extra depth of flavor. The *baharat* (spice blend) is simple: turmeric, cumin, and nigella. Dried apricots or dried plums add a tart note.

In Kurdistan, cooks prefer to use meat that is finely chopped (*gosht e narim* means chopped meat), not ground. You can start with a pound of flank or similar steak, or boneless lamb shoulder or chicken breast, and chop it, but I suggest you take the easy way, as I do, and use ground meat.   **SERVES 6**

¼ cup sunflower or extra-virgin olive oil

½ teaspoon turmeric

2 teaspoons ground cumin

1 teaspoon nigella seeds or ground nigella

1 pound ground beef, lamb, or chicken

2 cups cooked or rinsed canned split peas (see The Precooked Beans Habit, page 82)

1 tablespoon tomato paste

¾ cup dried apricots or dried plums, coarsely chopped

3 medium waxy potatoes, peeled and cut into 1-inch-long wedges

About 6 cups water or broth (see headnote)

2 teaspoons sea salt, or to taste (less if using salted broth)

ACCOMPANIMENTS

Flatbreads

Herb Plate (page 23)

Kurdish Black Rice (page 216), Kurdish Red Rice (page 217), or Basic Persian Rice (page 211)

In a wide heavy pot over medium heat, heat the oil until hot. Add the turmeric, cumin, and nigella and cook for a moment, stirring. Add the meat, split peas, tomato paste, and dried fruit and stir to expose all surfaces to the hot oil. Add the potatoes and enough water to cover by ½ inch and bring to a boil. Add the salt, partially cover, lower the heat, and simmer for 20 minutes, or until the potatoes are tender. Taste and adjust the seasoning if you wish.

Serve hot or warm with the flatbreads, fresh herbs, and rice.

SPICED BEEF SHANK

In Victorian times there was a tradition of spiced beef in England and North America, but it has largely disappeared. Spiced beef is not only delicious, but also a great way of using a tougher cut of meat (those that often have better flavor). I tasted this dish in Sulaymaniyah at the home of a political activist named Shler. The meat is simmered in spiced water, then set aside to cool. (I often cook it the day before I want to serve it.) Serve it in slices at room temperature as part of a meal, as I had it in Kurdistan, or use for open-faced or regular sandwiches.

I love having a supply of spiced beef on hand for unexpected guests or random hungry people. Serve it with plenty of good bread, plain or buttered, and something crunchy and fresh, such as sliced cucumber or pickles of some kind. Put out a condiment such as Georgian spice paste (*ajika*; see page 40 or 42) or Dijon mustard if you wish.   **SERVES 6 TO 8 AS PART OF A MEAL**

3 cups water

1 tablespoon whole cloves

1 teaspoon allspice berries

1 tablespoon cardamom pods, cracked

1 tablespoon black peppercorns

A 2- to 3-inch cassia (cinnamon) stick, broken into 2 or 3 pieces

3 or 4 large garlic cloves, coarsely chopped

1 teaspoon sea salt

About 2 pounds young beef or ethical veal shank or tendon, cut into short lengths by the butcher

Pour the water into a heavy pot, add the spices, garlic, and salt, and bring to a vigorous boil. Partially cover and boil for 10 to 15 minutes.

Add the meat, cover, and cook at a low boil until the meat is cooked through and tender, about 20 minutes. Remove the meat and set aside on a plate to cool to room temperature. (You can refrigerate it, in a sealed container, for up to 4 days.)

Serve the meat at room temperature, thinly sliced across the grain and arranged on a plate.

POACHED TONGUE

Tongue can seem intimidating if you have never cooked it, but it used to be a very normal cut for home cooks. It's still part of life in many places outside North America. When properly cooked and thinly sliced, it is tender and a pleasure to eat, rather like thinly sliced smoked meat. It must be poached until very soft, which takes 2½ to 3 hours. It's not possible to overcook tongue; if you're in doubt, let it cook a little more. The skin should be peeled off right away, while the tongue is still hot, or the job will be more difficult.

Tongue is usually served cold or at room temperature. Poach it ahead and store it in the refrigerator, bathed in the poaching liquid, so you can easily slice it thin and use it in anything from sandwiches to salads (see Yerevan Tongue Salad, page 198).

I used Jennifer McLagan's poached tongue recipe in her book *Odd Bits* for guidance; this recipe follows her method but with a different set of flavors in the poaching liquid.

BAKU, AZERBAIJAN—*A small inviting square in an area of the old city not yet transformed into expensive apartments and shops (left). A carpet laid on the cobblestone street outside a shop in the old city (right).*

1 small beef tongue (2½ to 3 pounds)

1 medium onion, coarsely chopped

1 tablespoon sea salt

4 whole cloves

8 allspice berries

1 thyme sprig or ½ teaspoon dried thyme (optional)

2 bay leaves

1 cassia (cinnamon) stick, broken in half

Place the tongue and onion in a large pot. Add water to cover by about 2 inches and the salt and bring to a boil. Skim off and discard the foam or scum that rises to the surface. Toss in the cloves, allspice, thyme, if using, bay leaves, and cassia stick, lower the heat to maintain a strong simmer, and cook, partially covered, until the tongue is very tender, 2½ to 3 hours. Top off the water if the level drops below the top of the meat, and turn the tongue over after about 1½ hours. To test for doneness, use a fork to pierce the tongue at both the thick end and the tip—it should slide in easily in both places.

Lift the tongue out of the broth and onto a plate or cutting board; set the poaching liquid aside. It is much easier to slide the skin off the tongue when it is hot. Work with a bowl of ice cubes nearby so you can cool your fingers from time to time, or use latex gloves to protect your hands from the heat. Start at the thick (throat) end of the tongue and use a small knife to pry an edge of the skin loose. Take hold of the loose edge with your fingers and then peel the skin off. It will come off in large strips. Trim off and discard any fat or gristle (there will be some at the thick end of the tongue).

Strain the poaching liquid into a container with a lid. Place the tongue in the broth, cover, and refrigerate for at least several hours, until completely chilled. It can be refrigerated for up to 4 days.

To use the tongue, slice crosswise as thin as possible.

YEREVAN TONGUE SALAD

This is my reconstruction of an appealing dish that I ate at a restaurant in Yerevan called Karas. It's made with slices of tender poached tongue tossed with red pepper, onion, and herbs.

The crunch of the red bell peppers and the cornichons is a nice contrast with the tender slices of tongue. If you don't want to use cornichons, try another pickle, such as Iranian-style pickled radishes, and chop them. Sorrel, with its lemony edge, is a great addition, along with the fresh tarragon or coriander.   **SERVES 6 AS AN APPETIZER OR A SIDE DISH**

1 onion, thinly sliced

About 1½ teaspoons sea salt

About ½ pound poached baby beef or veal tongue (see Poached Tongue, page 196), chilled

1 medium red or yellow bell pepper, cored, seeded, and cut into strips about ¼ inch wide and 1 inch long

10 cornichons, halved lengthwise (see headnote)

2 tablespoons red wine vinegar, or to taste

1 teaspoon sunflower or extra-virgin olive oil

About 2 tablespoons fresh tarragon leaves or chopped fresh coriander

3 or 4 sorrel leaves, cut into chiffonade, or substitute 2 tablespoons chopped fresh flat-leaf parsley plus 1 teaspoon ground sumac

Place the sliced onion in a bowl and sprinkle on about 1 teaspoon salt. Let stand for 15 minutes. Rinse the onion thoroughly in a sieve and gently squeeze it dry. Set aside.

Thinly slice the tongue, cut the slices into narrow bite-size strips, and transfer to a shallow bowl. Add the onion, bell pepper, and cornichons.

Mix the vinegar and oil with about ½ teaspoon salt and pour over the salad. Turn and toss gently. If you have the time, set aside for 30 minutes, loosely covered, to allow the tongue to absorb the other flavors and come to room temperature.

Just before serving, taste for salt and adjust if necessary. Sprinkle on the fresh herbs and toss again.

BEEF STEW WITH ONION AND TOMATO

KHARCHO

Kharcho is classic comfort food from Georgia. It's originally from mountainous Samegrelo and has the punchy flavors characteristic of that region. The beef cooks with onions and tomatoes. A paste of ground walnuts blended with garlic and spices enriches the gravy.

Though *kharcho* is usually served with breads, either Boomerang Breads (page 255) or *khachapuri* (page 251), I like serving it with rice.   **SERVES 6 TO 8**

¼ cup sunflower or extra-virgin olive oil

4 cups chopped onions (4 to 5 medium onions)

About 2 pounds stewing beef or pot roast, cut into bite-size pieces and trimmed of gristle and excess fat

2 tablespoons tomato paste

About 2½ cups water

2 cups chopped tomatoes (about 5 medium) or chopped canned tomatoes

1 cup finely ground walnuts

½ cup hot water

4 garlic cloves, crushed

1 tablespoon Georgian Spice Blend (page 28)

1 teaspoon cayenne (optional)

About 2 teaspoons sea salt

Freshly ground black pepper

¼ cup fresh coriander leaves

In a large heavy pot, heat the oil over medium-high heat. Toss in the onions and cook for a few minutes, until just starting to soften. Add the meat and stir, turning to expose all surfaces of the meat to the hot oil. Add the tomato paste and 2 cups water and bring to a boil, then lower the heat and simmer, partially covered, for 30 to 40 minutes.

Add the tomatoes and another ½ cup water and cook, partially covered, until the meat is tender, another 1 to 1½ hours. Stir again.

Once the meat is tender, place the walnuts in a bowl, add the hot water, and stir to blend to a paste. Add the garlic, spice blend, cayenne, if using, salt, and pepper to taste, then add the paste to the stew and stir in. Simmer for another 10 minutes. Taste for seasoning and adjust if necessary. Serve the stew sprinkled with the coriander leaves.

KURDISH FRIED CHICKEN IN BROTH

I love this style of cooking chicken for both its flavor and its ease. The chicken is cut into pieces and rubbed with salt and lemon juice, kind of a quick marinade, before being shallow-fried until golden. But there's no worry about whether the frying cooks the chicken completely, because it then simmers in water with a little onion, turmeric, and cumin until tender and cooked through.

Serve with rice and fresh herbs.   **SERVES 6 TO 8**

2½ to 3 pounds bone-in chicken legs and/or breasts, chopped into 1½-inch to 2-inch pieces

About ¼ cup fresh lemon juice

2 teaspoons sea salt, or more to taste

About 1½ cups sunflower or extra-virgin olive oil for shallow-frying

2 medium onions, grated

½ teaspoon turmeric

1¼ teaspoons ground cumin

¼ cup finely chopped fresh coriander or scallions, or a mixture

ACCOMPANIMENTS

Flatbreads

Kurdish Red Rice (page 217) or Kurdish Black Rice (page 216)

Herb Plate (page 23)

Place the chicken pieces in a large bowl, add the lemon juice, and turn the chicken to expose all surfaces to the juice. Add the salt and rub it onto the chicken pieces. If you have time, refrigerate, covered, for an hour or two to marinate.

About an hour before you want to serve the chicken, place a wide heavy skillet over medium heat. Add oil to a depth of ¼ inch. Once the oil is hot, lift the chicken pieces out of the marinade (reserve the marinade) and carefully slide them into the oil. (If your pan is too small to hold the chicken comfortably, use two pans or cook in batches, adding a little more oil if necessary.) Fry, turning the pieces from time to time, until the chicken is well touched with gold, about 15 minutes.

Lift the chicken pieces out of the oil and transfer to a large pot. Add the onions, the reserved marinade, and water to barely cover. Bring to a boil and toss in the turmeric and cumin, then lower the heat and simmer gently for 45 minutes or so, until the chicken is cooked through. (If you taste the broth early in the cooking, you will find the cumin too strong, but once it has finished simmering, the flavors come together.) Taste for seasoning and adjust if necessary.

Serve the chicken in its broth, topped with a sprinkling of chopped coriander and/or scallions. Set out plenty of flatbreads, the rice, and the herb plate.

Kurdish Fried Chicken in Broth, with Barberry Rice (page 215).

NEAR TBILISI, GEORGIA—*A casual spread of cheese, wine, and more set out in a farmhouse kitchen.*

WARMTH AT THE TABLE IN TBILISI

Late one spring afternoon, a friend and I made our way to dinner at the apartment of a family that I'd met only the week before. They live in the Tbilisi suburbs, in a tall apartment-block landscape like that of many former Soviet cities.

The blocks are charmless on the outside, and access is usually through a cement entryway that leads to a chipped concrete staircase, and perhaps to an elevator that may or may not work.

We climbed up to the fourth floor and found the apartment of our hosts, which was charming and inviting. The table had been set with plates, glasses, and clay ewers of Georgian wine, as well as with some of the dishes that were to be part of our meal: *khachapuri* (cheese-filled flatbreads; see page 251), Boomerang Breads (page 255), two kinds of *ajika*, red and green (see pages 42 and 40), a leafy green salad, and more.

In Georgia, an enormous effort goes into preparing food and laying a generous table for friends and family—and occasional strangers from afar like me. Though the work, almost all of it done by women, is long, it happens not in a rush but with a kind of easy stamina. Supper will be ready when it's ready, not at some exact preappointed time. The waiting time will pass with conversation and joking around. It's all part of a kind of unstructured style in Georgia that I find welcoming and relaxing.

After a while, our hosts brought more dishes to the table and we all sat down to the feast. Gia was *tamada*, or table host, and he proposed the first toast of the evening, the classic opener, "To God." We went on from there to eat and drink and tell stories. Several late arrivals were specially toasted in welcome. The toasts, the joking, the food explanations (translated for me by my friend Tamar), and the shifting conversations during the meal were all part of an in-the-moment delight. To Georgians, what matters most is coming together to eat and drink, finding pleasure and warmth at the table.

CLASSIC POMEGRANATE-WALNUT CHICKEN STEW

FESANJUN KHORESH

Ask an Iranian about Persian food, and for sure you'll be told about *fesanjun*. People have strong feelings about it. I took a cookbook with me to Iran, Margaret Shaida's classic *The Legendary Cuisine of Persia*, published in 1992. Her recipe for *fesanjun* puzzled me, because it calls for sugar as well as onion. When I found myself in Farahnoz's kitchen (see Caspian Interlude, page 140), I asked her about the sugar. "Oh, she must be from Tehran!" she said immediately. "*Fesanjun* is from here, from the north. It should be sour, with no sugar or onion, and intense with pomegranate."

This recipe follows her advice. Pomegranate molasses cooks down with ground walnuts to make a dark, intense sauce, and the chicken cooks in the sauce for about 45 minutes.

Cooks and eaters also differ about the texture of the walnuts: Should they be finely ground, or instead left a little coarser?

Serve this as the centerpiece of a meal, with Basic Persian Rice (page 211) or another plain rice.   **SERVES 6 TO 8**

SAUCE

2½ cups (8 ounces) walnuts or walnut pieces

4 cups lukewarm water

½ cup pomegranate molasses

½ teaspoon ground cassia (cinnamon)

1 teaspoon sea salt

CHICKEN

3½ pounds bone-in chicken legs, each cut into 4 pieces (with a cleaver or sharp heavy knife), or 2½ pounds boneless legs and breasts, cut into large bite-size pieces, skin removed

About 1½ teaspoons salt

Generous grinding of black pepper

To make the sauce, grind the walnuts in a food processor or other grinder until they are fine crumbs, not a powder. Place them in a bowl, add the lukewarm water, and stir to mix thoroughly. Set aside.

Place a wide heavy pot over medium heat. Add the pomegranate molasses and heat, stirring, until it starts to bubble. Add the water-walnut blend and stir as it all comes to a boil, then lower the heat and cook at a low boil for about 1 hour, uncovered. Check occasionally to make sure that the sauce is not burning as it cooks down, just thickening a little; add another ½ to 1 cup water if necessary. The sauce will darken in color as it cooks, and the oil from the walnuts will rise to the surface.

Meanwhile, make the chicken: If using skin-on chicken, pull off the skin and set aside for another purpose if you wish.

Place the chicken in a bowl, sprinkle on the salt and pepper, and toss to distribute the seasonings. Cover and refrigerate.

Once the sauce has cooked for a full hour, it should have reduced to about 2½ cups. (The sauce can be made up to 1 day ahead to this point. Bring back to a low boil before proceeding.)

Add the cassia and salt to the sauce, then add the chicken, partially cover the pot, and bring back to a low boil. If the sauce does not cover the chicken, add a little water so that it does. Cook partially covered, stirring occasionally, until the chicken is cooked through, about 45 minutes for bone-in chicken and a little less for boneless.

Serve hot or warm with rice.

DUCK FESANJUN

Prepare the sauce as above, cook at a low boil for about 1½ hours, until reduced to 2½ cups, and set aside. On the skin side of boneless duck breast (about 2 pounds total), make parallel slashes through the skin to the fat. Rub on salt and pepper. Heat a cast-iron skillet over medium heat and place the breasts skin side down. Gradually raise the heat to high as they cook for 7 to 8 minutes, releasing their fat; add some of it to the sauce. Set the breasts aside to rest for 10 minutes. Slice thinly and cut into bite-size pieces. Just before you want to serve, reheat the sauce, then add the duck and cook for 2 or 3 minutes.

CHICKEN GIBLETS IN SPICED WALNUT DRESSING

KUCHMACHI

Kuchmachi, a kind of warm meat salad, is aromatic with spices and rich with walnut paste. The chicken version includes livers, hearts, and gizzards, but since gizzards are no longer readily available, they're optional in this recipe. (The pork and beef versions include hearts, livers, kidneys, spleen, and lungs. If you want to make the beef or pork version, you will need to increase the cooking time.)

The giblets simmer until tender, then are dressed with a sauce of ground walnuts blended with spices and a little vinegar. My Georgian friends tell me that dried thyme is an essential ingredient, but I have seen recipes that call for summer savory rather than thyme.

Serve this as a main course with a vegetable dish and a fresh salad alongside, or serve as an appetizer with bread. **SERVES 4 AS A MAIN COURSE, 6 TO 8 AS AN APPETIZER**

½ **pound chicken livers**

½ **pound chicken hearts**

¼ **pound chicken gizzards (optional)**

2 **tablespoons sunflower or extra-virgin olive oil**

2 **red onions, 1 thinly sliced, 1 finely chopped**

About 1½ **cups water**

1 **bay leaf**

3 **small garlic cloves, 1 sliced, the others coarsely chopped**

¾ **cup walnuts or walnut pieces**

1 to 2 **tablespoons white or red wine vinegar, to taste**

1 **tablespoon Georgian Spice Blend (page 28)**

1 **teaspoon dried thyme or summer savory**

1 **teaspoon powdered dried red chiles or cayenne**

1½ **teaspoons sea salt, or to taste**

¼ to ½ **cup loosely packed chopped fresh coriander or tarragon**

Thoroughly wash the chicken livers, hearts, and gizzards, if using, and pat dry. Chop into ½-inch pieces and set aside.

In a wide heavy pot, heat the oil over medium heat. Add the sliced onion and cook, stirring occasionally, until very soft but not at all tinged with color. Add the chopped giblets and stir for a minute to coat with the hot oil. Add 1½ cups water, the bay leaf, and the sliced garlic and bring to a boil, then partially cover and simmer until the giblets are very tender, about 1 hour.

Meanwhile, grind the walnuts to a powder in a food processor or grinder. Add the remaining garlic to the walnuts and process briefly. Set aside in a small bowl.

Left: **EASTERN GEORGIA**—*A rooster and four hens tethered at a village market.*
Right: **TBILISI, GEORGIA**—*Walnuts for sale at one of the city's many markets.*

Remove the pot from the heat, stir in the walnut-garlic paste and the vinegar, and transfer to a large bowl. Stir in the spice blend, thyme or savory, chiles, and salt. Let stand for 30 minutes before serving, to give the flavors time to blend.

Just before serving, stir in the finely chopped onion and the fresh herbs. Serve at room temperature.

QUICK KUCHMACHI

Although *kuchmachi* is traditionally slow-simmered, I have also experimented with a faster method. The flavor is not as deep, but it's a very acceptable version.

Cook the onions as above. Toss in the chopped giblets, bay leaf, and garlic clove and add just ½ cup water. Cook uncovered over medium-high heat, stirring frequently, until the giblets are just cooked, about 5 minutes. Remove from the heat, add the walnut-garlic paste, vinegar, spices, thyme or savory, and salt, and stir thoroughly.

Turn out into a bowl and let stand for 30 minutes to give the flavors a chance to blend. Just before serving, add the chopped onion and fresh herbs.

RICE AND OTHER GRAINS

RICE IS AN HONORED AND BELOVED STAPLE in the Persian culinary world, from Iran to Azerbaijan and Kurdistan, and Persian rice cookery is in a class of its own. In Iran, rice grows near the Caspian Sea in Gilan Province and near Shiraz. The Persian rices used in savory dishes are long-grain and resemble basmati but, Iranians will tell you, are better than basmati; basmati is the closest equivalent available in North America.

Basic Persian Rice (*chelo*; page 211) is the model for the other flavored Persian rice dishes in this chapter. The rice is soaked, then briefly boiled and, finally, steamed. The bottom crust, *tahdig* in Persian, is a special treat, put out with the rice. In Azeri *plov* (a word related to *polo*, *pulao*, *perloo*, and *paella*), the rice is usually cooked using a method very similar to that for Persian *chelo*.

Among the Kurds of Kurdistan, rice is daily fare, eaten with bread and simply flavored (see Kurdish Black Rice, page 216; Red Rice, page 217; and Golden Rice, page 218). Kurdish rice, *birinji kurdi*, is completely unlike Persian rice, as it's short- to medium-grain, like Mediterranean rices; the cooked rice dishes resemble risotto but include a delicious bottom crust. Rice is grown in Iraqi Kurdistan but not exported; Arborio or Baldo is the best substitute.

Rice is more important among western Armenians than for people from eastern Armenia, for whom wheat is the staple. Armenian cooks work with wheat in many ways: to make soups and pilafs (see Emmer Mushroom Pilaf, page 231) as well as the festive traditional dish *herissah* (see page 232), where it's blended with lamb or chicken in a hearty kind of main-dish porridge.

In Georgia both wheat and corn rule. The smooth-as-silk Georgian dish called *ghomi* (see page 234), made of white cornmeal, is like a sleek version of polenta, and a favorite in my house.

Previous pages: **YAZD, IRAN**—*Bags of long-grain basmati-style rice for sale, all of them marked "Product of India."*

BASIC PERSIAN RICE

CHELO

This rice sets the standard for rice cookery from Azerbaijan to northern India. It is tender and moist, every grain separate and perfect, with a crust at the bottom of the pot that is crisp and flavorful. The Persian word for that crust is *tahdig*.

This recipe is the master recipe for the Persian rice dishes that follow. They all use the same method for cooking the rice; the variations come with the different ingredients used to flavor it. The constants are rice and time: You need to start soaking the rice at least 2 hours before you serve it.

Use high-quality rice: Persian long-grain rice or basmati rice, both of which can absorb a lot of water. The rice is washed and then soaked in salted water for at least an hour. The soaking gives the rice a chance to absorb water, which in turn contributes to even cooking.

After the soaking comes parboiling: The rice is sprinkled into a large pot of boiling salted water, as if it were pasta. This step requires attention, for the rice can take as little as 5 minutes or as long as 10 to 12, depending on its age and quality. The rice should be cooked just until it is no longer raw but not fully cooked; the centers of the grains are no longer hard and chalky, but the rice is still chewy, not tender.

The last step is steaming: A heavy pot is lined with a layer of rice mixed with yogurt and perhaps egg, or with flatbread or potato (see A Note on Crust), and the (remaining) rice is mounded on top in a conical shape. The lid is sealed tightly and the rice steams gently for 30 minutes over low heat. The process may seem complicated the first time you try it, but you'll understand the reason for each step once you taste the results. And once you've made it a few times, cooking perfect Persian-style rice will become an easy habit. **SERVES 8**

3 cups (1¼ pounds) **Persian or basmati rice**

Sea salt

2 to 3 tablespoons **plain yogurt,** preferably full-fat

1 medium or large **egg**

¼ cup **sunflower oil or butter-ghee**

About 2 tablespoons **butter,** cut into small chunks

2 to 3 tablespoons **Saffron Water** (page 27; optional)

continued

Wash the rice: Place it in a pot, pour on cold water generously, and swish it around, then drain in a sieve; repeat three more times, or until the water remains clear. Place the rice in a bowl, add water to cover by 2 inches, and stir in 2 tablespoons salt. Set aside to soak for at least 1 hour; drain.

Fill a large heavy pot with about 4 quarts water and bring to a boil. Add 1 tablespoon salt, bring back to a boil, and sprinkle in the rice. Stir gently and bring back to a boil. After 2 to 3 minutes, start testing the rice for doneness: It is ready when the center of the grains is no longer brittle but is still chewy, not fully cooked. Check the rice frequently and once it's done, usually 4 to 5 minutes after it comes back to a boil (but it can take longer), drain in a sieve and set aside for a moment.

Mix the yogurt and egg together in a medium bowl. Stir in about 1 cup of the parboiled rice. Place the pot back over medium-high heat, add the oil or ghee and 2 tablespoons water, and heat until hot. Sprinkle the yogurt-rice mixture onto the sizzling oil and water, and mound the remaining rice on top in a conical shape. Use the handle of a wooden spoon to make four or five holes in the rice and sprinkle the chunks of butter over the rice. Cover the pot with a heavy lid or a lid wrapped in a cloth to help seal it well and steam the rice for about 3 minutes. Reduce the heat (move the pot to another burner if using an electric stove) to very low and cook for 25 minutes or so; the rice should be tender and fluffy. Remove from the heat.

The crust will come up more easily if you place the bottom of the pot in cold water for a couple of minutes (fill the sink with several inches of cold water). Mound the cooked rice on a platter. If using the saffron water, scoop about 1 cup of cooked rice into a bowl, add the saffron water, and stir to mix; set aside and sprinkle the saffron-tinted rice on top. Lift out the crust in pieces and place them around the edges of the steamed rice.

A NOTE ON CRUST: Different cooks have definite preferences about *tahdig*. I prefer a crust made with rice mixed with yogurt and egg. You can use either yogurt or egg rather than both. Other people instead place a layer of thin flatbreads in the oiled pot to make the crust, or perhaps some thinly sliced parboiled potatoes, before mounding the rest of the rice on top. Instructions for all options follow.

CRUST CHOICES: Instead of the egg and yogurt, you can use just yogurt (about ¼ cup) or just egg (1 extra-large or 2 medium), with ¾ cup rice. For a potato crust, use sliced parboiled potatoes or grated potatoes, enough to cover the bottom of the pot, on their own or mixed with a little yogurt or an egg. For a flatbread crust, line the bottom of the pot with a layer of thin bread (a split pita or a thin lavash, for example). (Or see Jairan's Chicken Plov, on page 224, for

YAZD, IRAN—*A man carrying a bag of rice he just bought stops at a shop in the bazaar that specializes in pots of all kinds.*

another type of flatbread liner.) Place the potatoes or bread on the hot oil and water before mounding the rest of the rice on top.

BROWN BASMATI CHELO

Use the same method to cook brown basmati, but omit the saffron water. The rice will take 14 to 18 minutes to parboil. Sprinkle on about 3 tablespoons water along with the butter chunks. Steaming will take about 45 minutes. Because the top layer of brown rice is often a little more chewy, sample from a little lower in the pot to test for doneness after the steaming.

HERBED PERSIAN RICE

POLO SABZI

PHOTOGRAPH ON PAGE 164

Polo sabzi is layered with finely chopped herbs as it steams, which make it aromatic as well as beautiful. (You can substitute dried herbs if fresh are not available; use about 2 tablespoons each of two different herbs and mix them with the parboiled rice before steaming it.) It's always served at Nou-Roz, the Persian New Year, celebrated at the spring equinox.

Leftovers keep well and can be reheated in a pan with a little hot water to steam them. Or lightly toss in hot oil, with the addition of a few chopped fresh greens to perk things up. **SERVES 6 TO 8**

3 cups (1¼ pounds) basmati rice, washed and drained

Sea salt

2 to 3 tablespoons plain full-fat yogurt

1 medium or large egg

3 cups finely chopped mixed fresh herbs, such as coriander, flat-leaf parsley, dill, and scallions (choose two or more)

1 garlic clove, minced, or ¼ cup minced fresh garlic chives

2 tablespoons sunflower oil or butter-ghee

2 to 3 tablespoons butter, cut into small chunks

2 to 3 tablespoons Saffron Water (page 27; optional)

Place the rice in a large pot and add water to cover by 2 inches. Stir in 2 tablespoons salt and let the rice soak for an hour or two; drain.

Bring a large pot of water to a boil. Add 1 tablespoon salt and bring back to a vigorous boil. Sprinkle in the soaked rice, stir, and bring back to a boil (add the dried herbs here, if using). Boil the rice until slightly softened but not cooked through, 3 to 5 minutes. Drain in a fine sieve and set aside for a moment.

Mix the yogurt and egg together in a medium bowl. Scoop up about 1 cup rice and mix it into the yogurt-egg mixture; set aside.

Combine all the chopped greens and the garlic or garlic chives in a bowl and mix well.

Place a wide heavy pot over medium-high heat. Add the oil or ghee and 2 tablespoons water and heat until sizzling. Sprinkle on the yogurt-rice mixture, then sprinkle on about 1 cup of the remaining rice and top with about one-third of the chopped greens. Continue alternating layers of rice and greens, mounding the rice in a conical shape, ending with rice. Poke four or five holes in the rice with the handle of a wooden spoon. Sprinkle on the chunks of butter. Cover the pot tightly (wrap the lid in a cotton cloth if necessary) and steam the rice over high heat for another minute. Reduce the heat to very low and cook for 30 minutes or so, until the rice is very tender and fluffy.

Set the pot in a sink filled with 2 inches of cold water and let stand for a couple of minutes. (This will help the bottom crust release.) If using the saffron water, scoop about 1 cup of cooked rice into a bowl, add the saffron water, and stir gently to mix; set aside. Mound the rest of the cooked rice on a large platter and sprinkle on the saffron-tinted rice. Lift out the crust in pieces and place them around the edges of the steamed rice.

HERBED BROWN BASMATI POLO

Brown rice is not at all traditional for *polo*, but I do love it. Follow the directions for the herbed rice above but omit the saffron water. The rice takes longer to cook: Allow a generous hour. The rice will take 14 to 18 minutes to parboil. Sprinkle on about 3 tablespoons water along with the butter chunks. Steaming will take about 45 minutes. Because the top layer of brown rice is often a little more chewy, sample some from a little lower in the pot to test for doneness after the steaming.

BARBERRY RICE (ZERESHK POLO)

Photograph on page 201

Tart barberries give flavor and color to Basic Persian Rice (page 211). Soak 1 cup dried barberries in water for 30 minutes and drain. Follow the directions for the herbed rice above, but instead of layering in chopped herbs, mix the drained barberries in with the parboiled rice before mounding it on top of the crust mixture. Cook and serve as above.

KURDISH BLACK RICE

BIRINJI RASH PHOTOGRAPH ON PAGE 84

This is one of my all-time favorite ways of cooking rice. With the simple addition of walnuts and pomegranate molasses, the rice is transformed into a richly flavored dish that's like a lush risotto. Astonishing. Though its name in Kurdish means black rice, the rice is not actually black but just darkened by the flavorings in the cooking water. Serve as part of a vegetarian meal or alongside roast chicken, with a salad. **SERVES 6**

2 cups (¾ pound) Arborio or Baldo rice

4 cups water

5 tablespoons pomegranate molasses

3 tablespoons sunflower or extra-virgin olive oil

2 or 3 shallots, finely chopped (about 3 tablespoons)

1 tablespoon sea salt

¾ cup walnuts, chopped into small pieces

Wash the rice thoroughly in several changes of cold water; drain in a sieve. Pour 4 cups water into a bowl and stir in the pomegranate molasses. Set aside.

Place a wide heavy pot over medium-high heat. Add the oil, toss in the shallots, and stir. Cook until translucent. Add the pomegranate molasses mixture, raise the heat, and bring to a vigorous boil. Add the salt, then add the walnuts and rice. Bring back to a strong boil, stir, and cook, uncovered, until the water level is just at the top of the rice, about 5 minutes.

Cover the pot, reduce the heat to very low, and cook for 12 to 15 minutes, until the rice is tender. The texture will be like risotto, a thick-flowing mass. Remove from the heat, stir briefly, and set aside, covered, to rest for 10 to 15 minutes.

Serve the rice from the pot. There will be a layer of rice stuck to the bottom of the pot. The pot scrapings are delicious and a sought-after treat.

KURDISH RED RICE

BIRINJI SUR

This is the simplest of the Kurdish home-style rice dishes. The tomato gives it a slightly tart edge, so it's good with plain grilled meat or with slightly sweet dishes, such as those with beets or sweet potatoes, or with grilled onions.

Include a generous Herb Plate (page 23) with the meal; the greens are beautiful next to the tinted rice.   **SERVES 6**

2 cups (¾ pound) Arborio or Baldo rice

4 cups water

3 tablespoons tomato paste

3 tablespoons sunflower or extra-virgin
   olive oil

2 or 3 shallots, finely chopped
   (about 3 tablespoons)

1 tablespoon sea salt

Wash the rice thoroughly in several changes of cold water; drain in a sieve. Pour 4 cups water into a bowl and stir in the tomato paste. Set aside.

Place a wide heavy pot over medium-high heat. Add the oil, toss in the shallots, and stir. Cook until translucent. Add the tomato mixture, raise the heat, and bring to a vigorous boil. Add the salt, then add the rice. Bring back to a strong boil, stir, and cook, uncovered, until the water level is just at the top of the rice.

Cover the pot, reduce the heat to very low, and cook for 12 to 15 minutes, until the rice is tender. The texture will be like risotto, a thick-flowing mass. Remove from the heat, stir briefly, and set aside, covered, to rest for 10 to 15 minutes.

Serve the rice from the pot.

KURDISH GOLDEN RICE

BIRINJI ZERDE

Golden rice is tinted yellow with turmeric and cooked in chicken broth rather than water. It can include meat, but the versions I tasted in Kurdistan were served with meat alongside the rice rather than in it. It's rather like risotto, not in terms of the cooking technique, but because the broth gives the rice a risotto-like lushness.

I find it easiest to use the method I learned from home cooks in Kurdistan: I simmer two chicken legs in about 5 cups water with a chopped onion for an hour or so, lift out the chicken, and use that cooking liquid (plus extra water if needed) as the broth for cooking the rice. Serve the rice with chicken, grilled meat, or a hearty bean dish. Accompany with an Herb Plate (page 23) and a chopped salad or a vegetable dish. **SERVES 6**

2 cups (¾ pound) Arborio or Baldo rice

3 tablespoons sunflower or olive oil

2 or 3 shallots, finely chopped (about 3 tablespoons)

4 cups unsalted chicken broth, homemade (see headnote) or store-bought

1 small onion, minced, if using store-bought broth

1 teaspoon turmeric

½ teaspoon ground cumin

½ teaspoon ground coriander

1 tablespoon sea salt (or about 1 teaspoon if using salted broth)

Wash the rice thoroughly in several changes of cold water; drain in a sieve.

Place a wide heavy pot over medium heat. Add the oil, toss in the shallots, and cook, stirring occasionally, until translucent, a couple of minutes. Add the broth, raise the heat, and bring to a vigorous boil. If using store-bought broth, add the minced onion. Add the spices and salt, bring back to a strong boil, and add the rice. Bring back to a strong boil, stir, and cook, uncovered, until the water level is just at the top of the rice.

Cover, reduce the heat to very low, and cook for 10 to 15 minutes, until the rice is tender and plump. Remove from the heat and stir gently. Cover and let stand for 10 to 15 minutes before serving.

SULAYMANIYAH, KURDISTAN—*This well-stocked rice shop in the Sulaymaniyah bazaar sells rice from many places, including India, the United States, and Uruguay, as well as many kinds of tea.*

NORTH OF KERMAN, IRAN—*The view from the train windows on our overnight journey to Mashad. Much of the way the countryside is bare and dry due to the drought Iran has had since 2008.*

TRAIN CONVERSATION

On the overnight train from Kerman in southern Iran to Mashad, in the north, I was lucky to meet an English-speaking young woman named Fereshteh as we both sipped an early-morning tea in the dining car. My time with the five women in

my compartment (see Train Journey, page 290), none of whom spoke much English, had left me with many questions she was happy to answer.

I asked her whether her mother ever spoke about the impact of the Islamic Revolution on women of her generation, especially educated women in the cities. Overnight, they had gone from relative autonomy, with the freedom to go to parties and go out by themselves, dressed as they wished, to being subject to rules about clothing and decorum, in a sense persecuted for being women. My understanding of the period came from other conversations and from Azar Nafisi's *Reading Lolita in Tehran*. Fereshteh said her mother didn't talk about it. Was it too painful?

I asked if she, Fereshteh, ever chafed under the restrictions: having to cover herself with a head scarf and manteau, for example. Well, she said, things have improved. "Now I can work at the university and I can travel on my own on this overnight train to see my husband [whose job was in Mashad]. Things are still evolving," she went on. "In Iran, we now mistrust revolutions. We realize that evolution is better than revolution." I didn't want the conversation to end, but eventually the outskirts of bustling Mashad came into view, and it was time to make my way back to my compartment through the crowded narrow aisles of the train cars. Families were gathering themselves, groups of men leaned against the windows looking out, women adjusted their chadors and head scarves, and slowly we lurched to a halt in the station.

BAKED PERSIAN RICE

TAHCHIN

This version of Persian rice is stunning, a meal-in-one of aromatic chicken (or lamb; see the variation) encased in a flavorful crust of basmati rice. It's a golden "cake" that is turned out onto a plate and served warm or at room temperature, sliced into wedges. *Tahchin* makes great finger food for a picnic or a casual gathering. Serve with salad and a side dish such as Eggplant Borani (page 62).

The chicken is marinated in yogurt flavored with dried orange peel and then buried in the rice to cook. The festive version of the dish is lush with butter, but for a home-cooked meal on a weeknight, you may want to use a little less butter.

SERVES 8

FILLING

3 tablespoons sunflower oil or butter

½ cup minced onion

About 1½ pounds boneless chicken legs or breasts, or a combination, cut into bite-size pieces

3 tablespoons fresh lemon juice

1 teaspoon sea salt

2 teaspoons dried orange peel (see Glossary)

½ cup plain full-fat yogurt

1 large egg

RICE

3 cups (1¼ pounds) basmati rice

Sea salt

5 to 8 tablespoons melted butter (see headnote)

Up to 24 hours before you want to serve the dish, make the filling: Place a heavy skillet over medium heat and add the oil or butter. Toss in the onion and cook for a minute or two, until translucent. Add the chicken and cook, stirring occasionally, for 10 minutes. Add the lemon juice and salt, half cover, and cook over medium-low heat for 10 minutes. Remove from the heat and let cool to room temperature.

Meanwhile, place the orange peel in a small saucepan, add 2 cups water, bring to a boil, and boil for 2 to 3 minutes. Drain. Place the peel back in the saucepan, add 2 cups water, and bring to a boil. Remove from the heat and set aside to soak for 5 to 10 minutes, until the peel is well softened.

Drain the orange peel and mince it. Place the yogurt in a medium bowl and mix in the peel. Add the chicken, cover, and marinate in the refrigerator for at least 3 hours, and up to 24 hours.

At least 3 hours before you want to serve the dish, wash the rice well in several changes of water and place in a bowl with water to cover by 2 inches. Add 2 tablespoons salt, stir well, and set aside to soak for 1 to 2 hours.

Preheat the oven to 375°F. Use some of the melted butter to generously oil a deep 12-inch casserole or other heavy ovenproof pot with a lid.

Using a slotted spoon, lift the chicken out of the marinade and set aside on a plate. Add the egg to the marinade, whisk to mix well, and set aside.

Drain the rice. Bring a large pot of water to a rolling boil. Add 1 tablespoon salt, bring back to a boil, and add the rice. Cook until the rice is no longer brittle but is still chewy, not fully cooked. Check the rice frequently, and once it's done, usually about 5 minutes after it comes back to a boil, drain it in a fine sieve.

Add 3 cups of the rice to the egg-marinade mixture and mix well. Transfer the mixture to the buttered casserole, spreading it over the bottom and 1½ to 2 inches up the sides of the pot. Distribute the chicken pieces over the rice, leaving a 1-inch border all around. Spread the rest of the rice over the chicken, covering it completely, and smooth the top. Drizzle on 3 tablespoons or more of the melted butter.

Cover the pot with a heavy lid and bake for 45 minutes. Lower the heat to 350°F and bake for another 45 minutes. The top of the rice should be golden brown.

Fill your sink with 2 inches of cold water and place the casserole in the water for 5 minutes; this will help the rice crust release from the pot.

Remove the pot from the water and slide a knife around the sides of the pot to help release the rice. Place a large plate or platter over the casserole and invert it, so that the *tahchin* falls onto the plate. Serve hot or at room temperature.

TAHCHIN WITH LAMB

Substitute 1½ pounds boneless lamb shoulder or leg, cut into bite-size pieces, for the chicken. Cook with the onion, as above, but after the lamb has cooked for 10 minutes, add ½ cup barberries (see Glossary) and ¼ cup water, or ¼ cup pomegranate molasses diluted with ¼ cup water to the pan, then cook for 15 minutes at a low simmer. Let cool and proceed as above, but omit the orange peel.

JAIRAN'S CHICKEN PLOV

Plovs have "special dish" status in Azerbaijan. The rice requires a little care and so does the simmered chicken, but it's well worth it. This is a great dish to make for a crowd or for a celebration. I learned it from Jairan in Lahich.

Start by putting the rice on to soak about 4 hours before you want to serve. Once you have your prep done, cooking the rice and assembling the dish takes about an hour. The crust is different from the crusts in the other rice dishes in this chapter—it's made of a dough that bakes under the rice.

In this dish, the most important detail is the way the onions are sliced and cooked. They are sliced very thinly lengthwise, as opposed to the usual crosswise slices. Cut this way, they melt into the chicken.

A classic side for *plov* and other rice-and-meat dishes is Tart-Sweet Apricot and Raisin Relish (page 33). Put out a plate of trimmed scallions and sprigs of fresh herbs, such as coriander, basil, and mint; you could also or instead include watercress or arugula. Serve a salad of chopped tomato and cucumber, such as Baku-Style Tomato Salad (page 49), or put out a bowl of lightly salted thick yogurt. **SERVES 8**

RICE

4 cups (generous 1½ pounds) basmati rice

Sea salt

2 tablespoons sunflower or vegetable oil

¼ teaspoon saffron threads, soaked in ¼ cup hot water

CHICKEN

About 3 pounds chicken legs or breasts, or a combination

About 4 cups water

8 medium or 5 large onions

12 dried sour plums, or substitute 12 small or 8 large tomatillos

About ¼ cup (4 tablespoons) sunflower oil, butter, or butter-ghee

2 teaspoons turmeric

2 teaspoons sea salt, or to taste

CRUST

1 large egg

Scant ½ cup plain full-fat or reduced-fat yogurt

1 teaspoon sea salt

About 2½ cups all-purpose flour

continued

SHEKI, AZERBAIJAN—*Vendors in the main market in Sheki sit in long lines next to their vegetables and herbs, which gleam with freshness. The woman in the foreground has a bag of barberries; several jars of preserves; a large bunch of basil; bags of tomatoes, peppers, and eggplants; and a large squash.*

Left: **SHEKI, AZERBAIJAN**—*A butcher stands outside his small shop not far from the main bazaar.*

Right: **TBILISI, GEORGIA**—*Shallots for sale in Deserteri Market.*

Place the rice in a wide bowl and add water to cover by 2 inches. Set aside to soak for 2 hours.

Using a cleaver, chop each chicken leg and/or breast into several pieces. Pull off the skin and discard. Put the chicken pieces in a wide heavy pot, add 2 inches of water, and bring to a boil over medium heat. Reduce the heat and simmer, partially covered, for about 30 minutes. Set aside.

Meanwhile, remove the tough outer layers of the onions. Cut them lengthwise in half and then slice them lengthwise into very thin slices, almost like shreds. (You should have about 6 cups sliced onions.) Set aside.

If using sour plums, place them in a bowl, rinse, and drain. Cover with water and set aside to soak for 10 to 20 minutes. If using tomatillos, remove their papery husks, rinse, and cut in half or into quarters; set aside.

Place a wide heavy skillet over medium heat and add the onions without any oil. Cook, stirring occasionally, for 5 to 10 minutes; lower the heat a little if necessary to prevent the onions from sticking or changing color—you just want them to release some of their moisture. Add the oil, butter, or ghee, sprinkle on the turmeric, and stir the onions to coat them with oil or butter. Partially cover and cook over medium to medium-low heat, stirring occasionally, for 10 to 15 minutes. You don't want the onions to change color, just to gradually soften.

Add the drained sour plums or the tomatillos and cook, partially covered, for 10 minutes, lowering the heat if necessary to prevent the onions from burning and using a wooden spatula to scrape the bottom of the pan and keep them from sticking. Remove from the heat and set aside in a bowl.

Pour the cooking liquid from the chicken into a bowl. Arrange the chicken pieces evenly in the pot and strew the onions and plums or tomatillos over the top. Add the chicken cooking liquid and the salt, and bring to a boil over medium-high heat. Reduce the heat to medium-low, partially cover, and simmer for 30 minutes. Set aside (refrigerate, covered, if the wait will be longer than an hour).

Meanwhile, make the crust: Mix the egg, yogurt, and salt in a bowl. Add about a cup of the flour and stir, then add more flour, folding and kneading it in, until you have a soft, smooth dough. Lightly dust the dough with flour, place it on a lightly floured surface, and flatten it into a disk. Then continue to flatten with your palm, or use a rolling pin, until you have a round that has the same diameter as the pot you will use to cook the rice. Cover loosely.

An hour before you want to serve the dish, fill a large heavy pot with hot water and bring to a boil. Add about ¼ cup salt and bring back to a boil. Drain the rice and rinse well with cold water. Add the rice to the boiling water and bring back to a boil, stirring gently to ensure that no rice sticks to the bottom of the pot. It will take from 5 to 10 minutes for the rice to cook to almost done. Test by lifting out several rice grains and biting them; they should be almost cooked through, with no starchy chalkiness. Drain the rice in a large sieve.

Rinse out the pot and place it over medium-high heat. Add the 2 tablespoons oil and take the pot off the heat. Fold in a flap of dough on all four sides of the circle of dough, place the dough in the center of the pot, and unfold the flaps so that the bottom of the pot is covered with dough. Use a small thin glass to cut as many rounds as possible in the dough. Place the pot back over medium-high heat.

Add half of the rice to the pot, mounding it, and pour over half the saffron liquid. Add the remaining rice, mounding it into a conical shape, and pour on the rest of the saffron liquid. Poke four or five holes in the rice with the handle of a wooden spoon.

Cover the pot tightly (wrap the lid of the pot in a cotton cloth if necessary). Reduce the heat to very low and cook for about 45 minutes, until the rice is tender and fluffy. Set aside to rest for 10 minutes, until ready to serve.

Just before serving, gently reheat the chicken mixture. Taste and adjust the seasoning if necessary.

Mound the rice onto a platter and place the rounds of dough around the edge of the platter (the dough scraps are usually discarded). Serve the chicken in a separate bowl, or ladle it onto the platter of rice and serve the extra gravy in a separate bowl.

THE ARMENIAN WORLD
OF WHEAT

Wheat is the food of life in Armenia, as it is in the rest of the region. Over the centuries, Armenians have discovered many ways to work with it, apart from using wheat flour to make bread.

An early type of wheat, known in English as emmer, is an important ingredient there. Emmer (see Glossary) is now widely available in North America. The Armenian name is *hajar*. It cooks much more quickly than modern wheats and so it can be used in soups without presoaking (see Dried Apricot Soup with Wheat Berries, page 97), or to make risotto-like dishes called *pilav* (see Emmer Mushroom Pilaf, page 231).

In Armenia, soft wheat berries are used to make *tsavar*—precooked dried wheat berries. Until recently, it was made in the villages, but now people buy ready-made *tsavar* at the market. The traditional village processing involved washing the grain, cooking it in water, and then leaving it out in the sun to dry so it could be stored safely.

Tsavar is used in a number of ways. Whole *tsavar* is cooked with meat and then mashed to make *herissah*, often called the Armenian national dish, which is a kind of meat porridge (see page 232). *Herissah* can also be made with soft wheat berries that have not been transformed into *tsavar*, but the cooking time is longer. Bulgur (*gorgot*) is also made from *tsavar*: the dried wheat berries are pounded into flakes, which makes the grain even quicker to cook. Coarse bulgur (*hushor*) is used for pilafs and dolmas (see Cabbage Rolls Stuffed with Beans and Tart Fruit, page 124), and finer bulgur (*gorgudak*) is used for tabbouleh, especially in western Armenia. *Tsavar* is also the basis of *po-khinze*, a precooked flour made by toasting the cooked dried wheat berries and grinding them.

Po-khinze is a practical ingredient, for it needs very little additional cooking (very like Tibetan *tsampa*, which is the barley

Left: **YEREVAN, ARMENIA**—*The two essential types of wheat in Armenia are* hajar, *a form of emmer (left), and* tsavar, *precooked wheat berries (right). The best substitute for* tsavar *is soft wheat berries (see Armenian Herissah, page 232).*

Right: **GEORGIA**—*A batch of Georgian Boomerang Breads (page 255) in a small rural bakery, lying on their sides to cool.*

equivalent). In Armenia, *po-khinze* is combined with water to make a gruel or porridge called *khasheel*, among other dishes. The porridge is sweetened with honey, sugar, or some kind of preserved fruit or sweet fruit syrup and enriched with butter and yogurt, and sometimes walnuts.

Wheat is also part of many ritual dishes at certain holidays. A few weeks before Easter, for example, which is the time of resurrection for Christian Armenians and also the season of the Zoroastrian New Year in the Persian world (see page 36), Armenian families, like Georgian families, sprout wheat berries. A plate of the sprouted wheat, vibrantly green, is used as a centerpiece on the Easter feast table, usually with eggs on top, signifying resurrection and new life.

EMMER MUSHROOM PILAF

HAJAROV PILAV

Emmer is an early variety of wheat that cooks up quickly; it has an inviting homey taste and is a staple in Armenia. Farmers are starting to grow it again in North America. Here it is used in a dish that is a cross between pilaf and risotto.

You can make this with just mushrooms, or you can include a little ground meat. Instructions for both are given below.   **SERVES 4 TO 6**

2 tablespoons sunflower or vegetable oil

2 tablespoons butter-ghee or butter
(1 tablespoon if using meat)

2 medium onions, thinly sliced
(about 1 cup)

½ pound ground pork, beef, or lamb
(optional)

½ pound (¼ pound if using meat)
mushrooms, chopped: cremini, button,
or portobellos (about 4 cups)

2 teaspoons dried thyme

1 cup (scant ½ pound) emmer wheat
berries, washed well and drained

2½ cups water or light broth

1½ teaspoons sea salt, or to taste
(less if using salted broth)

Generous grinding of black pepper

2 to 3 tablespoons chopped fresh tarragon
or mint, or substitute 2 teaspoons
Mint Oil (page 19)

OPTIONAL ACCOMPANIMENTS

About 2 cups plain thick yogurt
(see Glossary), lightly salted

Herb Plate (page 23)

Place a wide heavy skillet or heavy pot over medium heat. Add the oil and butter; when the butter melts, swirl to coat the pan. Toss in the onions and cook until translucent. Add the meat, if using, the mushrooms, and thyme and cook, stirring occasionally, until the meat has changed color and the mushrooms are starting to soften, about 5 minutes. Add the emmer and water or broth and bring to a boil. Add the salt and bring back to a boil, then lower the heat slightly to maintain a strong boil and cook for 5 minutes.

Cover the pan, lower the heat, and simmer for 30 minutes, or until the emmer is very tender and cooked through. The finished dish should be slightly soupy, like a very thick risotto.

Taste and add salt if needed and the pepper. Stir in the herbs or oil. Serve hot or warm, with yogurt on the side, and the herb plate if you like.

Emmer Mushroom Pilaf, with thick yogurt and an array of fresh herbs.

ARMENIAN HERISSAH

Herissah, often called the national dish of Armenia, is served at Easter and on festive occasions. Cooked wheat berries and chicken or lamb are ground together to a coarse puree. The result is warming and sustaining, like so many of the grain dishes in the repertoire. *Herissah* is a close cousin of the *harissa* of Iran (not to be confused with the North African chile paste called harissa).

In Armenia, *herissah* is traditionally made with *tsavar*, precooked dried wheat berries (see The Armenian World of Wheat, page 228), but those can be hard to find in North America; use soft wheat berries instead (soft wheat cooks a little more quickly than hard wheat) or emmer wheat berries (see page 231).

Start preparing the dish at least 5 hours before you want to serve it. Or cook the wheat berries and meat a day ahead and refrigerate until needed.

You can dress up *herissah* with loads of chopped fresh herbs, or put out a generous herb plate. **SERVES 8**

2 cups soft wheat berries or emmer wheat berries, washed well and drained

6 to 7 cups water

1½ pounds boneless lamb shoulder or leg; 2 to 2½ pounds bone-in lamb shoulder, trimmed of excess fat; or 2½ pounds chicken legs and/or breasts

1 onion, quartered

1 teaspoon dried thyme or 2 fresh thyme sprigs

2 bay leaves

About 10 black peppercorns

2½ teaspoons sea salt, or to taste

About ¼ cup dry red wine (or white wine if using chicken) or 2 tablespoons pomegranate molasses (optional)

Freshly ground black pepper

ACCOMPANIMENTS

Herb Plate (page 23)

Lemon wedges

Chopped cucumber and/or chopped tomato

2 cups plain full-fat yogurt, lightly salted

Place the wheat berries in a large heavy pot, add 5 cups water, bring to a strong boil, and boil for 10 minutes. Remove from the heat, cover, and let stand for at least 2 hours, or as long as overnight.

Bring the pot of wheat berries back to a boil and cook at a medium boil until the berries are tender and yielding to the bite, about 1 hour (if using emmer, the cooking time will be a little shorter). Add more water if necessary to prevent burning or sticking. Set aside.

Meanwhile, place the lamb or chicken in another large pot and add water to cover. Add the onion, thyme, bay leaves, and peppercorns and bring to a boil.

Partially cover, lower the heat to maintain a gentle boil, and cook until the meat is tender, about 45 minutes (a little longer for bone-in lamb). Lift the lamb or chicken out of the pot and into a large bowl. Strain the stock and set it aside. If using meat on the bone, remove the meat from the bones; discard the bones. (The cooked wheat berries, the meat, and the stock can be refrigerated overnight in separate well-sealed containers.)

When ready to proceed, place some of the wheat berries and meat in a food processor and process to a slightly coarse paste; you may need to add a little of the reserved stock to help with the processing. Working in batches, continue processing until you have ground all the wheat and meat together, then process for a few minutes more to get a reasonably smooth paste.

Transfer the paste to a large heavy pot. Add the remaining stock and the salt, stir, and bring to a low boil over medium heat. I like to add a splash of red wine or pomegranate molasses at this point, though it is not traditional. Cook for another 5 minutes. Add pepper to taste, and adjust the seasoning if necessary.

Serve in individual bowls and put out the accompaniments so guests can help themselves.

NORTH OF YEREVAN, ARMENIA—*A rural gas station in high plateau country. The light is bright and harsh here, and the shadows sharp-etched in a way that reminds me of Tibet and Wyoming.*

GEORGIAN POLENTA

GHOMI AND ELARGI

I love *ghomi,* even though I didn't grow up with polenta or grits. In the western part of Georgia, particularly in Emereti, as well as in the Georgian-influenced areas across the border in Turkey, corn has been an important staple for centuries. Corn flour is used to make corn flatbreads, and to make this soft cornmeal dish that, at its best, is smooth and silky and completely irresistible.

Ghomi takes about an hour and a half to cook. It's traditionally made in a heavy cauldron-like pot called a *kardala;* my heavy Le Creuset pot is ideal. It can be served plain to accompany any meal, but it's most often served with slices of *suluguni,* a smoked cheese, set into it. The dish is then called *elargi.* Instructions for both follow. Serve hot or warm, as a main dish with a vegetable side, or to accompany roasted or grilled meat. Leftovers of *ghomi* and *elargi* are delicious sliced and fried in hot oil (see A Note on Leftovers). **SERVES 8**

GHOMI

2 cups medium-coarse cornmeal, preferably white

7 to 8 cups hot water, or as needed

1 tablespoon sea salt, or to taste

¼ cup fine corn flour, preferably white

FOR ELARGI

About ¼ pound *suluguni* cheese (see Glossary), or substitute mozzarella or smoked Gouda, sliced into rectangles about 1 inch wide, 2 inches long, and ¼ inch thick

Place the cornmeal in a large bowl and add water to cover generously. Swirl the water and cornmeal with your hand and drain in a fine sieve. Repeat twice.

Place the cornmeal in a heavy pot with 5 cups of the hot water. Bring to a vigorous boil, cover tightly, reduce the heat to the lowest setting, and cook for 15 minutes.

Remove the lid and stir. The mixture will have come together into a smooth porridge. Raise the heat a little and start stirring and smoothing it with a wooden spoon or spatula every couple of minutes. After about 15 minutes, it will have thickened. Add another 2 cups water, lower the heat a little, and stir occasionally to make sure that it's not sticking.

After another 15 minutes, start stirring fairly constantly to help the starches break down and to smooth out the mixture. If the *ghomi* gets very thick, so that it's barely pourable, add another cup or so of water.

TBILISI, GEORGIA—*Corn kernels of many colors at the market. Corn originated in the Americas and came to the Caucasus sometime in the last four hundred years. It soon became a valuable crop, especially in western Georgia, displacing millet.*

Once the cornmeal is tender (after about another 10 minutes), stir in the salt. Sprinkle on the corn flour, stir it in, and cook for another 15 minutes, stirring and smoothing the *ghomi* fairly constantly; again, add more water if you need to. The texture should be like that of a thick applesauce. Taste for salt and adjust the seasoning if necessary. Pour into a wide shallow bowl.

If you want to make *elargi*, place the slices of cheese in the *ghomi*, standing them on their long sides in rows. The hot *ghomi* will melt them a little.

A NOTE ON LEFTOVERS: Like polenta, *ghomi* lends itself to a second cooking. Pour leftovers into a rectangular container so they can be easily sliced the next day, cover, and refrigerate. Heat a little sunflower or olive oil in a heavy skillet and fry the slices briefly, turning them once, until lightly browned on both sides and warmed through. Serve with a fried egg on top or with a salad.

FLATBREAD HEARTLAND

BREAD IS LIFE IN GREATER PERSIA:
Flatbreads are eaten every day as the
accompaniments to meals. For centuries,
they were the most important source of
sustenance for most people.

In Iraqi Kurdistan, home cooks make fine,
thin unleavened breads called *nane-tire*
(see page 240), baking them on the curve of
a *saj*, a dome-shaped metal pan set over a fire.
The breads are used to wrap foods or pick
them up, as traditionally in Kurdistan people
eat with their hands.

A yeasted version of the Kurdish *saj* breads,
called *lavash*, is the bread of Armenia, and

similar breads are made in bakeries in Kurdistan, Azerbaijan, and Iran (see photo, page 243).

In Azerbaijan, Armenia, and Kurdistan, fine unleavened flatbreads are folded over chopped greens or other fillings to make large half-moon-shaped hand pies that are like inviting baked sandwiches. See the recipe for Azeri *kutab* on page 245. Georgian cheese-filled breads, called *khachapuri* (page 251), are rich and satisfying; both home cooks and bakeries make them. Bakeries in Georgia also make distinctive crusty, boomerang-shaped tandoor-baked breads with pointed ends (see page 255).

In Iran, two remarkable breads have pride of place: *sangak* and *barbari* (see Bread in Iran, page 258). Most bread is made in bakeries except in some rural areas, where women bake bread at home. Homemade versions of *sangak* and *barbari* are included here (see pages 261 and 267).

These days in the Persian culinary world, almost all bread is made with white or unbleached white flour. In earlier times, breads would have been made with less-refined flour, so you will find occasional suggestions in some of these recipes for including whole-grain flour.

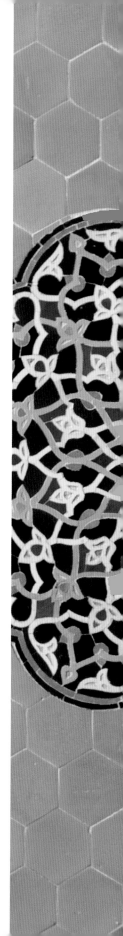

Previous pages: SULAYMANIYAH, KURDISTAN—*An older Kurdish man selects flatbreads at a bakery in the bazaar. Families go through stacks of flatbread in a day.*

BULGUR BREADS

NANE SAUER

I learned a lot about bulgur breads from several Kurdish women I met in the town of Sulaymaniyah in Kurdistan. This recipe includes an enticing spice blend. Bulgur breads are delicious on their own, chewy and flavorful, and they also pair well with soft fresh goat cheese and with strong cheeses such as aged cheddar.   **MAKES 8 FLATBREADS, ABOUT 8 INCHES IN DIAMETER**

2 cups medium or fine bulgur

¼ teaspoon ground cumin

¼ teaspoon ground nigella

⅛ teaspoon ground fenugreek

½ cup minced onion

1 teaspoon sea salt

2 cups hot water

About 1 cup unbleached all-purpose flour, plus extra for surfaces

Combine the bulgur, spices, onion, and salt in a bowl. Pour over the hot water and stir to mix, then cover and set aside for 30 minutes.

Add ½ cup of the flour and start pressing and mixing the dough. As you press and work it, the bulgur, softened by the hot water, will start to get sticky and turn into a dough. If your bulgur is very fine, you may need only ½ cup flour, but with coarser bulgur, you will need to add a full cup of flour and knead it thoroughly and firmly so that it develops into a dough. Set the dough aside, covered with plastic wrap, to rest for at least 30 minutes or as long as 3 hours.

Thirty minutes before you want to bake, place a baking stone or unglazed quarry tiles on a rack in the upper third of the oven. Preheat your oven to 450°F.

Turn the dough out onto a lightly floured surface, pull it together into a block, and cut it into 8 equal pieces. Using floured palms, flatten each one into a disk. Use a rolling pin to roll out 2 or 3 disks (as many as will fit in your oven) into 8-inch rounds. Use a flour-dusted peel or the back of a baking sheet to transfer the breads to the hot stone or tiles. Bake for about 2 minutes on each side, until touched with color; use a long-handled spatula to turn them over. Remove them, once done, to a cotton cloth and wrap them in it so they will stay supple. Repeat with the remaining breads.

KERCHIEF FLATBREADS FROM KURDISTAN

NANE-TIRE

This is the bread that I watched Hoshida's daughter Dila make one day in Halabja (see Kurdish Welcome, page 67). She made a huge quantity of large, fine, supple breads, enough to feed her household and her mother's for about a week. This recipe makes breads that are smaller than Dila's and thus more easily managed in a North American kitchen. Dila baked on a *saj*, a kind of domed griddle, like an upside-down wok, for which I substitute a cast-iron skillet.

Unleavened *saj*-baked breads like this are called *nane-tire* by the Kurds; the same name is also used by the Khamseh, a nomadic people in southern Iran—see Nomad Encounter, page 190. Lavash, a similar-looking bread, is usually leavened; see the variation. This recipe calls for a little fine bran, to mimic the higher-extraction flour that Dila used for her bread dough, but it's optional. If you omit the bran, you'll just need a little less water. (If your bran is rather coarse, put it in the food processor and grind it to a finer texture.)

The kneading technique is special: It calls for a stretching of the dough that's rather like the pastry-making technique called *fraisage* (see photo, page 242). For rolling out the breads very thin, it's best to use a tapered rolling pin.

MAKES ABOUT 16 THIN FLATBREADS, ABOUT 9 INCHES ACROSS

4 cups unbleached all-purpose flour

Scant ½ cup finely ground bran (optional; see headnote)

1½ teaspoons sea salt

About 1¾ cups lukewarm water

Place the flour, bran, if using, and salt in a large bowl or a large food processor. If working by hand, add about half the water and stir, then slowly add the rest and stir and fold to incorporate it. If using a processor, with the machine running, slowly pour the water through the feed tube. The dough should come together into a ball; continue processing for another 15 seconds.

Turn the dough out onto a lightly floured surface and knead it: Flatten it slightly, fold it in half, and give it a half turn before flattening it and folding it again. Repeat for a few minutes, until the dough is fairly smooth and not sticky.

Stretch the dough: Hold one end of the dough against the work surface with one hand and use the heel of your other hand to rub and push the rest of the dough away from you, stretching it until just before the point where it feels like it might tear (see photo, page 242). Fold the dough over itself and repeat. Continue this stretching-kneading until the dough feels extremely smooth and less tight than at the start, 8 to 10 minutes (yes, I know that's a long time!). Set the dough aside to rest for an hour, or as long as 3 hours, in a large plastic bag.

Meanwhile, figure out your cooking arrangement: If you have a *saj*, use it. I use an 11- or 12-inch cast-iron skillet. You could also use a cast-iron griddle.

Turn the dough out onto a lightly floured work surface. Use a dough scraper or a large sharp knife to cut it in half, then cut each half into 8 equal pieces (by cutting the pieces in half and then in half again twice more). Roll each of them under your palm on the lightly floured surface to make a rough ball and flatten gently. Set them aside on your work surface, loosely covered.

Place your *saj* or pan over medium-low heat. While it heats, start rolling out your first bread. Flatten it with your palm, then with a rolling pin (see headnote). Working from the center outward and rotating the dough a quarter turn after each stroke, roll it out to a circle 9 to 10 inches in diameter. If the dough springs back, let it rest for a moment while you start rolling out a second bread. Then return to the first bread and roll it out a little more; or, if you prefer, pick it up between your palms and stretch it a little over the back of your hands. The dough should be very thin, almost translucent.

Place the stretched bread on the hot surface of the pan, and continue rolling out portions of dough, all the while keeping a close eye on the bread that is cooking. Cook it on one side only, lifting it to check for color on the underside; it should show small touches of pale brown in about a minute. If it colors more quickly than that, lower the heat slightly. Lift up the cooked bread, lay it on a cotton cloth, and cover with another cloth.

Continue rolling out and baking the remaining pieces of dough, stacking them on top of each other and covering them so that they stay soft and supple.

Serve warm or at room temperature. Once the breads are exposed to the air, they will dry out and crisp up. You can eat them like that or sprinkle on a little water to soften them.

continued

NOTE: When the breads dry out, they become very brittle and break into large flakes. You can gather these up and use them to make the bread-cheese pie the Armenians call *banrakhash* (see the recipe on page 272).

LAVASH

You can make a leavened version of this bread using the Home-Style Bread Dough (page 254). The breads will be slightly thicker than the Kurdish flatbreads; in Iran, they are called *lavash* or *taftoon*, and in Armenia, they're *lavash*. They're traditionally baked in a tandoor oven, but a baking stone in a 450°F oven is a good substitute. Turn the risen dough out onto a lightly floured surface and divide it into 4 pieces, then cut each of those into 4 pieces. Shape into balls, flatten them with the palm of your hand, and set aside to rest, loosely covered, for 10 minutes. Stretch one piece between your hands, or use a rolling pin, as above, until it is a very thin round or oval about 9 inches across. Place it on a floured peel or the back of a baking sheet and transfer to the hot baking stone. The bread will bake in about 2 minutes. Remove and repeat with the remaining dough. Wrap the baked breads in a cotton cloth to keep them soft.

 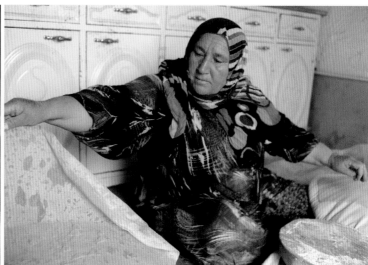

Above: HALABJA, KURDISTAN—*Pulling and stretching the dough to develop it for Kerchief Flatbreads (page 240; left). Dila lifts a paper-thin bread off the* saj *after it cooks for about a minute (right). She makes over a hundred breads at a time, shaping and baking them one by one, on the roof of her house.*

Opposite: MASSOULEH, IRAN—*A tandoor baker flings a baked lavash onto his pile. He uses the oblong pillow to transfer stretched dough onto the oven walls.*

HALF-MOON HAND PIES

KUTAB · KALANA

The unleavened dough of the Kurdish *nane-tire* is used to make supple filled breads called *kalana* in Kurdistan and *kutab* in Azerbaijan. The most common filling is chopped greens (scallions and fresh herbs), but in Azerbaijan I also encountered cheese-filled *kutab*, as well as breads stuffed with pumpkin. You can use one filling for all the breads or mix and match them; quantities of each filling below are for 16 breads.

Two filled breads with a bowl of soup make a satisfying meal.   MAKES 16 HALF-MOON-SHAPED FILLED FLATBREADS

FILLINGS

Greens: 4 packed cups finely chopped greens, a mix of any or all of these: scallions, coriander, tarragon, dill, and other herbs, sprinkled with 1 teaspoon salt

Pumpkin or squash: About 3 cups mashed cooked pumpkin or squash, mixed with a tablespoon of sunflower or extra-virgin olive oil or melted butter and seasoned with salt and a little ground cumin

Cheese: 2 cups crumbled aged goat cheese or feta, mixed with ½ cup fresh chopped tarragon or a generous 2 tablespoons dried mint

Dough for Kerchief Flatbreads (page 240), allowed to rest

About ¼ cup melted butter or butter-ghee for brushing

Mix together your filling ingredients of choice.

Turn the dough out onto a lightly floured surface and divide it into 16 equal pieces, cutting it first in half and then each half into 8 pieces. Roll out one piece to a round about 9 inches in diameter. Put it aside to rest while you roll out a second round, then return to the first one and roll it out a little more, to close to 10 inches across; you want it to be as thin as possible. Set aside for a moment.

Heat a large heavy griddle or skillet over medium heat for several minutes. Rub the skillet with a lightly oiled paper towel or cloth, then return to shaping the breads.

Place about ¼ cup packed chopped greens, a scant ¼ cup pumpkin or squash, or about 2 tablespoons cheese filling on one half of a dough circle, leaving a ½-inch margin at the edge. Fold the dough over to cover the filling, flatten lightly with the palm of your hand, working from the folded edge outward to press out any air, then press the edges together to seal well. Use a pizza cutter or a knife to trim the curve to a tidy edge; this also helps seal the edge. Transfer the bread to the hot skillet. Continue shaping the next bread as the first one cooks. The bread should get touched with pale brown on the bottom in about 1½ minutes; if it starts to get darker patches sooner than that, lower the heat slightly. Once it is light brown, turn it over and cook the second side until touched with color. Remove and brush with a little melted butter or ghee. If not serving the breads right away, wrap them in a cotton cloth to keep warm.

Continue shaping and baking the remaining breads. If you make them ahead and want to rewarm them, reheat in the skillet, or wrap in foil and place in a 300°F oven for 5 to 10 minutes. Brush the warmed breads with a little more melted butter or ghee if you wish.

ARMENIAN GREENS HAND PIES (ZHINGALOV HATS)

Armenian versions of these half-moon pies, called *zhingalov hats*, are a specialty of the disputed Nagorno-Karabakh region. They're made with a yeasted dough and filled with lightly cooked greens: finely chopped leeks and scallions with fresh herbs. Use well-risen Home-Style Bread Dough (page 254) instead of the unleavened dough. Cut it into 16 pieces and follow the instructions above for shaping, rolling the dough out very thin. Bake as above, or on a baking sheet in a 400°F oven.

HALABJA, KURDISTAN— *Dila sprinkles chopped scallions and herbs onto a stretched round of bread before folding it in half and cooking it on the* saj, *in the background.*

CHEESE-FILLED PASTRIES

PENOVANI

These beautiful rich pastries are sold street-side and in markets in Georgia. Make them as appetizers, or pair them with a Persian *ash* (or other hearty soup) or a bean stew for a warming dinner.

If it's winter and you don't have access to fresh herbs, you can substitute about 1 tablespoon dried dill or dried mint, and you'll want to add a generous amount of freshly ground pepper.   **MAKES 16 PASTRIES, ABOUT 2½ INCHES SQUARE**

1 packed cup crumbled or grated cheese: a mix of feta and mild cheddar

½ cup minced fresh tarragon, dill, mint, or scallion greens

1 teaspoon freshly ground black pepper (optional)

½ teaspoon cayenne (optional)

Georgian-Style Flaky Pastry (recipe follows)

Place a rack in the upper third of your oven and preheat the oven to 425°F. Lightly oil a baking sheet.

Put the cheese in a bowl, add the herbs and black pepper or cayenne, if using, and mix well. Set aside.

Cut the dough into 4 equal pieces. Set 3 aside, loosely covered with a cloth or plastic.

Lightly flour your work surface. Flatten the remaining piece of dough into a square (the dimensions don't matter, because you'll be rolling it out thinner later on). Cut in half lengthwise and then crosswise to yield 4 equal pieces. Set 3 pieces aside, loosely covered.

Use a rolling pin or your floured palm to flatten and stretch the remaining piece of dough into a square about 4 inches on a side. Scoop up 1 tablespoon of the filling and place it in the center of the square. Pick up one corner and fold it over to the center of the cheese, repeat with the opposite corner, and pinch them together. Do the same with the other 2 corners. Pinch the open slits lightly at the bottom (the corners of your pastry) to make sure the cheese won't flow out of the corners, leaving the rest of the slit open. Set on the lightly oiled baking sheet. Repeat with the other 3 dough squares, then repeat with the remaining dough. Use a second baking sheet if necessary, or bake in batches.

Bake for 20 minutes, or until the pastries are lightly touched with gold and the bottoms are firm and almost crisp. Transfer to a rack or a plate and serve warm.

continued

GEORGIAN-STYLE FLAKY PASTRY

Puff pastry meets baklava in a yeasted dough that is a pleasure to work with. It makes a tender wrapping for cheese-filled pastries and other savory pastries, and for sweet pastries too. Make it at least 2 hours and up to 2 days ahead, then refrigerate it to chill and settle.

I start with cold butter and grate it on a box grater, but you can instead use very soft butter. The important thing is that you be able to spread the butter easily onto the dough. The butter between the layers of dough causes the pastry to puff as it bakes, and the result is very tender. **MAKES ABOUT 1½ POUNDS**

1 cup lukewarm water

1 teaspoon active dry yeast

1 teaspoon sugar

3 cups unbleached all-purpose flour, plus extra for surfaces

½ teaspoon sea salt

8 tablespoons (1 stick) unsalted butter, grated or very soft

Place the water in a medium bowl, add the yeast, sugar, and 1 cup of the flour, and stir well. Set aside for at least 20 minutes, and preferably several hours.

Add the remaining 2 cups flour to the mixture, stirring and turning to incorporate it. Sprinkle some flour on your work surface. Turn out the dough and knead briefly, until the dough is soft but no longer sticky, incorporating flour from the work surface as necessary.

Sprinkle a little more flour on your work surface and use your hands or a rolling pin to flatten the dough into a rectangle about 18 by 12 inches, with a long side toward you. Spread one-quarter of the butter over the center and right side of the dough, covering two-thirds of the surface, all the way to the edges, as you would for puff pastry. Fold the unbuttered third over to cover the center, and then fold again, as you would a letter, so you have three layers of dough separated by two layers of butter. Flatten the dough again with lightly floured hands and rotate it 90 degrees, so that again a long side is facing you. Repeat the buttering and folding, flattening, and rotating three more times, using one-quarter of the butter each time and reflouring your work surface and your hands as needed.

Fold the dough in half and flatten it a little. Fold it in half again in the other direction, and flatten it a little. Seal it in plastic wrap and refrigerate it for at least 2 hours, and for as long as 2 days.

Use the chilled dough to make the cheese-filled pastries, or fill it with the apricot-nut filling from the *paghlava* recipe on page 283 or with a very thick fruit jam, such as Apricot Moraba (page 318), using about 1 tablespoon filling per pastry.

NEAR KERMAN, IRAN—*A couple picnicking in Shazdeh
Garden (meaning Prince's Garden), near the village of Mahan.
Cascading fountains flow through the garden, cooling the air.*

CHEESE-FILLED QUICK BREADS

EMERETI KHACHAPURI

With a little practice, these quick-bread versions of Georgian *khachapuri* can be mixed, shaped, and baked in less than an hour. As with many quick breads, they are best eaten hot and fresh, for they toughen a little as they cool. These are made with a blend of all-purpose and pastry flour, to replicate the softer flour used in Georgia; use either white or whole wheat pastry flour.

Many people in Georgia don't have ovens, so they cook their *khachapuri* in a skillet on the stovetop. See the Note for stovetop cooking instructions.

MAKES 8 CHEESE-FILLED ROUNDS, ABOUT 7 INCHES ACROSS

FILLING

4 ounces mild or medium white cheddar, Monterey Jack cheese, or mozzarella, grated (about ¾ cup packed)

4 ounces feta cheese, crumbled into small pieces (about 1 cup packed)

1 large egg

2 tablespoons plain full-fat yogurt

About ¼ cup finely chopped fresh mint or tarragon (optional)

Generous grinding of black pepper

DOUGH

2½ cups all-purpose flour, plus extra for surfaces

2 cups plain full-fat yogurt

1½ cups white or whole wheat pastry flour

1¼ teaspoons salt

1 teaspoon baking powder

About 2 tablespoons melted butter for brushing on (optional)

Place one rack in the center of the oven and another one in the upper third. Preheat the oven to 425°F. Set out two baking sheets.

To make the filling, in a small bowl, mix together the cheeses, egg, and yogurt. Add the herbs if you wish and the pepper and mix well. Set aside.

To make the dough, place 2 cups of the all-purpose flour in a large bowl, add the yogurt, and stir to mix well.

In another bowl mix together the pastry flour, salt, and baking powder. Add to the yogurt-flour mixture and mix in thoroughly. Turn out onto a floured surface and knead for several minutes, until very smooth, incorporating more flour as necessary.

Cut the dough into 8 equal pieces (cut it in half, then cut each piece in half and half again). Roll each piece into a ball between your lightly floured palms. Set all but one aside, loosely covered.

continued

Lightly flour your work surface and flatten the remaining dough ball into a round with the floured palm of your hand. Turn the dough over and use a rolling pin to roll it out to a round about 8 inches in diameter. Place 2 tablespoons of filling in the center of the round. Pick up one edge of the dough between your thumb and forefinger and gently place on top of the mound of filling. Repeat with another edge about 1½ inches farther around, pleating the dough over the filling. Repeat all the way around, so the mound of filling is covered by pleated layers of dough; the dough is a little fragile, so you need to work gently to keep the cheese from breaking through. Press down gently on the mound to seal it and send the filling out to the edges of the bread. Turn it over and press again gently, then use your rolling pin with a light touch to roll the dough, working from the center outward, to about a 7-inch round that is less than ½ inch thick.

Transfer to a baking sheet, seam side down. Repeat with 3 more rounds.

Prick each bread four or five times with a fork and put the baking sheet on the top rack in the oven to bake for about 15 minutes. Repeat with the remaining dough and filling, placing the second baking sheet on the center rack. When the breads on the first sheet are firm to the touch and very slightly tinged with color, after about 15 minutes, remove from the oven and move the second sheet to the upper rack to bake until done.

Transfer the baked breads to a cloth-lined basket, brush with butter if you wish, and cover to keep them warm. *Khachapuri* are often cut into quarters and served that way; leave them whole or cut them as you wish.

NOTE: Stovetop versions of *khachapuri* are traditionally cooked on a clay surface called a *ketsi*, but a lightly oiled cast-iron or other heavy skillet does a fine job (though it's best to work with two skillets). Heat a little sunflower or extra-virgin olive oil or butter-ghee in each skillet over medium heat. Swirl to coat the surfaces and add one or two breads to each. Cook until firm and touched with color, about 10 minutes; turn them over after about 5 minutes. Keep the first batch warm in a cloth-lined basket while you cook the remaining breads.

KHACHAPURI MANY WAYS

One day I drove east out of Tbilisi into the green hills to visit the farm of Ana Mikadze-Chikvaidze, a cheesemaker and altogether lively personality. When I arrived, two of her friends were in the kitchen making *khachapuri*, using a variety of different fillings. The rest of the group sat outside on the grass talking and drinking Georgian red wine. Soon platters arrived stacked with wedges of hot fresh *khachapuri* of many kinds. I felt as if I'd landed in a cheese and bread paradise.

That day broadened my idea of what could go into *khachapuri*. Here are two other fillings. Use them to stuff the quick *khachapuri* dough (above) or the yeasted version (below).

FOUR-CHEESE KHACHAPURI Combine different cheeses that you like, a mix of three or four sharp cheeses totaling 1¾ packed cups, with chopped fresh tarragon, mint, or dill, or a little dried mint, and 1 large egg.

MUSHROOM, TARRAGON, AND SCALLION KHACHAPURI Cook about 1 pound chopped mushrooms in butter with a little minced scallion. Season with salt and pepper and let cool, then add ½ cup packed chopped fresh tarragon or coriander and minced scallions.

YEASTED KHACHAPURI
These are more tender and keep better than the quick *khachapuri*. Use the Home-Style Bread Dough (page 254), well risen. Divide the dough into 12 pieces and fill with 1 heaping tablespoon filling. Shape and fill the breads as above. Let stand for 15 minutes after shaping them before you bake them as above, in the upper third of the oven. The breads will bake in about 12 minutes.

NEAR TBILISI, GEORGIA—*A plate of khachapuri filled with a mix of cheese and herbs (left), stove-top baked, and cut into wedges just a moment before, at the farmhouse of Ana Mikadze-Chikvaidze, a cheesemaker and cheese researcher (right).*

HOME-STYLE BREAD DOUGH

Cooks in rural places in the three Caucasus countries often live far from a baker and so they still make their own breads, as their mothers and grandmothers did. The difference is that these days they have access to dry yeast and are happy for the certainty it gives.

If you have the time to let your dough do a long, slow rise, cut the yeast back to ½ teaspoon (or use a sourdough starter) and let the bread rise overnight in a cool place. It will have a more complex flavor.

This is a basic white-flour bread dough that is very like the doughs I saw women making (at home and in small bakeries) in Armenia, Georgia, and Azerbaijan. They don't put in an egg or any dairy product. And they make the dough quite wet and soft, so that the breads are tender, moist, and a little airy.

Use this to make the Georgian Boomerang Breads (opposite), Lavash (page 242), Armenian Greens Hand Pies (page 246), or the yeasted-dough version of *khachapuri* (page 253).   **MAKES ABOUT 2 POUNDS DOUGH**

2 cups lukewarm water

1 teaspoon sugar or honey

1 teaspoon active dry yeast

2 cups unbleached all-purpose flour, plus extra for surfaces

2 cups pastry flour or whole wheat pastry flour, or an additional 1¾ cups unbleached all-purpose flour

2 teaspoons sea salt

Place the water in a large bowl, add the sugar or honey, and stir, then add the yeast and stir. Add 2 cups of the all-purpose flour, stirring until you have a smooth batter. If you have the time, set aside for an hour or two, covered.

Add the pastry flour (or additional all-purpose) and salt and stir and turn to incorporate. Flour your work surface generously with all-purpose flour and turn the dough out. Knead until smooth, satiny, and still soft, incorporating flour only as necessary to prevent the dough from sticking. You want a moist dough. Transfer to a clean bowl, cover with plastic wrap, and set aside to rise for about 3 hours, until more than doubled in volume.

BOOMERANG BREADS

DEDAS PURI

These Georgian breads are baked in the Georgian version of a tandoor oven, called a *toné*, in bakeries all over the country. They look like small boomerangs. A *toné* is a wide barrel-shaped oven, gas-fired from below. The fire heats the inside walls, then the flame is lowered and the breads are laid onto the hot walls using a pillow, just as *naan* are baked in central Asia and northern India. But, unlike the long rectangular or oval breads of central Asia, Georgian tandoor breads have pointed ends. As tandoor bakers do in Iran and other places, Georgian bakers use a hook to grab the breads and a kind of scraper to help detach them from the oven wall (see photo, following pages).

You can bake these breads at home on a baking stone, but they need to be much smaller than those from bakeries—about 16 inches long, rather than more than 24 inches—so that they fit easily into a regular oven. The breads are fun to eat warm: Cut a slit in the side of the bread and slide in some cheese or slices of salami. **MAKES 8 FLATBREADS, ABOUT 15 INCHES LONG**

Home-Style Bread Dough (opposite), risen
Flour for surfaces

Cornmeal for dusting (optional)

Pull the risen dough together and turn it out onto a lightly floured surface. Cut it into 8 pieces. Roll each into a cylinder about 8 inches long and set aside to rest for 15 minutes, loosely covered.

Place a baking stone or unglazed quarry tiles on a rack in the upper third of your oven. Preheat the oven to 450°F. Lightly dust a peel or the back of a large baking sheet with flour or cornmeal.

Work with one dough at a time on a lightly floured surface: With floured fingertips, press on the dough to flatten it and then pull on either end to stretch it to about 12 inches long. Fold it in half lengthwise. Flatten it with your fingertips and pull on both ends to stretch them to a point. Transfer the bread to the peel and then to the baking stone or tiles.

Repeat with a second bread if there is room on your stone or tiles. Bake until touched with brown and cooked through, about 7 minutes. Transfer to a rack to cool for a moment, then wrap in cotton cloth to keep warm. Repeat with the remaining dough.

NEAR MANAVI, EASTERN GEORGIA—
A village baker lifts boomerang-shaped dedas puri off the hot walls of her low tandoor oven, called a toné in Georgian. Behind her, shaped dough rests on a shelf before being stretched and baked.

BREAD IN IRAN

There's a kind of reverence surrounding two of the breads of Iran. One is the classic breakfast bread called *barbari*, with a ridged browned top, and the other is *sangak*, the chewy, textured "pebble bread" that most often accompanies lunch and supper.

Both *sangak* and *barbari* are large flatbreads, made in bakeries in special ovens. These days the ovens are heated with gas. At a *sangak* bakery, all that's made is *sangak*, and *barbari* bakeries are equally specialized.

The traditional oven of a *sangak* bakery has a tall, narrow opening, and inside the cavern of the oven is a wall of gravel sloping upward toward the back. *Sang* means stone or pebble in Persian, so *sangak* refers to bread baked on a bed of stones. The wet dough is stretched onto a wet peel and laid onto the slope of hot gravel in the oven. When they are lifted out of the oven, the breads have a deeply dimpled bottom surface that often has a few pebbles embedded in it. The baker gives the breads a firm tap or two to dislodge the clinging stones before hanging them on a nail or laying them on a rack.

In the big cities of Iran, though, many *sangak* bakeries have modernized. A modern *sangak* oven has no pebbles, but instead a rotating baking surface that has rows of small manufactured bumps on it. Baking is quick, and the breads are quite standardized in shape, color, and texture.

A *barbari* oven is more like the large hearth ovens of traditional European-style bakeries. The distinctive thing about *barbari* is the shaping of the bread, rather than the oven. Before it is laid on a peel and placed on the hot hearth, the bread is brushed with a thin starchy paste and scored with parallel lines of dents along its length. The paste results in a very appealing browned surface. And the lines of dents create a lovely texture of alternating soft ridges and crisper "valleys." Bakers used to create the dents with their fingertips, and some, like the *barbari* bakers in Massouleh (see photo, page 263), still do. But most bakers now "dock" the breads with a sharp-toothed metal tool (see photo, page 260).

It's possible to make reasonable versions of both *sangak* and *barbari*

TABRIZ, IRAN—*Sangak bread is baked on a slope of pebbles, a few of which may get embedded in the bread. The rack they're laid on to cool has over time accumulated its own deep layer of pebbles that have dropped out of the breads.*

Left: **ISFAHAN, IRAN**—*Sangak bakers work with long peels to lay the moistened and shaped dough onto a slope of hot pebbles in the oven. Note the baked bread hanging on nails against the wall.*

Right: **YAZD, IRAN**—*A metal roller that bakers use to dock or pierce barbari breads creates lines of dents along their length.*

in a home oven if you have a baking stone and, for making *sangak,* a supply of small stones (though you can make it without pebbles; see the variation on page 262). The bakery breads in Iran are very large. These versions are smaller, both so they can fit into a home oven and because smaller breads are easier to handle. Homemade Persian flatbreads come close to the bakery versions, and the process of making them gives a real appreciation of the baker's art. I urge you to give them a try.

BAKER'S NOTES: If you have a starter going, use it rather than the yeast and lengthen the proofing times as necessary.

The flour used in Iran is a little softer than most North American all-purpose flour. It's more like European bread flour, at 10 to 11 percent protein. You can use all-purpose, but I like to mix all-purpose and pastry flour. The result is bread that is more tender and closer to the texture of the breads in Iran. There the ovens are very hot and the climate is dry, so the breads' surfaces tighten and firm up immediately. Once you tear off a piece of bread and bite into it, the surface may be firm and a little dried out, but the crumb is tender.

PERSIAN PEBBLE BREAD

NAAN-E-SANGAK

People line up at *sangak* bakeries in the late morning, waiting for bread to take home to the family for the noontime meal. The breads are huge, sometimes four feet long and nearly two feet wide, dimpled golden sheets that soon stiffen in the dry air. People carry stacks of them home in their arms, or they may fold them for easier carrying. The breads are cut or torn and eaten with the noon and evening meal, used as wrappers for grilled meats or torn into smaller pieces to scoop up mouthfuls of vegetables or sauces, and snacked on to assuage hunger at any time.

If you don't want to hassle with stones or pebbles, you can finger-dent the dough; see the variation on page 262. Otherwise, you need a thick bed of pebbles on a rimmed baking sheet. (If the pebbles are in just a single layer, the dough drapes around them and too many of them become embedded in it.) I had thought that the stones needed to be rounded river stones, but in fact in Iran the bakers use regular sharp gravel. Smooth-surfaced stones are easier to dislodge from the breads, but if your only source is gravel with some sharp shapes, it's fine.

You will also need a sturdy baking sheet to hold your bed of gravel. The larger the baking sheet, the larger the breads you can make. Also see Baker's Notes, opposite.   **MAKES 8 THIN, BUMPY FLATBREADS, ABOUT 16 INCHES LONG AND 3 TO 4 INCHES WIDE**

3 cups lukewarm water

1 teaspoon active dry yeast

3 cups fine whole wheat flour (if you can't get finely milled flour, sift the flour to remove the coarsest bran)

1 cup pastry flour

About 3½ cups unbleached all-purpose flour

4 teaspoons sea salt

1 cup sesame seeds

Twenty-four to 36 hours before you want to bake the breads, place 1 cup of the water, ⅛ teaspoon of the yeast, and 1 cup of the whole wheat flour in a large bowl and stir until you have a smooth batter (or poolish). Cover the bowl with plastic and set aside to ferment for 18 to 24 hours.

About 5 hours before baking the breads, stir the poolish (some water may have separated out), then add the remaining 2 cups lukewarm water and the remaining scant teaspoon yeast and stir again. Add the remaining 2 cups whole wheat flour, the pastry flour, and 2 cups of the all-purpose flour and stir to make a smooth batter. Add the salt and another cup of all-purpose flour and stir and turn to incorporate.

Turn the dough out onto a heavily floured surface (use another ½ cup or so of flour) and knead for 5 to 8 minutes, incorporating flour only as needed. You want the dough to be somewhat soft, not stiff, but no longer sticky. Transfer to a clean bowl, cover with plastic wrap, and set aside to proof for about 5 hours. The dough should double in volume.

Half an hour before you want to start baking, place a baking stone or quarry tiles on a rack in the upper third of your oven. Place the baking sheet of stones (see headnote) on it. Preheat the oven to 500°F.

After the oven has preheated for 15 minutes, shape the breads: Put out a bowl of water so you can moisten surfaces and prevent the breads from sticking to the peel. Gently release the dough from the sides of the bowl and pull it together. Moisten your work surface with water and turn out the dough. Cut it in half and then divide one half into 4 pieces; loosely cover the other half. Depending on the size of your baking sheet, you may be able to bake 2 breads at a time. You can use a peel or the back of a baking sheet to transfer the breads onto the hot stones, or just drop them onto the stones with your hands.

Moisten the peel or back of the baking sheet with water. Pick up one piece of dough with both hands and move your hands apart to stretch it to 15 or 16 inches long. Touch the bottom surface of the bread against the wet countertop to moisten it and lay the dough on the peel, with one end hanging over the front edge by about an inch. Quickly sprinkle on 2 tablespoons sesame seeds, then transfer the bread to the oven, using the hanging end to "catch" the dough on the far side, and slide the peel away as you lay the bread on the hot stones. Alternatively, hold one end of the bread in each hand and place the stretched bread on the hot stones.

Bake until the bread begins to color on top, about 8 minutes. Meanwhile, if your baking sheet will hold 2 breads, shape a second one and slide it onto the stones. Remove the baked bread using a wide spatula or tongs, and place on a rack to cool; rap the bread to dislodge any clinging stones, or pick them out. Repeat shaping and baking the remaining cut dough pieces, and then the remaining dough.

FINGER-DENTED BREADS

This technique is very like that used by Afghani bakers for making tandoor naan, but this dough is wetter (more hydrated), so the dents result in a bottom surface with dimples that are like those in pebble-baked *sangak.*

MASSOULEH, IRAN—*Bakers in the village shape barbari bread every day, a huge production. Here, instead of a metal roller (see photo, page 260), the bakers rely on the traditional technique, denting the breads with their fingertips.*

As above, place a baking stone or quarry tiles in the oven and preheat. Set a bowl of water by your work surface. Divide the risen dough as above. Wet your fingertips and, starting at one end of one piece of dough, working with stiff fingers and sharp jabs, make repeated deep dents all over the surface. Open the oven door, pick up the dough on the back of your hands or on your palms, pull them apart gently to stretch the bread to about 15 inches long, and lay it directly on the hot baking stone. If you have room, shape and bake a second bread alongside. Bake as above. Repeat with the remaining dough.

MASSOULEH, IRAN—Barbari *bread for breakfast, with honey and a pot of black tea.*

VILLAGE BREAKFAST

On my first trip to Iran, I flew to Tehran and immediately headed out of the city by car. The driver spoke little English, so as we inched along in heavy rush-hour traffic for nearly two hours (a reminder that the city is huge and prosperous),

I used the time to learn Arabic numbers. The car license plates and the driver together were my teachers. Finally we turned onto the highway that leads to Shomal, "the north," and left the worst of the traffic behind. The road cut through the steep mountain barrier that separates the dry central Iranian plateau from the humid Caspian Sea area to the north. As we approached the Caspian, the air grew softer, and soon the windshield was sprinkled with rain. It was after ten at night by the time we followed a narrow winding road uphill and came to a muddy clearing. We'd arrived at the village of Massouleh.

A man was there to meet me, with a flashlight against the dark and a strong shoulder for my bag. We walked along a muddy path in the rain, the flashlight casting shadows here and there. There were puddles to dodge, stone steps to go up, and more steps, and darkness all around. Finally he pulled out some keys and opened a heavy wooden door. This was my room, a large space carpeted with layers of thick rugs, where I'd be staying for the next couple of days. My host told me there'd be breakfast in the morning, and off he went.

Tired from journeying, and chilly in the damp air, I crashed on one of the beds under a load of quilts. Next morning, bundled in layers of wool, I opened the shutters and looked out to see a tightly packed steeply terraced village in shades of slate gray and clay brown, darkened with rain and softened with mist.

My host knocked at the door and came in with a tray of breakfast. Ah, my first meal in Iran, extra welcome because I hadn't eaten since noon the previous day. On the tray were large pieces of *barbari* bread hot from the oven, as well as fresh cheese, honey, a pot of tea, a tea glass, and a bowl of sugar cubes. I ate all the bread and cheese and drank all the tea.

And then I went looking for the bakery.

BARBARI BREAD

NAAN-E-BARBARI

Barbari has ridges down its length and is often topped with a scattering of nigella or sesame seeds. It's the classic breakfast bread in Iran. *Barbari,* like the word *barbarian,* comes from a root word that means foreigner. There are many theories about where the bread originates. People in Iran told me that the best *barbari* bakers come not from Iran, but from a valley in Afghanistan.

I am indebted to an Iranian-American baker named Omri who posted a lot of information about *barbari* on a website called The Fresh Loaf (see Bibliography). His notes were a great help as I was trying to figure out a home-style *barbari* recipe.

In Iran, bakers use a 10-percent-protein flour; I use a blend of pastry flour and all-purpose to mimic that. You can use a sourdough starter to leaven it if you have one going. Otherwise, follow the directions below. **MAKES 16 FLATBREADS**

3 cups lukewarm water

1 teaspoon active dry yeast

1 cup whole wheat flour or unbleached
    all-purpose flour

2 cups pastry flour

About 2 cups unbleached all-purpose
    flour, plus extra for surfaces

4 teaspoons sea salt

About 1½ cups wheat bran

About ⅓ cup sesame seeds or about
    1 tablespoon nigella seeds (optional)

FLOUR PASTE TOPPING

1 cup water

About ¼ cup all-purpose flour, sifted

Place 1 cup of the lukewarm water in a large bowl. Add ⅛ teaspoon of the yeast and stir. Add the whole wheat or all-purpose flour and stir well to make a smooth batter; this is your poolish. Cover with plastic and set aside for 18 to 24 hours to ferment.

The next day, the poolish should have bubbles in it and some water may have separated out; just stir it back in. Add the remaining 2 cups lukewarm water and the remaining scant teaspoon yeast and stir. Add the pastry flour, 1 cup of the all-purpose flour, and the salt and stir in one direction to incorporate the flour. When you have a smooth batter, sprinkle on another cup of flour and stir and turn to incorporate it.

continued

Flour your work surface with another cup or so of flour and turn out the dough. Knead for 7 to 10 minutes, incorporating the flour as necessary, until you have a satiny-smooth dough; it should be tender and soft. Place the dough in a clean bowl and cover with plastic to prevent it from drying out. Set aside in a cool place to rise for 5 or 6 hours, until doubled in volume.

Put out a baking sheet or tray and sprinkle with flour. Turn the dough out onto a lightly floured surface. Fold it a couple of times and cut it in half, then cut each half into 8 equal pieces. Shape each one into a ball under your palm or using both hands, and set on the floured baking sheet, leaving 1½ to 2 inches between the balls of dough.

Cover loosely with plastic wrap and set aside to proof for an hour or so. To test, wet a fingertip and poke it into one of the dough balls; the dent you make should remain rather than bouncing back.

Meanwhile, 30 minutes before you wish to bake, place a baking stone or quarry tiles on a rack in the upper third of your oven and preheat it to 500°F. Put out a peel or an upside-down baking sheet.

To make the flour paste topping, pour the water into a small saucepan and bring to a vigorous boil, then reduce the heat to very low. Start whisking the water and at the same time use your other hand to sprinkle a little of the flour into the water. Continuing to whisk to prevent lumps, add a little more flour, and then a little more, whisking. After about 3 tablespoons of flour and a few minutes whisking, you should have a milky-to-clear paste that's quite liquid, and a little sticky. It will thicken more as it cools, and you want it to be loose and spreadable. Set the paste aside to cool completely.

Cover a roughly 15-by-18-inch area of your work surface with the wheat bran. Carefully move 8 of the dough pieces onto it, trying not to deflate them. As you move them, they will stretch a little; shape them gently to pull each one into a slightly rectangular pillow shape. Let stand for 10 minutes.

Place the pan of cooled flour paste and a pastry brush by your work surface, as well as a bowl of water.

Start shaping the breads 10 minutes after the oven has reached temperature. Brush some paste onto each of the 8 portions of dough with a very light hand. You want to be sure that you don't deflate the dough as you shape it. Dip your fingertips into the water and make a continuous line of deep vertical dents in one piece of dough down its full length, about ¼ inch from the edge (see photo, opposite). Leaving a ¼-inch space (this will become a puffed ridge in the baked bread), repeat, wetting your fingertips again before making another parallel line of dents, poking vigorously. Repeat until you get to within ¼ inch or so of the other edge. Sprinkle on sesame seeds generously or a few nigella seeds if you wish.

continued

Carefully slide your hands under the dough and lift it onto the peel, pulling your hands apart to stretch it lengthwise; it should end up being 3 to 4 inches wide and 12 to 15 inches long. Don't worry if it has the odd hole; that just gives even more interesting texture. Quickly slip it onto the hot baking stone, leaving room for one or two more breads if possible. Repeat with another dough or two—whatever you have room for on your baking surface. Bake the breads until the top is well browned, about 8 minutes. Remove the breads from the oven and place them on a rack to cool, or wrap in a cotton cloth to keep them warm and moist. Repeat with the remaining pillows of dough. As you move the breads from the bran surface into the oven, transfer the 8 remaining dough pieces onto the bran so they have time to rest before being shaped.

Repeat the shaping and baking process with the remaining dough; remember to carefully brush on the paste before you start making the dented lines in the breads.

To serve, cut or tear the breads crosswise into smaller lengths and stack them, or put out the whole breads and invite guests to tear off pieces as they wish.

NOTE: To reheat the breads, place cut pieces of bread in a wet paper bag and heat in a 300°F oven for about 10 minutes.

SHIRAZ, IRAN—Posing for a photo in the garden at the tomb of the famed Persian poet Hafez (see Fountains and Gardens, Picnics and Poetry, page 169).

BREAD FRITTATA

DEDAS KHARCHO

For this traditional Georgian way of transforming old bread into succulent eating, cubes of dried bread are tossed in hot oil with onions and water and cooked until softened. Quantities are flexible. Whisked egg is stirred into the mass of soft bread and onion to make a kind of frittata. Serve with a green salad, or sliced tomatoes and cucumbers, or pickled peppers, for breakfast or brunch or for a light meal at any time.

This is best made with artisanal bread or a mix of breads with a good firm crust and crumb. **SERVES 4 OR 5**

About 3 tablespoons sunflower or
    extra-virgin olive oil

1 large onion, chopped (about 1½ cups)

4 to 5 cups 1-inch cubes dried bread
    (tough crusts trimmed)

1 medium or 2 small tomatoes, coarsely
    chopped (optional)

6 large eggs

1 teaspoon sea salt, or to taste

About ¼ cup chopped fresh tarragon,
    coriander, or sorrel (optional)

Freshly ground black pepper

Heat the oil in a wide deep skillet or wide heavy pot over medium heat. Toss in the onion and cook until translucent, 4 to 5 minutes. Add the bread cubes and turn and stir to expose them all to the hot oil, a minute or two. Add water to cover and bring to a boil, then reduce the heat to medium-low and cook, uncovered, until the bread is well softened and most of the water is absorbed, 3 to 5 minutes. If using tomatoes, add them a couple of minutes after the water comes to the boil.

Meanwhile, break the eggs into a bowl, add the salt, and whisk well. Stir in the chopped herbs, if using, and pepper to taste.

Add the eggs to the bread mixture and stir a little to distribute them. Cook for a minute or two, until the eggs have just set. Turn out onto a platter and serve.

OLD-BREAD CHEESE PIE

BANRAKHASH

Until recently, during wintertime in Armenia, most people living in villages and on farms had access only to what they had put away in their pantry and cold storage, as well as to milk and cheese and bread. Cooks needed to figure out interesting ways of making full use of the ingredients available, and that inventiveness resulted in a number of ways of cooking with dried-out flatbreads.

Banrakhash is rather like a pizza made of leftover bread. Cheese and leftover lavash or other thin breads are layered into a baking pan with some chopped onion, and doused with melted butter, then topped with beaten egg and cream before being baked. The dish is a rich and hearty way to use leftovers, and to warm body and soul on a cold night.

This recipe comes from a place that has seen hard times, the Gyumri area, which lies between Armenia's capital, Yerevan, and the southern Georgian region called Javaheti. In December 1988, a massive earthquake devastated the city of Gyumri, and the breakup of the Soviet Union a couple of years later stripped Armenia of jobs and income.

But things are looking up. Recently I met an American man who had started an IT company in Gyumri. As he says, it's hard to export products from a landlocked country like Armenia, but software, the product of Armenians' brains and ingenuity, is very exportable. The company is prospering and Gyumri is turning into a small IT hub, a reason for optimism in a country where optimism can be in short supply.

You will need a round or square baking pan 10 to 12 inches across. This is an improvised dish that accommodates the tools and ingredients available, so if your pan is smaller, just add another layer to use up all your bread and cheese.

Serve this as a main dish to accompany a soup or a bean stew. Put out an Herb Plate (page 23) or some cooked greens to balance the richness of the cheese pie. Leftovers are great the next day, served at room temperature or rewarmed in a low oven. **SERVES 6 TO 8**

2 tablespoons sunflower or extra-virgin olive oil

1 or 2 onions, thinly sliced

About 1 pound dried-out lavash or other thin flatbreads (if you have pita, split the breads to make thin layers)

About ⅓ pound chopped cheese: a mix of pot cheese, feta, or other salty, crumbly cheese and string cheese or medium cheddar

8 tablespoons (1 stick) butter, melted

1 medium or large egg

About ¼ cup light cream

KHOR VIRAP, NEAR YEREVAN, ARMENIA—*A family leaving church with a newly christened baby. One of the most revered sites in Armenia, Khor Virap is an ancient monastery in the shadow of Mount Ararat, within sight of the Turkish border.*

Place a rack in the upper third of the oven and preheat the oven to 375°F.

Place a heavy skillet over medium heat. Add the oil and toss in the onions. Fry, stirring occasionally, until translucent and softened. Set aside.

Line a 10- to 12-inch baking pan or dish (see headnote) with some of the bread, overlapping the pieces so the surface is completely covered; it's fine if some of the pieces come up the side of the pan.

Sprinkle on about a quarter of the cheese. Add another layer of bread. If the bread is very dry and brittle, sprinkle on a tablespoon or two of water. Sprinkle on more than half the remaining cheese and half the cooked onions. Add another layer of bread pieces. Again, if they are extremely dry, sprinkle on a little water. Top with the remaining cheese and onions and cover with another layer of bread. Pour the melted butter over and let stand for a moment.

Whisk the egg and cream together and pour over the top of the dish. Place the pan in the oven and bake for about 25 minutes, until the top is touched with brown and the top layer of bread has crisped up. Let cool for 15 minutes before cutting and serving.

NOTE ON OPTIONS: You can include a light sprinkling of nigella seeds on one or two of the cheese layers, or a dusting of dried mint or scattering of fresh tarragon. You can also use this dish as an opportunity to use up tired ends of dried cheese that may be hanging around your refrigerator, making it an even more useful dish for leftovers.

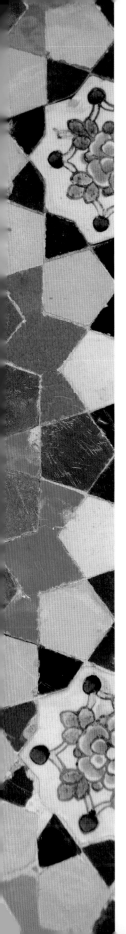

A TASTE FOR SWEET

MOST PEOPLE IN THE PERSIAN CULINARY region eat sweet treats as a break in the day, with tea or coffee, juice or water, rather than at the end of a meal. The sweet may be something baked, like a cookie or a pastry, but it could also be a spoonful of thick jam (see Apricot Moraba, page 318, and Carrot Moraba, page 321, in the fruit chapter) or a pudding. There are several Persian puddings here, smooth and creamy; they make elegant desserts.

Cookies and other sweetmeats are served at times of celebration—at Nou-Roz (New Year's), for example, and at birthdays and weddings. Iran is famous for its cookies, each city or region having its own specialties. I've included the diamond-shaped cookies from the city of Yazd called *baqlava* (see page 295), which are drenched in sweet syrup, and several others that are Nou-Roz classics.

In Georgia and Armenia, home cooks work with layered pastry to make treats that are sometimes flavored with nuts and dried fruit and always rich with butter (see Armenian Puff Pastry Cake, page 287). The strudel-like rolled pastry called *paghlava* from Georgia (see page 283) is a distant cousin of the more familiar baklava of the eastern Mediterranean.

And finally there's a Persian-style halvah from southern Iran, made not with sesame paste, as it is in Arab countries, but with toasted flour and butter flavored with sweet ripe dates.

Tea is the everyday drink, the lubricant of conversations in bazaars and at home, in Iran, Azerbaijan, and Kurdistan. Many Persian and Azeri households keep a large samovar, full of hot water, ready to wet the tea leaves in a pot or to dilute the strong brew already in the pot.

People in the region drink their tea without milk, sweetened with sugar. Sometimes it's spiced with cardamom or a spice blend (see Tea from the Caspian and Spice Blend for Tea, page 302). Black tea is the standard in Iran and the rest of the region, but there is green tea too. In Georgia and Armenia, coffee made

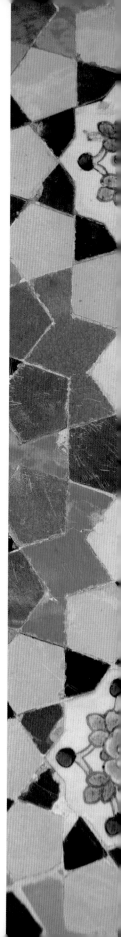

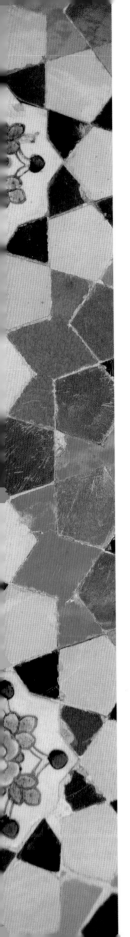

in the Armenian way (see page 305), an intense hit of sweet flavor and caffeine, is the more likely hot drink, though tea is always an option.

In warm weather, yogurt makes a favorite cold drink: Plain yogurt is mixed with cold water and ice, sprinkled with a little dried mint, perhaps, and lightly salted (see page 309). It's very refreshing.

Previous pages: MELIKGYUGH, ARMENIA—*Freshly home-baked gata (Armenian Puff Pastry Cake; see page 287). I was lucky to arrive in this small village near Mount Aragats and be invited in by Tsayhlik on a day she was baking.*

Above: YAZD, IRAN—*There's a painted mural on a wall at this little park in central Yazd, with palm trees offering some shade. A group of men sitting here chatting and drinking tea together invited me to join them.*

ROSE WATER PUDDING

FERENI

This delectable pudding is smooth and creamy, lightly perfumed with rose water and topped with chopped pistachios. The pistachios are optional, but they complement the rose water beautifully. **SERVES 6**

2 cups whole milk

2 cups light cream

¼ cup rice flour

½ cup sugar

1 tablespoon rose water

About ½ cup shelled pistachios, ground to a coarse powder (optional)

Mix the milk and cream in a bowl. Pour ¼ cup of the mixture into another bowl.

Sift the rice flour into the smaller amount and whisk thoroughly to make a smooth paste. Slowly add another cup or so of the milk mixture, whisking so that there are no lumps. Transfer to a large heavy saucepan and add the remaining milk mixture, whisking to prevent lumps. Set over medium-low heat and stir in the sugar. Add the rose water and continue cooking, whisking often, until the mixture thickens, about 30 minutes. Taste and add a little more rose water if you like.

Pour into individual bowls or a large serving bowl. Set aside to cool a little, then cover and refrigerate for several hours or overnight to thicken. Serve chilled.

If you'd like to top the pudding with the ground pistachios, sprinkle them on just before serving, when the pudding has thickened.

PERSIAN RICE PUDDING

SHIR BERENJ

Rose water, cardamom, and pistachios play together enticingly in the creamy Persian version of rice pudding. Simple seduction.   **SERVES 6**

¾ cup short-grain rice or broken rice (see Glossary)

4 cups whole milk

¾ cup sugar, or more to taste

3 tablespoons rose water, or more to taste

½ teaspoon ground cardamom

About 12 pistachios, coarsely chopped (optional)

Wash the rice well, place in a heavy pot with the milk, and bring to a boil. Lower the heat, partially cover, and simmer, stirring occasionally, until the rice softens and most of the liquid has been absorbed, about 1 hour. The pudding will have a soft, slightly soupy texture.

Stir in the sugar, rose water, and cardamom and cook, stirring, for 10 minutes. Taste and add a little more sugar or rose water if you wish. Let cool to room temperature.

If you like, top the pudding with the pistachios just before serving.

From left to right: ISFAHAN, IRAN—*Pistachios close up, and women buying pistachios at the bazaar;* **SHEKI, AZERBAIJAN**—*at the market, with barberries above, bright plump rose hips and garlic below;* **KASHAN, IRAN**—*stills for making rose water (for which Kashan is famous) and carpeted benches for customers to sit on while they sample the waters and sip tea.*

MASHAD, IRAN—*The tomb of Imam Reza in far northeastern Iran is the holiest place in the country, a destination for about twenty million pilgrims annually. The huge complex consists of courtyards, mosques, and meeting places built around the tomb, which is marked by the golden dome.*

MIRRORS AND PATTERNED LIGHT

When I visited the lovely shrine of Shah Chirag in Shiraz, a place of pilgrimage and one of the holiest sites in Iran, I picked up a flower-sprigged white chador from a bin of chadors, and draped it over my head so it covered me from head to toe. I clutched it closed at the front with one hand and passed through an archway into the graceful courtyard.

From there I went through the curtained women's entrance into the mausoleum of Amir Ahmed. (He was the brother of Imam Reza, the much-revered seventh imam, whose shrine is in Mashad.)

Inside was a different world. A high mesh metal grille divides the men's and women's sections. The large white marble sarcophagus, protected by a metal grille, is set midway in the shrine so that it's accessible from both the men's and women's sides. I walked forward past black-chadored women. Many sat on rugs on the ground praying, while others crowded around the sarcophagus, kissing the grillwork and touching it, some crying. Over the loudspeaker, a preacher was telling a story of the martyrdom of one of the imams, and as the story moved toward a tragic crescendo, many women burst out sobbing and rocked to and fro.

All this was happening in a place of light and beauty, with the black forms of the women reflected in fantastically complex mirrored tiling, a mosaic of triangles, squares, and diamond shapes that covered the walls and ceilings and gleamed and glinted in the light from glass chandeliers. The effect was dizzying, disorienting, and also thrilling in a way I can't explain.

I sat down by a wall, letting the sounds and feelings wash over and through me. The echoing sound of the preacher's hoarse voice lamenting, the women's sobs and heartfelt anguish, and the thousands and thousands of mosaicked reflections that amplified sound and movement were like waves of human pain. I realized that I too felt the ache of grief and that I had become part of it all. Human pain and suffering, the hurts that we each experience in our lives, found expression and release in this outpouring of grief for the imams

SHIRAZ, IRAN—*A fellow tourist took this photo of me outside the shrine of Shah Chirag, a beautiful mirrored place of worship and veneration. The shrine provides cotton chadors for women visitors; upon leaving, I just put my chador back into the bin.*

who died long ago and who are revered in Shia tradition.

I don't know how long I sat there, feeling like a piece of flotsam being swept up by tides of emotion. Even as a nonbeliever, the experience of being in the shrine with all that intensity left me cleansed through.

APRICOT-WALNUT PASTRY

PAGHLAVA

The name of this terrific pastry from Georgia is *paghlava,* but it's not the baklava of Turkey or Syria and Lebanon; it's more like a cross between a strudel and baklava, with layers of pastry alternating with nuts and dried fruit. It's a cousin of the Armenian puff pastry called *gata* (see page 287) and the Persian *baqlava* cookies from Yazd on page 295.

The pastry, freely adapted from a recipe in Julianne Margvelashvili's book *The Classic Cuisine of Soviet Georgia,* is tender and easy to work with. It's rolled out, covered with chopped dried apricots and walnuts, rolled up like a Persian rug and baked, then sliced once cooled.

This is especially delicious topped with heavy cream. **SERVES 10**

PASTRY

1¼ cups all-purpose flour, plus extra for surfaces

⅛ teaspoon baking soda

8 tablespoons (1 stick) very cold butter

⅓ to ½ cup sour cream, or substitute full-fat plain yogurt

1 to 2 teaspoons regular or pearl sugar for glazing

FILLING

1 large egg, separated

¾ cup sugar

1 cup finely ground walnuts

1 cup chopped dried apricots (pieces about the size of small raisins)

¼ teaspoon ground cardamom

Place the flour and baking soda in a bowl and grate the butter into it. Rub the flour and butter together to make crumbs. Add ⅓ cup of the sour cream or yogurt and mix gently. Try to pull the pastry together; if it is too dry, add a little more sour cream or yogurt and mix to make a slightly soft dough.

Pull the pastry together into a ball and flatten into a thick disk. Seal in plastic and refrigerate until you are ready to use it.

Preheat the oven to 375°F. Line a baking sheet with parchment paper or grease it lightly.

Whisk the egg white in a medium bowl; set aside 1 teaspoon of the white. Add the sugar, walnuts, apricots, and cardamom to the remaining egg white and mix well. Set aside.

continued

Place a cotton cloth on your work surface and dust it with flour. Flatten the pastry gently on the cloth. Use a rolling pin to roll it into a rectangle measuring about 15 by 20 inches, with one of the 15-inch sides nearest to you. Spread the filling on it, leaving a generous 1-inch border on the side farthest away from you and a ½-inch border on the other three sides. Beat the egg yolk and brush it onto the exposed pastry edges. Use the cloth to lift the edge of the pastry nearest you and roll it up like a jelly roll. Place seam side down on the lined baking sheet.

Brush the top of the pastry with the reserved egg white and sprinkle on a teaspoon or two of sugar. Bake for 20 to 25 minutes, or until well touched with gold. Let cool for at least 30 minutes before slicing.

Left: *Rolled out and spread with the filling, the pastry is being brushed around the edges with egg yolk, which helps seal in the filling.*

Opposite: *The baked pastry has been sliced after it cooled completely. Note that sulfured apricots will be bright-colored and attractive, as in these photos. But I prefer to use the duller brown unsulfured ones for their flavor. Chopped, partially cooked apple in place of half the apricots is also delicious.*

ARMENIAN PUFF PASTRY CAKE

GATA

This pastry is an Armenian national treasure. Everyone has his or her favorite version. *Gata* is made with a dough similar to puff pastry that is filled with a lightly sweetened butter paste. I learned how to make *gata* from a hospitable, generous woman named Tsayhlik who lives with her family in a small high-altitude Armenian village below Mount Aragats.

Gata is often made as individual puff pastry rectangles. Tsayhlik made those and also *gata* in other shapes. This is the one I find easiest to make and serve: It's a round of puff pastry with a buttery cardamom-scented filling. Serve it cut into wedges. **MAKES 2 LARGE FILLED PASTRIES; EACH SERVES 8**

DOUGH

2 medium or large egg yolks

1 cup lukewarm water

1 tablespoon cider vinegar or white wine vinegar

12 tablespoons (1½ sticks) butter, softened

¼ teaspoon sea salt

About 3 cups all-purpose flour, plus extra for surfaces

LAYERING

8 tablespoons (1 stick) butter, well softened

1 tablespoon all-purpose flour

FILLING AND TOPPING

¾ cup sugar

6 tablespoons butter, well softened

½ teaspoon ground cardamom

3 tablespoons all-purpose flour

¼ teaspoon baking soda

1 egg, beaten, for brushing on top

To make the dough, place the egg yolks, water, vinegar, butter, salt, and 2½ cups flour in a bowl and stir until you have a smooth, loose dough. Add another ½ cup flour and stir and fold it in.

Turn the dough out onto a lightly floured surface and knead it briefly, incorporating more flour if necessary. You should have a soft, tender dough. Transfer to a clean bowl, cover with plastic wrap, and let rest for 1 to 3 hours, whatever is most convenient.

continued

To make the layering mixture, place the butter in a bowl and stir in the flour, blending well. The butter should be very soft, so that the mixture can be spread easily. Set aside.

Turn the dough out onto a lightly floured surface. Use your hands or light strokes of a rolling pin to stretch it out to an 18-inch square. Spread half the layering mixture onto two-thirds of the dough, leaving one-third bare. Fold the bare third over the buttered surface (as if you were doing the first fold of a business letter), then fold the remaining buttered dough over that, to give you a rectangle about 18 by 6 inches. Rotate the dough 90 degrees and repeat, spreading on the rest of the mixture and then doing the same "envelope fold," so that you have an almost square shape.

Press the dough down lightly with your hands to flatten it a little, and fold it again in thirds. Cut it in half crosswise to give 2 almost-square pieces. Pinch together the cut edges of each piece, then flatten each gently with the palms of your hands to make a rounded square about 7 inches in diameter. Set aside in the refrigerator to rest for 30 minutes.

Place one rack just above the center of your oven and another about 3 inches below it. Preheat the oven to 425°F. Line two baking sheets with parchment paper.

To make the filling, combine the sugar and soft butter in a bowl. Mix with a wooden spoon until well blended. Add the cardamom, flour, and baking soda, and stir to blend completely. Divide the crumbly filling between two small bowls.

Dust a work surface lightly with flour. Place one of the dough pieces on it and, with light strokes of a rolling pin, roll it out to a circle about 16 inches in diameter. Sprinkle half of the filling evenly on the circle, leaving a 2- to 3-inch border; break up any lumps as necessary. Pick up the edge at one point and pull it over to the center of the circle. Still holding on to that first piece, pick up the edge 2 inches farther along and pull it over to the center, pleating the dough, and continue until you have pulled the dough up to completely enclose the filling. Press the pleats together to seal. Turn the pastry over, reflouring the work surface lightly if necessary, curve your hands around the edges to shape it into a smooth round, then roll it out a little more, again using light strokes from the center outward, to flatten it to a circle 12 inches in diameter. Transfer to one of the lined baking sheets. Repeat with the second half of the dough and the remaining filling.

Prick the top of the pastries all over with a fork in a decorative pattern (see photo, opposite). Pricking the dough helps to keep it from ballooning as it bakes. Brush the beaten egg generously over the top of the pastries.

Place one baking sheet on each oven rack and bake for 20 minutes, or until the pastries are well touched with golden brown; rotate the sheets at about the

10-minute mark. The pastries are fragile until they cool, so let them cool for at least 30 minutes on the baking sheets, then use the parchment paper to transfer them to a rack or a platter. Don't worry if they puffed up while baking; once you start slicing them, the top crust will settle back down onto the rest.

Serve at room temperature, cut into wedges.

MINI GATA

Instead of dividing the dough in half after the folding process, cut it into 4 pieces. Pinch the cut sides to seal them, press down lightly to flatten slightly, and set aside. Proceed as above: Roll out to 11-inch rounds, then fill and shape into 4 pastries about 8 inches in diameter. Remember to prick the top surface. The smaller pastries will bake more quickly than the larger versions, so check for doneness at about 15 minutes. Switch oven racks at about the 8-minute mark, as above.

ARMENIA—*The pastry is pricked and flattened in an attempt to prevent the top layer from puffing up as it bakes, but somehow it seems to nonetheless. Once you cut the first slice, the top settles back down, as you can see on page 286.*

TRAIN JOURNEY

After some confusion about my ticket, I rushed out onto the train platform in Kerman just a few minutes before the train was due to leave and climbed aboard at the nearest door. My berth was in a compartment two cars farther up, it turned out,

so as the train creaked out of the station, I slowly made my way there, passing compartments full of men and boys, and clusters of men standing in the corridor and looking out the windows. I was a surprise to them, visibly foreign, with my badly arranged head scarf, saying "Excuse me" and giving apologetic smiles as I threaded my way through. A door, another car, this one with women and families still stowing luggage and getting settled, and then at last my compartment. The other five passengers, women, were already there. We were going to be together for about fifteen hours, for this was the overnight train from Kerman, in southern Iran, to Mashad, in northeastern Iran.

I felt shy, and so did they. We smiled at each other in encouragement and they showed me where to put my bag. I learned that my companions were a mother and daughter who were traveling to a cousin's wedding, and a three-generation group: grandmother, daughter, and granddaughter.

The wedding-goers were both strikingly beautiful, the mother in her mid-forties, I guessed, and the daughter in her mid-twenties. The daughter spoke a little English and understood more. Like many young women I'd seen in Iranian cities, she was wearing narrow Band-Aid strips on her face: one over the bridge of her nose and another across the front of her nose just above her nostrils. This badge of recent plastic surgery seems to be worn with no embarrassment in Iran, and often, with some pride. In the first hour or two of the trip, I saw her checking under the strips, using a hand mirror to see how well her scars were healing, then carefully sticking them back on. Like most young women in Iran, she wore lots of makeup and had beautifully manicured hands.

The three-generation family had a different vibe. The grandmother wore a black chador, and under that she had a head covering. She and her daughter wore no makeup and were dressed for

YAZD, IRAN—*I met these women in a public garden. They were tourists from other parts of Iran. Like many educated Iranians, they spoke good English, which was a pleasure for me.*

YAZD, IRAN—*A young woman and her grandmother shopping together in the bazaar. Note her relatively light and pretty head covering, and the contrast with the older woman's traditional layers of black-on-black topped by a chador.*

comfort rather than style. Perhaps they came from a more rural or working-class background; I didn't know enough about the social signals to be able to decipher them. The granddaughter was about eighteen, fresh-faced and shyly intrigued with me. Eventually she tried out some English and I some Persian, and we made friends.

The wedding-goers chatted occasionally, but mostly the daughter was on her cell phone, texting and playing games, trying to make the time pass. Was she looking forward to the wedding? Was she hoping to meet a man? Or did she already have a man whom she'd left behind?

The train moved on north, lumbering across the desert-like landscape of central Iran as the light turned golden with sunset dust-glow before night fell.

The grandmother pulled packages of cookies, nuts, and dried fruit out of her bag and offered them around. Everyone

produced containers of cooked rice and other food. I had brought only nuts, dried fruit, and some bread. We offered and shared, accepted and demurred, doing the dance of politeness with each other. The others wanted to know my age, my matrimonial status, where I was from, what my job was. When I told them my husband had left the marriage, we all rolled our eyes together and laughed. "Men!" we were saying to ourselves, each in her own language. And everyone relaxed into the journey.

There was a curtain over the glass in the door, so we could be comfortable, without worrying too much about our head coverings. But men—conductors and tea sellers—came by from time to time, first knocking, then sliding the compartment door open, and each time they did, there'd be a rustling and a reaching, to make sure that head scarves were in place and clothing arranged.

Eventually we settled into our berths, and the lights were out by ten. The train stopped several times in the night, with a screeching of metal and the thump of doors opening and closing. At one of those stops, the mother and daughter wedding-goers slipped away.

When early-morning light came, I wanted to see the countryside, but the blinds would be down until we were all dressed, so I headed down the train in search of tea. The landscape had become hilly and green, and the sky was a deep central Asian blue. Flocks of sheep and goats grazed in the morning light.

DATE-NUT HALVAH

HORMAH BERESHTE

Halvah is a chameleon, taking on different identities depending on which culture is making it. It's always a sweet treat and often contains nuts as well as some enriching butter or oil. The word *halvah* is from the Arabic, and it means sweet. In Arab cultures, halvah is most often made from sesame seeds. But in Persian tradition, it's made of wheat flour or semolina that is cooked in butter or ghee and sweetened and flavored in various ways, then served in small bites to accompany tea or coffee, or water.

One evening when I was staying in southern Iran, Afsar, my host, and her daughter made this simple halvah. It's a dense hit of flavor, with sweetness that is not overwhelming and a little crunch from chopped nuts.   **SERVES 8**

¾ cup all-purpose flour

6 tablespoons butter, melted, plus a little more if needed

¾ cup walnuts or pistachios, or a blend, processed to fine crumbs

1 cup pitted dates, finely chopped

Pinch of ground cassia (cinnamon; optional)

About 20 walnut pieces, lightly toasted (optional)

Place a wide cast-iron skillet or heavy pot over medium heat, add the flour, and cook, stirring constantly with a wooden spoon so the flour toasts evenly, without scorching. You'll soon start to smell the aroma of toasting grain. Keep stirring, and when the flour has changed color slightly, add the butter and stir it into the flour. Lower the heat. Add the ground nuts and mix in. Add the chopped dates. Use the spoon to smear and smooth them, blending them into the paste. It will take 5 to 10 minutes to get them very smooth and integrated. Add a little more melted butter if necessary to help everything blend. Remove from the heat and taste; there should be no raw flour taste. Let cool slightly.

Lightly oil a large dinner plate or a 9-inch square baking pan. When the halvah is cool enough to handle, transfer it to the plate or pan. Use the back of an oiled spoon or your wet or oiled fingertips to press it out evenly, smoothing the surface. The paste should be about ½ inch thick. Sprinkle on the cassia or press the toasted walnuts on top if you wish. Refrigerate to set to a firm fudge texture, at least 30 minutes, or as long as a day.

Cut the halvah into squares or diamonds to serve.

*Diamond-shaped Oasis Baqlava (right) and pale
rounds of Cardamom Cookies (left; page 296).*

OASIS BAQLAVA

The oasis city of Yazd in the center of Iran is best known for its Zoroastrian fire temple, its underground water channels and astonishing Water Museum, and its distinctive architecture. But among Iranians, it is also famous for cookies and other sweets. These diamond-shaped cookies are cut from a thin, almond-rich cake baked in a small sheet pan and then drenched in rose water syrup. They're very attractive, and very delicious. This is an adaptation of a recipe I was given by Jennifer Klinec, author of *The Temporary Bride: A Memoir of Love and Food in Iran*; it comes from her mother-in-law, who lives in Yazd.

Serve the cookies with tea or coffee, or with a tart iced *sharbat*, made with either bitter orange (page 332) or tamarind (page 328).

SYRUP AND TOPPING

¼ teaspoon saffron threads

1 cup sugar

⅓ cup water

2 teaspoons honey

¼ cup rose water

About ¼ cup ground pistachios

COOKIES

6 tablespoons unsalted butter,
    at room temperature

½ cup sugar

3 large eggs

¼ cup rose water

¼ teaspoon ground cardamom

1 cup all-purpose flour

1 teaspoon baking powder

1 cup ground almonds

Place the saffron threads in a small bowl, add 1 tablespoon hot water, stir, and set aside for 30 minutes.

Place a rack in the center of the oven and preheat the oven to 340°F. Line a quarter sheet pan or a 9-by-13-inch baking pan with parchment paper, or use a nonstick pan. (If you have only a large baking sheet, you can use that; the dough holds its shape.)

To make the cookies, use a mixer, or a large bowl and a wooden spoon, to blend the butter and sugar together until smooth. Beat in the eggs one by one. Beat in the rose water and cardamom.

Mix the flour and baking powder together in a bowl and sift into the butter mixture, stirring and mixing as you do so. Add the ground almonds and beat until well mixed.

continued

Scrape the batter into the sheet pan and smooth the top. (If using a large baking sheet, spread the batter out to a 9-by-13-inch rectangle.) Bake for 35 to 40 minutes, until firm to the touch and golden on top. Set aside to cool completely.

Meanwhile, make the syrup: In a small saucepan, combine the sugar with the ⅓ cup water and the saffron water, stir well, and bring to a boil over medium heat, stirring occasionally. Cook at a medium boil for 5 minutes, or until the syrup has started to thicken. Remove from the heat, stir in the honey and rose water, and set aside.

Cut the cooled cake, in the pan, into diamond shapes about 1½ inches long. Pour over the syrup and set aside to soak for 10 to 15 minutes.

Sprinkle on the ground pistachios before removing the cookies from the pan.

CARDAMOM COOKIES

PHOTOGRAPH ON PAGE 294

These classic cookies from the Persian tradition, made with rice flour, egg yolk, sugar, and butter, are a rather special version of shortbread cookies. More tender than cookies made with wheat flour, they melt in your mouth. They are also a little more brittle and require careful handling once baked.

The classic version is made with white rice flour and topped with chopped pistachios. I use brown rice flour, because it gives a more melting texture to the cookies, and I top each cookie with pine nuts instead of pistachios.

MAKES ABOUT 40 COOKIES

½ pound (2 sticks) unsalted butter, melted and cooled to tepid

1 cup confectioners' (icing) sugar

1 large egg yolk

¾ teaspoon ground cardamom

2 cups brown or white rice flour (see headnote)

Pinch of sea salt

About 3 tablespoons pine nuts

Place the butter and sugar in a medium bowl and stir or whisk together until smooth and pale. Stir in the egg yolk and cardamom. Add 1½ cups of the flour and the salt and mix in thoroughly. Add the remaining ½ cup flour and stir and fold until completely mixed in. The dough will be stiff and pasty.

Transfer to a plastic bag and seal well, or wrap in plastic wrap. Refrigerate for at least 2 hours, or as long as 24 hours.

Place racks just above and just below the center of the oven and preheat the oven to 350°F. Line two baking sheets with parchment paper, leaving an overhang over the short ends. (This makes it easier to lift the paper and cookies off the sheet after baking.)

Cut the cookie dough into 4 pieces, and place 2 back in the refrigerator while you work with the others. Cut off or pull off a generous teaspoon of dough and roll it into a ball with your hands. Place it on one of the lined baking sheets and flatten slightly; don't worry about perfect shaping, since the cookies will spread as they bake. Repeat with the remaining dough, leaving 1 inch between the cookies.

Once you have filled one sheet, top each cookie with several pine nuts, place on the upper oven rack, and bake for 17 to 20 minutes, or until the edges of the cookies start to turn golden.

Meanwhile, shape the remaining dough and place the baking sheet on the lower oven rack. Switch it to the upper rack once the first sheet of cookies has baked.

The cookies are very fragile when they come out of the oven. Carefully transfer the parchment paper, with the cookies on it, to a rack so they can cool and firm up. After about 20 minutes, they can be lifted off the paper and transferred to a plate or to an open cookie tin to cool completely—or grabbed and eaten right away.

ROSE WATER COOKIES

NANE NAKODCHI

These aromatic cookies are one of the classic seven sweetmeats that are included on the table during Nou-Roz, the Persian New Year. Seven is an auspicious number, and so at Nou-Roz there are seven good-luck foods, the *haft-sein*.

The cookies, which are about ¾ inch thick and about 1 inch across, have a sandy texture and a subtly enticing rose-water and cardamom flavor.

The main ingredient is roasted chickpea flour. If you can find only unroasted chickpea flour, you'll need to briefly dry-roast it before making the cookies (see the Note opposite). Because the dough must be very smooth and fine-textured, the flour is then triple-sifted before being combined with the oil, sugar, and aromatics.   **MAKES ABOUT 30 COOKIES**

**1½ cups superfine sugar
    (see Note on Sugar)**

1½ cups sunflower oil

2 teaspoons ground cardamom

2 teaspoons rose water

**4 cups roasted chickpea flour
    (see Note on Roasting Chickpea Flour),
    triple-sifted, plus extra for surfaces**

About ¼ cup slivered pistachios

Sift the sugar into a medium bowl. Add the oil, cardamom, and rose water and stir for about 2 minutes, until very smooth. Add the chickpea flour and stir and turn until the flour is completely incorporated. Use your hands to fold the dough on itself several times to make sure it is fully blended.

Lightly dust your work surface with chickpea flour and turn out the dough. Pull it together into a lump and flatten it into a smooth disk about ¾ inch thick. Cut the disk in half. Wrap each piece in plastic and refrigerate for at least 1 hour, or for as long as a day.

Place a rack in the center of your oven and preheat the oven to 300°F. Line a baking sheet with parchment paper.

These cookies are usually made in the shape of a clover leaf, but you can use any small cookie cutter (1 to 1¼ inches across). I find the clover-leaf shape a little finicky to work with, so I cut out round cookies. Place one piece of chilled dough on a work surface lightly dusted with chickpea flour and cut out cookies. Use a spatula to transfer them to the baking sheet, leaving ¾ inch between the cookies.

Gather the dough scraps, pat into a ¾-inch-thick piece, and cut out a few more cookies. Repeat with the second piece of dough.

Sprinkle a few pistachio slivers on each cookie, pressing very slightly so they stick. Bake for about 25 minutes; the underside of the cookies should be touched with pale brown. Let the cookies stand on the baking sheet for about 10 minutes before moving them, because they are very crumbly when they first come out of the oven. Then use a spatula to transfer them to a fine-mesh rack to cool completely.

NOTE ON SUGAR: Granulated sugar is too coarse for these cookies, so look for sugar labeled "fine granulated," "superfine," "castor," or "quick-dissolving."

NOTE ON ROASTING CHICKPEA FLOUR: Set a wide cast-iron or other heavy skillet over medium heat. Add the flour and turn and stir it with a spatula as it heats, making sure to scrape the bottom to prevent the flour from burning. Once it is aromatic and starting to get a hint of color, in about 5 minutes, remove from the heat and continue to stir and turn for another couple of minutes to prevent scorching. Transfer to a bowl and let cool before using (you can speed up the process by spreading the flour out on a baking sheet).

NOTE ON SHAPING BY HAND: Although the cookies are traditionally made as described above, from a firm chilled dough that is cut out into shapes, I often like to make a slightly softer dough and shape the cookies by hand. They're less uniform, less perfect looking. (They would not meet with approval from a Persian mother-in-law, I imagine.) I use about ¼ cup less chickpea flour and mix and chill the dough as above. To shape, I cut off small pieces of dough, about 1 tablespoon each, and roll them between my palms into balls (about 1 inch in diameter). Then I place them on the parchment paper and press down a little to flatten them slightly; I press on the pistachio shards at the same time. They take the same amount of time to bake into sometimes-irregular rounds.

TEA WITH SUGAR IN IRAN

Black tea in a glass, with a bowl of rough-cut sugar cubes alongside, is the go-to beverage in Iran. Tea has been grown near the Caspian Sea, in the northern province of Gilan, for more than a hundred years. (Before that, it was imported from

India and China.) The best Iranian tea is aromatic and memorable.

Until about 150 years ago, coffee held sway in Iran. But now tea rules, though coffee is making a comeback in Tehran. Teahouses (*chaikana*) are places to meet friends, conduct business, and take pleasure in the day while lounging on wide benches (called *takht*) covered with carpets. Men, families, and, nowadays, groups of women chat and take their ease, as Persians have done for centuries (see Fountains and Gardens, Picnics and Poetry, page 169).

Tea is part of breakfast (to wash down *barbari* bread; see Village Breakfast, page 265) and is drunk as part of business, to welcome guests, or as a pause in the day. Even "ordinary" tea at a café or on the train is a special drink. It may be made in a samovar and poured from it, or instead the samovar may be filled with boiling water that is poured onto the tea leaves in your glass. The glass often has a saucer

under it. But that's all there is: a glass of tea, perhaps a saucer, and a bowl of lump or rock sugar. What's missing, for people from elsewhere, is a small spoon. And therein lies a tale or two.

In Iran people take sugar *with* their tea, not *in* their tea. Some hold a sugar cube in their teeth and sip the tea through it. Some just pop a sugar cube into their mouth and drink the tea while chewing on the sugar. Sometimes tea is served with a stick of sugar crystals or rock sugar, called *nabat* in Persian, that you can dip in your tea or just suck on as a sweet (see photo, page 370). In Yazd, I watched a sugar maker cooking sugar in a huge vat that would eventually be transformed into *nabat*, a long, hot process.

Occasionally an older person in Iran will dip a sugar cube into the tea and then take a bite of it. This is the story I was told to explain the practice: Sometime long ago (in the late 1800s, it seems), there was a dispute between the authorities and some of the foreign

EAST OF SHIRAZ, IRAN—*Hajji Hossein, the patriarch of a large nomad family (see Nomad Encounter, page 190), dips a cube of sugar into his tea before taking a first sip.*

(mostly English) sugar merchants about pricing. The authorities wanted the price to stay down, the merchants wanted a higher price. The authorities played hardball by having the mullahs at the mosques declare that sugar was *haram,* or unclean. Suddenly no one would buy sugar. This forced the merchants back to the negotiating table and eventually a deal was reached. But how to change the decree about sugar being *haram*? Simple: The mullahs declared that dipping sugar into tea made it clean.

TEA FROM THE CASPIAN

After our excursion to the seashore (see Caspian Interlude, page 140), Farahnoz made us tea back at the house from green tea leaves that had been grown nearby. She perfumed it lightly with cardamom. Here's my approximation of that warming afternoon drink. **SERVES 4**

About 5 cups water

4 cardamom pods

2 tablespoons green tea leaves

Lumps of sugar for serving

Bring the water to a vigorous boil in a teakettle. Pour a little into a teapot to warm it, and let the kettle stand for a minute to cool slightly.

Crack the cardamom pods with the side of a knife or in a mortar. Pour off the water in the teapot and add the cardamom pods and tea leaves, then add the hot water and stir. Cover and let steep for 5 minutes.

Pour into glasses or small cups. Serve with lumps of sugar.

SPICE BLEND FOR TEA

At a farm homestay near Shiraz, I was offered a glass of tea that was aromatic with a blend of cassia, powdered ginger, and black pepper, and a wonderful welcome.

You can make up a small amount of the spice powder (an *advieh,* in Persian) any time you're making tea, but it's easier to keep a jar of it on hand. Add ½ teaspoon powder to your glass or cup before you pour in the tea. Stir and let stand a moment to allow the flavors to blend. A little sugar will bring the aromas of the spices forward. **MAKES ABOUT 2 TABLESPOONS; ENOUGH FOR 12 CUPS OF TEA**

1 tablespoon ground cassia (cinnamon)

2 teaspoons ground ginger

½ to 1 teaspoon freshly ground black pepper

Mix the spices together in a small dry jar. Store in a cool place, out of the sun.

THERE'S NO SHIRAZ IN SHIRAZ

That's what I wrote in a message to a friend while I was in Iran. But appearances can be deceptive. As far as the nonreligious members of the population are concerned, the ban on alcoholic drinks in Iran is there to be ignored.

And that's a lot of people, I learned, mostly educated and more prosperous people.

"Have you tasted *arak*?" I was asked one day by a couple of young Iranian men. "No," I said, surprised. "I thought the whole country was dry." They laughed. "No, no, you can get anything here. You just have to know where to go. In the countryside, many people make their own wine and spirits. In Tehran, there's a number you can call and they'll deliver beer right to your apartment. It even comes chilled!"

The *arak* they gave me to taste (they'd made a quick trip down the street to buy it from their local "supplier") was a clear liquor, very alcoholic, that came in a recycled two-liter soft-drink bottle. They drank it straight, over ice. After a first sip, I diluted mine with sour cherry juice and water. Whew!

And I forgot to ask them for the phone number of the beer delivery people. . . .

SHIRAZ, IRAN—*A woman coming through a shop entrance near the bazaar.*

ARMENIAN COFFEE

SOORJ

An ongoing frustration for Armenians and people of Armenian descent is the way that the coffee they know as "Armenian coffee" is generally referred to as "Turkish coffee" by others. Given the painful history of Armenians with Turkey, it adds insult to injury. Coffee made this way is the standard in Armenian households, and is addictive. It is always served black, and always sweetened—a little or a lot, as you wish.

To make it well, you really need to learn in the kitchen of a person who makes terrific Armenian coffee. Second-best is to watch a video on the Internet.

You will need an Armenian coffeepot, a small metal pot with no lid and with a handle on one side, that can hold enough water to make two small cups of coffee. You can find one in an eastern Mediterranean shop or a specialty store. And the coffee must be very finely ground, to a powder. Espresso is not a substitute. You'll need a little sugar too.   **MAKES 2 CUPS**

2 heaping teaspoons fine-ground coffee beans

1 to 3 teaspoons sugar

2 cups cold water

Stir the coffee and sugar into the cold water in an Armenian coffeepot and place the pot over the heat. As it heats, the coffee will start to foam. Keep an eye on the rising foam as the coffee comes to a boil, and lift the pot off the heat before it spills over. Place back on the heat, let the foam rise again, and remove from the heat. Repeat a third time. Pour the coffee into two small cups, adding a little to each in turn, then adding a little more.

Serve immediately. When you get close to the bottom of your cup, where there is sludge, stop drinking. Coffee grounds, like tea leaves, have long been used to read fortunes. To read yours, turn the cup upside down on a saucer; most of the coffee sludge will fall onto the saucer. Turn the cup back over and read the patterns in the cup.

NOTE: At a café in Kurdistan, I had Armenian coffee that had been perfumed with a little cardamom. To do this, add about ⅛ teaspoon ground cardamom or 1 crushed cardamom pod per cup to the cold-water mixture.

Glasses of coffee with two slices of Armenian Puff Pastry Cake (page 287).

HONEY HOMELAND

I can't talk about sweetness in the Persian culinary region without including a note about honey. The valleys of Georgia are home to a special species of honey bees, *Apis mellifera caucasia*. They are also found in the valleys of Armenia, Azerbaijan, and eastern Turkey.

When I was traveling with friends in Kakheti, the fertile wine area in eastern Georgia, we came upon a group of beekeepers. Their hives were stacked high on the back of a huge tractor-trailer. The beekeepers park the truck near fields in bloom for a week at a time before moving on in search of new "pastures" for the bees. As the beekeepers checked some of the supers (the wooden boxes that are stacked in layers and that hold the honeycomb), moving carefully and deliberately, never rushing, we chatted with them quietly, so as not to disturb the bees. The men were happy that the sun was out and the weather warming after five or six cool rainy days. The warmth and sun made the bees livelier. We watched as they winged out to the flowering fields to get to work.

A couple of years later, I came upon a beekeeper in Azerbaijan, about an hour's drive out of Baku. His hives were set out in a hilltop meadow by a small wood. He seemed to be living all alone out there in that lovely lonely place, with big views, and only his cat for company.

Beehives at Ikalto Monastery, in eastern Georgia.

WEST OF BAKU, AZERBAIJAN—*This beekeeper lives in a small cabin with a great view in three directions and a ginger cat to keep him company.*

COOLING YOGURT DRINKS

THAN · AYRAN · DUGH · MATSOH · MATSONI

Yogurt is an important food throughout the Persian culinary region: It's an essential ingredient in Persian *borani* (see pages 55 and 62) and in yogurt soups (see pages 93 and 94), and it's also the base for a cooling drink with a long history. In Armenian, the drink is known as *than*; in Azeri, it's *ayran* or *dugh*. In some Kurdish languages, it's *matsoh*, while in others it's *dughas*; in Georgia, it's *matsoni*, and in Persian it's called *dugh* (sometimes transcribed *doogh*).

These days yogurt drinks are sold in plastic bottles, in many different versions, all over the region. Sometimes they're fizzy, with fermentation or with soda water, and sometimes smooth and flat.

Many people still make *dugh* at home. Plain full-fat yogurt is diluted with water or soda water and chilled with fragments of smashed ice. It often has a little dried mint added and/or a little toasted ground cumin. Some people include black pepper in their *dugh*. In the *Encyclopedia Iranica*, I came across a mention of a special version prized by mystics that includes an extract of hashish and is called *dugh-e wahdat* in Persian. A similar drink, called *bangab* (literally, bang-water), is made by adding an infusion of cannabis leaves steeped in water or milk. I have never been offered either one. **SERVES 6**

4 cups plain full-fat yogurt, chilled

3 cups cold tap water or soda water, or a mixture

½ teaspoon sea salt

1 cup chipped ice

2 teaspoons dried mint (optional)

1 teaspoon cumin seeds, lightly toasted and finely ground (optional)

Mix the yogurt, water, and salt in a pitcher and stir thoroughly to blend them. (Or use a blender.) Add the chipped ice just before serving. Sprinkle on or stir in the mint and/or cumin, if using. Serve in tall glasses.

HALABJA, KURDISTAN—*A small shop specializing in yogurt, yogurt drinks, butter, and fresh cheese.*

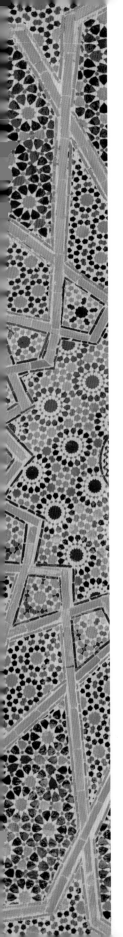

A WEALTH OF FRUIT

OF ALL THAT I LEARNED AND MARVELED AT on my first trip to Georgia for this book, twenty-four years after I'd been there in the Soviet era, it was the fruit that dazzled me the most.

The markets in Georgia were full of fresh and dried fruits, and gardens were filled with fruit and nut trees. On later trips to Iran, Armenia, Kurdistan, and Azerbaijan, I learned that throughout the region, at least in rural areas and small towns, family larders are a treasure-house of preserved fruits.

Cooks in the Caucasus, Iran, and Kurdistan have a deep understanding of the value of fruit. Most is used to make delicious syrups and juices, or preserved in a variety of other ways. *Moraba—*

sometimes written *"muraba"*—is the word all over the Persian culinary region for fruit preserved in syrup like thick jam (see Apricot Moraba, page 318, and Carrot Moraba, page 321).

The other Persian-world knockouts in the fruit department are *kompot* and *sharbat*. Here *kompot* means a fruit-flavored liquid, made of fresh fruit that steeps in water with a little sugar, leaching its lovely flavor into the water. In other words, it's a kind of slow-motion fruit tea (see pages 324 and 326). *Sharbat* is the word for a category of Persian drinks made with sweet fruit syrups diluted with water and served over ice (see pages 327–332).

People in the region also preserve fruit by drying it whole, or by cooking it down to make a puree and then drying it in thin sheets to make fruit leather, probably the earliest and simplest way of storing fruit over winter (see page 314). Tart dried fruits and fruit leathers are an ingredient in many savory dishes. All these inventive ways of preserving fruit mean that in the cold of winter, families have foods to eat that evoke the intense ripe flavors of summer. They're life-giving emotionally as well as culinarily.

Previous pages: **TBILISI, GEORGIA**—*Autumn in the markets of the Caucasus means ripe pears.*

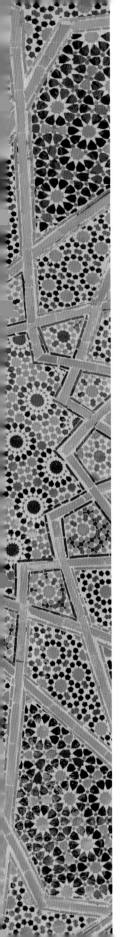

Winemaking may have come before all these methods of preserving fruit. It certainly came early; archaeological finds confirm that the ancestors of Georgians and Armenians were making wine thousands of years ago. In fact, the species of wild grape that is the ancestor of modern wine grapes is native to the Caucasus.

In Georgia and Armenia, many people still make wine at home, using traditional "natural" wine methods (see Wine in the Caucasus, page 336). They also make *cha-cha*, a kind of grappa-like liquor.

In Iran, some people make homemade liquor from raisins, a drink that's known as *aragh* or *arak*.

In Georgia, Armenia, and Azerbaijan, liquor distilled from other fruits and from grains is often referred to as vodka; that made from mulberries (*tut* in all the languages of the region; see Mulberry Country, page 339) is known as *tutovka*. *Tutovka* is often homemade and is usually drunk straight, chased with homemade or store-bought sour cherry juice or another tart-sweet fruit juice.

FRUIT LEATHER

LAVASHAK · TKLAPI · LAVASHANA · BASTEIGH · NAN QESI

Rolls and folded sheets of fruit leather of all types and colors are sold in markets throughout the Persian culinary region, but many home cooks in the countryside still make their own. The Persian word for fruit leather is *lavashak*; in Georgian, it's *tklapi*; in Azeri, *lavashana*; in Armenian, *basteigh* or *basteil*; and in Kurdish, *nan qesi*. This may well have been the earliest way that the people here preserved fruit. It requires no sugar, no jars or special containers—just a pot to cook the fruit and a flat surface where it can be spread to dry. The leather is important as a way of storing fruit flavor and intensity for use in the winter months.

My favorites are the unsweetened sheets of sour plum or sour cherry. I love their tart edge and intense flavor. Tart fruit leathers (e.g., sour plum, sour cherry, apricot) are used as flavorings in savory dishes; sweeter ones (e.g., peach and kiwi) are eaten as a snack.

Make this when stone fruits are plentiful and in season. You will need a heavy pot for cooking the fruit down, a blender or food processor for reducing it to a smooth puree, and some parchment paper-lined baking sheets for it to dry on.

The pureed fruit gets spread onto the parchment paper to dry. Then it can be stored for up to 6 months.

10 pounds plums, apricots, peaches, or nectarines, halved and pitted, or cherries, pitted

About 1 cup water
Sugar or honey (optional)

Place the fruit in a large heavy pot, add the water, cover, and bring to a boil over medium heat. Reduce the heat and cook at a low boil, stirring occasionally, until the fruit has completely softened and broken down, 15 to 20 minutes. Taste and decide if you want to add some sugar or honey. If you do, stir it in and cook the fruit a little longer to blend the flavors. Set aside to cool.

Working in batches, process the fruit in a food processor or blender to a smooth puree. Transfer to a wide bowl.

Line several baking sheets with parchment or wax paper. Pour the fruit puree onto the paper, spreading it to leave a small margin all around; it should be about ¼ inch thick, no more. Set out in the hot sunshine to dry, loosely covered with cheesecloth or a cotton cloth. Or, if you are in a rush or lack hot sun, heat your oven to about 160°F to dry the fruit. Leave it for about 5 hours, opening the oven

WEST OF BAKU, AZERBAIJAN—*Very near to the beekeeper pictured on page 307, I came upon a man selling rounds of fruit leather he pinned up on a clothesline. They glowed like pieces of thick stained glass as they waved and fluttered in the breeze.*

door occasionally to check on it and let out humidity, until dry and no longer sticky. (You'll notice that it shrinks as it dries.)

Rather than storing the large sheets, it's more practical to cut the fruit sheets into long strips 2 to 3 inches wide. Peel off the paper backing (sometimes it's stuck on), then place the fruit sheets back on the paper and cut the fruit and paper into strips. Loosely roll up the strips (the paper backing helps ensure that the fruit doesn't stick to itself) and store away from sun and heat in well-sealed plastic bags or other containers for up to 6 months.

TBILISI, GEORGIA—*Walnuts and hazelnuts are threaded on strings, then dipped in thick fruit syrup to make* churchkhela. *In the foreground are strings of apples.*

WALNUTS ON A STRING

CHURCHKHELA · KAGHSTR SAJUKH · SUJUKH

In autumn, when it was time to harvest grapes, walnuts, and hazelnuts, households in Armenia, Georgia, and Azerbaijan traditionally stored part of that harvest in the form of these odd, bumpy-looking "fruit candles." Nowadays, with more

people living in towns and cities, most *churchkhela* are made in quantity by specialists and sold in markets.

The process of making it involves stringing the shelled nuts on a thread and dipping them into *doshab* (see Glossary), the thickened grape juice that's yet another use for the grapes of the region. They're dipped many times, with pauses for each layer to cool and set a little before dipping again (like making candles). It's a brilliant storage method. The *doshab* acts like the fat in a confit: It seals in the nuts, thus preventing them from going rancid as well as protecting them from pests.

The "candles" are a treat to be sliced and enjoyed in the winter months. They also make great traveling food.

The *doshab* that's used in Armenia for making *kaghstr sajukh* is generally thickened with a lot of flour or cornstarch. (*Sajukh* means sausage, so these sausage-looking items are called "sweet" [*kaghstr*] *sajukh*.) In Georgia, much less thickener is used. The result is that the Georgian *churchkhela* have a sharper, more direct flavor, while the Armenian versions are milder and more muted in taste.

APRICOT MORABA

ARITCH MERABESE

In the attractive town of Sheki, tucked against the Caucasus Mountains in western Azerbaijan, I was served apricot *moraba*—a thick jam, called *aritch merabese* in Azeri—with tea. You take a sip of tea and then a little jam on a spoon as a sweet accompaniment.

You'll notice that this recipe calls for very little water, and that the pot is shaken to mix the jam, rather than stirred with a spoon, so that the apricots keep their shape instead of turning to mush. The whole process is more like candying apricots. The basic proportions are 1 pound sugar and a scant ⅓ cup water per pound of pitted fruit. You will need a scale, a canning funnel, and canning jars. **MAKES ABOUT 10 PINTS**

About 7 pounds fresh apricots,
  halved and pitted
1 teaspoon baking soda
About 6½ pounds sugar

2 cups water
3 tablespoons fresh lemon juice or
  1 teaspoon citric acid (see Glossary)

Place the apricots in a large pot and add water to cover. Add the baking soda and stir to dissolve it. Let the fruit stand for 30 minutes.

Drain the apricots in a colander, rinse thoroughly, and drain again. Weigh the fruit, then measure out the same weight of sugar.

Pour the 2 cups water into a large heavy nonreactive pot, add the sugar, and place over medium-high heat. Bring to a boil, stirring to dissolve the sugar (the mixture will be very thick). Add the apricots and shake the pot; do not stir. Bring back to a boil and boil for 10 minutes, shaking the pot occasionally. The syrup will foam up; lower the heat as necessary to prevent it from boiling over. Remove from the heat and use a heatproof spatula to scrape down the sides of the pot; otherwise, you will have a rim of crystallized sugar. Let stand for 10 minutes.

Put the pot over the heat and bring back to a boil, again shaking the pot rather than stirring. Boil for 15 minutes, shaking the pot occasionally. Remove from the heat and set aside to rest, covered loosely with cheesecloth, not a lid (the idea is that some of the water will evaporate). If the day is very dry, a

Apricot Moraba on homemade Persian Barbari Bread (page 267).

3- to 4-hour rest will be sufficient; if it is very humid, then let the *moraba* rest for 6 to 10 hours.

Sterilize ten 1-pint jars or twenty ½-pint jars, rings, lids, a canning funnel, and a ladle: Put them through a hot wash in a dishwasher, or wash them thoroughly in very hot soapy water and rinse well in hot water. Set them on a tray and place in a 200°F oven to air-dry.

Bring the *moraba* to a boil over medium heat, shaking the pot to prevent sticking, then shake the pot frequently as the *moraba* boils gently for 15 minutes. To test the *moraba*, drizzle a small spoonful on a cold surface. It should be thick, not runny. If it is not, cook for 5 to 10 minutes longer and retest.

Stir in the lemon juice or citric acid and cook for another minute. Remove from the heat.

Using the funnel, ladle the *moraba* into the clean, dry jars. Put on the lids and rings, but don't fully tighten the rings; let cool until you hear the lids pop (meaning they've sealed). Remove the rings and wipe the tops of the jars well. Replace the rings and tighten them. Label the jars and store in a cool, dark place for up to 1 year.

Left: **TATEV, ARMENIA**—*A classic Armenian breakfast of flatbread, tea, apricot* moraba, *butter, and crumbled white cheese.*

Right: **OUTSIDE SULAYMANIYAH, KURDISTAN**—*The Persian love of picnics is a feature of Kurdish culture. Here at a festival out in the country, a teapot and a kebab rest on the still-hot embers of a small wood fire.*

CARROT MORABA

MORABA YE HAVEEJ

The sweetness of carrots makes them ideal for *moraba*. Carrot *moraba* is a delicious very sweet Persian preserve that is traditionally flavored with cardamom and rose water. There's a lively citrus note from lemon zest and juice. Serve this as a spoon jam (see Glossary) or a sweet taste on a spoon, or use as you would any jam. **MAKES 2 CUPS**

1 pound carrots, preferably organic, peeled

1 large or 2 small lemons, preferably organic

1 cup water

2 cups sugar

5 cardamom pods, lightly crushed

1 tablespoon rose water

Sterilize two 1-cup jars, rings, lids, and a spoon or ladle: Put them through a hot wash in a dishwasher, or wash them thoroughly in very hot soapy water and rinse well in hot water. Set them on a tray and place in a 200°F oven to air-dry.

Shred the carrots on a box grater; you should have about 4 cups. Set aside.

Use a Microplane or a fine grater to zest the lemon(s). Set the zest aside.

Squeeze the juice from the lemon(s) (you should have about 3 tablespoons) and set aside.

Pour the water into a large heavy pot, add the sugar, and bring to a boil, stirring to dissolve the sugar. Add the zest and cardamom pods and boil for 10 minutes, then add the carrots and cook at a strong boil until they are softened and reduced to a tender thick mass, 12 to 15 minutes.

Add the lemon juice and the rose water, stir, and simmer for another minute.

Ladle the carrots and syrup into the clean, dry jars, distributing the liquid and solids evenly. Put on the lids and rings, but don't fully tighten the rings; let cool until you hear the lids pop (meaning they've sealed). Remove the rings and wipe the tops of the jars well. Replace the rings and tighten them. Label the jars and store in a cool, dark place for up to 1 year.

KUTAISI, WESTERN GEORGIA—*Apple blossoms in Dodo's amazing garden.*

KUTAISI GRANDMOTHER

Elene's grandmother Dodo is a slender woman in her nineties, stylish, intelligent, and entertaining. She lives in the family house in Kutaisi with her widowed daughter, her other granddaughter, and her jars of preserves, ready to welcome visitors.

She inhabits the present as well as multiple layers of the past, and wanders through the layers, alighting now here, now there. Because her life has been full of drama, with grand highs and tragic lows, at one moment she might be laughing with remembrance about the fur coat she wore when she visited Moscow with her husband before the Second World War, and the next minute weeping about the loss of her son by drowning.

The first *kompot* I ever tasted was at Dodo's house. She went to the cupboard and lugged over a very large sealed jar of peaches, pausing for us to admire it. The whole peaches were smooth globes, pale yellow tinted with pink. She unscrewed the lid and, with a small dipper, lifted out some liquid and poured it into a narrow glass. It was a tender pink, and tasted like I imagine the nectar of the gods might taste, lightly sweet, heavenly.

Dodo smiled with satisfaction at the blissed-out look on my face. She'd scored a hit, but of course she had never doubted that she would.

Dodo and her granddaughter Elene in the garden near the house.

PEACH KOMPOT

Kompot is the word used in Armenia, Azerbaijan, and Georgia for juices made from ripe fruit that has been steeped in hot water with a little sugar. *Kompots* are a treat in the cold months, a reminder of summer.

The summer after my first trip to Georgia for this book, the peaches in Toronto were fabulous. The peach *kompot* I had tasted in Georgia, made by Elene's grandmother (see Kutaisi Grandmother, page 323), was my inspiration for this recipe.

Get all your canning equipment ready first, and follow the canning instructions. Because the acidity of peaches is high, they don't need a very long boil in the canner, unlike lower-acidity foods.   **MAKES 3 QUARTS**

One 6-quart basket of peaches (about 10 pounds)

Sugar: 1 cup sugar per quart jar; ½ cup sugar per pint jar

SPECIAL EQUIPMENT

A canner, or very large tall pot at least 4 inches taller than your jars

A rack that fits in the bottom of the pot

1-quart or 1-pint glass canning jars; for each 6-quart basket of peaches, allow 3 large jars plus 1 small jar, or 7 small jars

New two-part lids for each jar

Tongs for lifting the jars out of the boiling water

A large heavy tray or baking sheet and a rack that fits on it; check to see how many jars fit at one time on the rack

Place a rack in the canner or tall pot. Wash the jars and lids in very hot soapy water and rinse well, or wash them in a dishwasher. Fill them partway with hot water and place them on a tray by your stovetop.

Bring a kettle of water to a boil. Fill the canner or pot about three-quarters full with hot water and place on the stove.

Wash the peaches well in hot water. Cut out any bruised patches and remove any stems. If you wish, peel them; I think it's prettier to leave the peel on (I leave in the pits too). If the peaches are too large to fit through the mouths of the jars, cut them into large pieces.

Empty the hot water from one jar and start to fill the jar with peaches, not forcing them or bruising the fruit. When the jar is half full, add half the sugar needed for that size jar (see above). Add more peaches to fill the jar, then add the rest of the sugar. Pour in boiling water from the kettle, pausing to allow bubbles to rise to the surface and filling the jars almost to the top; leave ½ inch of headspace. Put on the lid and screw on the ring. Repeat until you

ETCHMIADZIN, ARMENIA—
*Not far from Yerevan, the
mother church of the Armenian
Apostolic Church is a solemn
place. The Sunday I visited
the cathedral, the church
was packed with people of all
ages, including these candlelit
children.*

have filled as many jars as will fit in the canner. (If your kettle is empty before you have filled all the jars, then refill it and bring to a boil before continuing.)

Place the jars in the canner, being sure that they are level. The water should cover the jars by a generous 1 inch or more; add water if needed. Put on the lid, bring the water to a rolling boil, and boil for 10 minutes.

Place a rack on your counter or on a baking sheet. Using tongs, lift the jars out carefully, keeping them vertical, and place on the rack to cool. (If you have a second batch to do, repeat the jar-filling and -boiling process.)

After 10 minutes or so, you should hear each jar lid pop as it seals (see Note below). Once that happens, take off the rings and wipe off the rims of the jars. Put the rings back on and tighten them. Let the jars cool completely, label them, and store in a cool, dark place.

Let stand for at least 1 month before using; the liquid will gradually get infused with peach flavor. The peaches keep well for up to 1 year.

Serve the peach liquid as a special drink, or stir it into thick yogurt to make a sweet treat. Use the peaches in baking or add them to cereal for breakfast, or serve with yogurt or ice cream as a simple dessert.

NOTES: If any of your jars don't seal, remove the ring and lid, then replace them carefully and repeat the canning process by putting the jar back in the canner and boiling it for 10 minutes, immersed in water.

Sometimes you'll notice that a small amount of the sugar in the syrup crystallizes, making a layer of crystals near the bottom of the jar. Don't worry; it will dissolve over time.

FRUIT JUICES

AZERI KOMPOT

One night when I was staying with Jairan and her husband at their homestay in Lahich, in Azerbaijan, she dug out about a dozen one-quart jars. She carefully washed them and their lids in boiling water and set them out to dry.

She assembled piles of fruit, mostly pears from a neighbor's tree, but also some apples, blackberries, and purple plums from the garden, as well as a couple of pomegranates. She halved the plums and discarded the pits. She cut the pears into quarters, without removing the cores.

Then she was ready. Into each jar she put some fruit (10 to 12 halved plums, or several chopped pears) plus a cup of sugar and a handful of pomegranate seeds—a beautiful jeweled addition. She filled the jars to the top with boiling water. On went the lids, screwed tightly shut. She turned each jar upside down briefly to mix everything. Finally she laid all the jars on their sides on the floor in a cooler room, and covered them with a blanket. The juice would be ready to drink in a week, she told me, though it can sit for as long as six months.

Since then I've used her method for making fruit juices of all kinds. They are always delicious. I'd seen her mix and match, putting a handful of blackberries in with the pears, for example, and a couple of plums, so I took that kind of free-form approach too. It doesn't matter, really, what fruits you use, on their own or in combination. What is important is the amount of sugar: 1 cup sugar for a 1-quart jar. If the fruit is very tart, increase the sugar a little.

Dilute the juice a little if you wish (I like it with hot water), or drink it straight, or instead use it to flavor cocktails.

BERRY KOMPOT

In Armenia, I learned a slightly different way of making *kompot*. Anahit, whose welcoming apartment I stayed at in Yerevan, makes a fruit juice concentrate from raspberries and/or blackberries. She calls it her vitamin C for wintertime. After washing the fruit and letting it dry, she mixes it with sugar (about 1 cup sugar per pound of fruit) in a large bowl and then sets it aside in a cool place for 2 days, loosely covered with a cotton cloth, stirring it every so often. The sugar makes the berries release their liquid. After 2 days, the uncooked fruit and the liquid go into sterile jars, to be stored in the refrigerator or a cool pantry.

RHUBARB SYRUP
FOR SHARBAT

In Iran and Azerbaijan, syrups are made from fruit juice and sugar cooked down together and flavored with rose water or other aromatics. The syrups are used to make *sharbats*: diluted with cold water (still or sparkling) and served over ice cubes. A *sharbat* makes a welcome cooling refreshment in the heat of summer. Since I have a passion for rhubarb, this one, pale pink and tart-sweet, is one of my favorites.

I use less sugar than is traditional; you may want to increase the amount. The lemon juice adds surprising dimension. You can vary the aromatics, by using vanilla sugar, for example, or tossing a vanilla bean into the rhubarb as it cooks instead of using rose water. **MAKES ABOUT 2 CUPS; ENOUGH FOR 8 OR 9 SERVINGS**

1½ pounds rhubarb, sliced into approximately ½-inch pieces (about 5 cups)

1 cup water

2 cups sugar, or to taste

3 tablespoons fresh lemon juice

2 teaspoons rose water, or to taste

Place the rhubarb in a nonreactive pot, add the water and sugar, and bring to a boil. Lower the heat and cook at a strong simmer, stirring occasionally, for 20 minutes, or until the rhubarb has disintegrated. You should have about 4½ cups.

Pour the rhubarb into a fine-mesh sieve set over a bowl. Use the back of a large spoon or a spatula to press the rhubarb against the mesh so that the juice is squeezed out. Return the liquid to the pot; set the solids aside for another purpose (see Note). Add the lemon juice and simmer the liquid for 15 minutes to cook it down and concentrate it. Remove from the heat and add the rose water. Transfer the syrup to a glass jar and store in the refrigerator for up to 3 months.

To make *sharbat,* mix the syrup with cold water, using 3 parts still or sparkling water to 1 part syrup, or to taste. Serve over ice. Float a small sprig of mint or lemon balm on top if you wish.

NOTE ON RHUBARB SAUCE: The sweetened rhubarb pulp that remains after you've pressed out all the liquid is like a rhubarb version of applesauce, but much smoother on the tongue. Add a dollop to your morning yogurt or to a bowl of ice cream, or spread it on bread or toast like fruit butter.

TAMARIND SYRUP FOR SHARBAT

SHARBAT TAMBREH HENDI

Tamarind pulp, processed from the fruit of tamarind trees, is now widely available in Asian grocery stores. Often shipped from Vietnam or Thailand, it comes in dark brown blocks wrapped in clear plastic. Tamarind is a wonderfully versatile souring ingredient in savory dishes (see Fried Stuffed Fish, Bushir-Style, page 144), and it also makes a delicious *sharbat*.

Dilute the syrup with cold water or soda water, and serve over ice as a refreshing drink. Or stir it into mascarpone or ice cream. Or try it my favorite way, diluted with hot water to make a warming drink on a cold day. **MAKES 2 CUPS; ENOUGH FOR 10 TO 12 SERVINGS**

1 cup (½ pound) tamarind pulp

2 cups boiling water

2 cups sugar

Cut the tamarind pulp into small chunks, place in a bowl, and pour the boiling water over it. Stir with a fork and set aside to steep for 20 to 30 minutes.

Stir and mash the tamarind with a fork to break it up, then place a fine-mesh sieve over a bowl and pour the tamarind into the sieve. Use the back of a large spoon to press the pulp against the mesh and extract as much liquid and flavor as possible. Discard the coarse pulp in the strainer. You should have about 1½ cups thick liquid.

Transfer the tamarind liquid to a large measuring cup and add enough water to make 2 cups. Pour into a medium nonreactive saucepan and stir in the sugar. Bring to a boil over medium heat, stirring to dissolve the sugar; the mixture will foam up as it boils. Lower the heat to maintain a simmer, partially cover, and cook for 10 to 15 minutes, until reduced to about 2 cups. Cool and store in a glass jar in the refrigerator.

To make *sharbat*, add 2 tablespoons tamarind syrup to a glass filled with ¾ cup cold water, stir together, and add an ice cube. Taste and stir in a little more syrup if you wish. For a hot drink, use more syrup, about ¼ cup per cup of hot water.

LEMON SYRUP FOR SHARBAT

Because lemons are easily available year-round, lemon *sharbat* is a drink you can make any time. I freely adapted this from a recipe in *The Azerbaijani Kitchen* by Tahir Amiraslanov and Leyla Rahmanova. Note that you need to steep the lemon zest for at least 5 hours.

Because the zest is used as well as the juice, it's important to start with organic lemons. The saffron threads are optional, but they give a deeper yellow color to the *sharbat*.   **MAKES ABOUT 3 CUPS; ENOUGH FOR 12 SERVINGS**

6 or 7 organic lemons, scrubbed
¼ teaspoon saffron threads (optional)
1 cup hot water plus 1 cup water

1½ cups granulated sugar
¼ to ½ cup superfine (castor) sugar (optional)

Grate the zest from the lemons into a bowl. (Put the grated lemons in a plastic bag and refrigerate.) Add the saffron threads, if using, and the hot water and stir. Set aside, loosely covered, for at least 5 hours, or as long as overnight.

Pour the lemon zest liquid into a fine-mesh sieve or a cheesecloth-lined colander set over a bowl and discard the solids. Set the liquid aside.

Pour the remaining 1 cup water into a heavy saucepan, add the granulated sugar, and heat over medium heat, stirring to dissolve the sugar. Remove from the heat and set aside to cool to lukewarm.

Meanwhile, juice the lemons and pour the juice into a sieve set over a bowl; discard the pits and pulp. Add the lemon juice and the cooled sugar syrup to the steeped-zest water and stir well. Taste and add the superfine sugar, if desired; stir vigorously to make sure it completely dissolves.

Store in a well-sealed glass jar in the refrigerator.

To make *sharbat*, place an ice cube in a glass, add ¼ cup of the syrup and ¾ cup cold water, and stir. In winter, this makes a warming, healing hot drink on a cold night: Dilute a generous ¼ cup of the syrup with ¾ cup hot water in a mug and stir in a little honey or add a dash of rum to smooth it out.

BITTER ORANGE SYRUP FOR SHARBAT

Bitter oranges are called *naranj* in Iran, and originated in Persia.

In the West, our word for oranges comes from the original Persian name. Bitter oranges are sometimes called Seville oranges because they became known to the English via trade with Spain. They are used to make classic orange marmalade, and their peel is the flavoring in orange bitters and in a number of other dishes.

Until recently, bitter oranges were available for only a few weeks in the winter. But they are now being grown in California, so it's easier to find them and they are available for longer: late January until late March or early April. They are a little wild looking: bumpy and irregular shaped, with lots of seeds and often not a lot of juice. The juice they do have is precious. Use it in salad dressing in place of lemon or lime juice, or drizzle it on grilled fish or roasted chicken. Or use it to make this orange syrup, the base for a delicious *sharbat* that is citrusy and reminiscent of old-style lemonade, but with a generous orange undertone.

MAKES ABOUT 2½ CUPS; ENOUGH FOR 8 OR 9 SERVINGS

5 bitter oranges
1 cup water

2 cups sugar

Cut the oranges in half and juice them. Pour the juice through a fine-mesh strainer set over a bowl and discard the pulp. You should have a scant 1 cup juice. Set aside.

Fill two 1-cup jam jars with hot water and set aside.

Place the water in a nonreactive saucepan, add the sugar, and stir with a wooden spoon until the sugar is completely dissolved. Bring to a boil, add the orange juice, and bring back to a boil, then reduce the heat and simmer for 5 minutes. Remove from the heat. Empty the jars of water and pour in the syrup. Cover tightly and, once cooled, store in the refrigerator for up to 3 months.

To make *sharbat*, place an ice cube in a glass, add ¼ cup syrup and ¾ cup cold water or sparkling water, and stir.

Previous pages: *Sharbats, from left to right: Lemon, Rhubarb, and Tamarind (pages 329, 327, and 328).*

POMEGRANATE TECHNIQUES

There are many ways of eating a pomegranate, but my favorite is the way I learned in Iran, watching a Khamseh nomad man in the mountains east of Shiraz (see Nomad Encounter, page 190).

Here's his method: Pomegranates are full of juicy seeds held in place by bitter pith, and when the fruits are ripe and fresh, sucking the juice is the easiest and best way to eat them. Start by holding the pomegranate in your hands and squeezing it all over, pressing on it with your fingertips all over until it goes from being a tight-skinned fruit to feeling very soft. Feel for any firm places and press on them.

Poke a small hole in the fruit and immediately put your mouth over the hole and start swallowing the juice (it will spurt out if you're not careful). Suck and swallow some more. Keep pressing on the fruit as you suck, and keep rotating it around. The pressing breaks up the seeds, releasing their juice. As you continue to suck, the fruit will get more and more like a basketball that has lost its air, with dents and hollows and softness. Eventually, when it is very saggy, you can break the pomegranate open. Inside, the seeds will be a pale pink, having had their juice pressed and sucked out of them. There may be the odd renegade still-red seed or two; those you can eat one by one. At the end of the process, your pucker muscles will be a little tired, but you'll have had a delicious drink of fresh pomegranate juice without having had to deal with the messiness of the seeds and pits and membranes.

TO GATHER POMEGRANATE SEEDS FOR USE in recipes, my usual method is one I saw used by home cooks in Iran: Put out a bowl for the seeds. With a sharp knife, carefully cut a small—say, 1 inch—triangular piece out of the skin near the top and lift it off. Gently pull the seeds off the piece and put them in the bowl. Cut a second small piece and repeat. After that, you can pull the fruit apart, carefully, into several large fragments. Work with one piece at a time, gently detaching the

TWO HOURS WEST OF YAZD, IRAN—*Ripe pomegranates for sale by the side of the road in a small hamlet. I bought a bagful of them and then ate them the nomad way (see page 333) over the next few days. They were the best pomegranates I have ever tasted.*

seeds and letting them drop into the bowl. After you've finished, go through the seeds and discard any fragments of bitter white pith.

TO SQUEEZE A POMEGRANATE FOR FRESH JUICE, place it in a ziplock bag and roll it on a hard surface, pressing down firmly. Make sure you press on it all over. If the pomegranate splits, the juice will leak into the bag. If it doesn't, take it out of the bag and hold it over a bowl while you make a hole in the skin: The juice will start pouring out. Squeeze the fruit with your hands to press out more juice. Alternatively, you can remove the seeds as described above, clean off the pith, and process them in a blender or processor to break them down and release their juice. Place a sieve over a bowl, pour the blender contents into the sieve, and press on the solids to extract more juice. Discard the solids.

POMEGRANATE MOLASSES

ROBB-E-ANAR · NARSHARAB

Pomegranate molasses, also known as pomegranate syrup, is a concentrated, cooked-down version of pomegranate juice. *Anar* is the word for pomegranate in Persian and in most of the languages of the Persian culinary region. The word *robb* has traveled far. It's from Persian, and is also found in Georgian, Armenian, and Azeri, as well as in Kurdish. It came into English as *rob*, an old word that probably traveled to England after the Crusades, and old English cookbooks have recipes for various robs.

Many kinds of *robb* were on sale in the village of Massouleh, near the Caspian, when I was there, being bought by eager tourists from other parts of Iran. But pomegranate molasses is the most widely used version of *robb*: A dash of it adds a tart-sweet depth to soups and stews (it is often used in Persian *ash* dishes; see page 107), and it's also the basic flavoring in *fesanjun* (see page 204).

Now that bottled pomegranate molasses (see Glossary) is widely available in North America, it's no longer necessary to make it at home. But if you'd like to taste the homemade version, here are the instructions for making it.

It takes about 6 cups of pomegranate juice to make 1½ cups of molasses. Pomegranates vary from sweet to tart. Most juice available in North America is from sweet pomegranates.   **MAKES JUST UNDER 1½ CUPS**

**6 cups pure unsweetened
pomegranate juice**

Up to ¼ cup sugar (optional)
2 tablespoons fresh lemon juice (optional)

Place the pomegranate juice and sugar, if using, in a wide heavy pot. Bring to a boil, stirring if using sugar, and then cook for about 25 minutes at a medium boil. After about 20 minutes, you will notice that the volume is starting to decrease. Lower the heat and start stirring the molasses with a wooden spoon to prevent it from sticking. As it thickens, the syrup will have big smooth bubbles. Keep cooking until it has reduced to about 1½ cups, about another 20 minutes. (As the syrup cools, it will thicken further.) Taste it; the syrup should be tart and intense. If you like, you can increase the tartness by stirring in the lemon juice before you take it off the heat.

Pour into clean dry jars, seal, and store in the refrigerator for up to 1 month.

WINE IN THE CAUCASUS

It's impossible to imagine a feast in Georgia or Armenia without wine. Wine, both red and white, has been part of the culture in both countries for millennia. (And since the arrival of Christianity in both countries in the fourth century, red wine has

been the wine of the communion service.) There are many wineries in Georgia, but most often if you are eating at someone's house, you will be drinking wine that your hosts or someone in their family made.

Grapes are native to the Caucasus, and there are hundreds of varieties of wine grapes in the region, many of them very old. In Georgia, the best-known grape for red wine is the Saperavi. Whites include Kisi, Khikhvi, Rkatsiteli (also grown in Azerbaijan), and Tsolikouri. The grapes are used to make both "natural" wines and European-style barrel-aged wines.

It's only recently that people outside Russia have had any contact with wines from the Caucasus. The wines were sold locally and to the Russian market (although Armenian brandy had a following in the West). Collectivization of vineyards and industrial-style winemaking were imposed by the Soviet authorities in the 1930s. Many grape vines were torn up in the 1980s when Gorbachev, then leader of

the USSR, declared drunkenness a huge problem and restricted wine production and sales.

In the last thirty years, some local wineries and small winemakers have returned to traditional, more labor-intensive methods of winemaking, known as "natural" winemaking, which families had long used for making household wine for their own consumption. Wines from Georgia and Armenia, and from Azerbaijan too, are now finding markets in the rest of the world, and production of both natural wines and more Western-style wines has grown. Natural winemaking has become a fashion in other places, and natural wines now have a niche market.

Kvevris, large clay amphorae that are kiln-baked and lined with beeswax, are the essential tools of Georgian and Armenian makers of traditional wines. The Armenian word for *kvevri* is *karas*. The *kvevris* used for fermentation, when the must (grape liquid) sits with the mash, hold from 1,000 to 3,000 liters. They are buried in the ground, which keeps the temperature of their contents stable and cool enough for controlled fermentation. The grapes are pressed (traditionally by being trod on by a crowd of young people), and the pressed juice is stored with some of the mash (skins, seeds, and stems) in the *kvevri* to ferment for some months under a sealed lid (with a small pipe to vent carbon dioxide). The debris all sinks to the narrow bottom point of the *kvevri,* leaving the liquid clear. No additives are used in the red wines; the whites, which are a pale orange rather than white, do have added sulfites to stabilize them. After the early fermentation, the wine is transferred to smaller *kvevris* for aging.

Georgia's best-known wine region is in the east, in Kakheti, but western Georgia is now producing interesting wines too. In Armenia, most grapes are grown in the fertile, sheltered Arax River Valley and on the slopes above it. Other fruits are also used to make wines in Armenia. In the summer and fall months, the road near the village of Areni, east of Yerevan, is lined with small stands selling homemade fruit wines and liquors, as well as fruits and vegetables.

As in other wine-producing regions, the Georgians make a distilled drink from the fermented grape mash (like marc in France or grappa in Italy). The Georgian word is *cha-cha,* which is also the term for the fermented mash. Armenian brandy, distilled from fermented grape pressings, is made in a distillery in Yerevan.

Though Azerbaijan is a Muslim country, its wine industry is growing. European-style wines are produced from grapes grown in the Caucasus foothills and in the Kura River Valley near the inland city of Ganja. As in Georgia, many indigenous varieties of grapes are grown, as well as European varieties such as Pinot Noir.

TATEV, ARMENIA—*Three generations of a family were cooking gallons of tomatoes over a fire in their backyard when I walked by their house in this small hilltop village one sunny day. One of the brothers invited me to drink tutovka with them. Here they're making a toast to friendship.*

MULBERRY COUNTRY

The climate in the Persian culinary region suits all kinds of fruit trees, including mulberries. And in places in the Caucasus, there are still enormous mulberry orchards, remnants of a time when people living near the mountains raised silkworms;

the fresh leaves would be gathered in huge piles to feed the worms. I met a man of about fifty in Sheki, Azerbaijan, who remembered gathering mulberry leaves when he was a child.

The Silk Museum in Tbilisi gives some idea of how complex, and also how beautiful, the process of raising silkworms used to be. It was a domestic industry; individual households raised silkworms and sold the thread to silk factories, where it was woven into fabrics and rugs. There is still a silk factory in the town of Sheki and orchards of mulberry trees in the valley below the town. But these days, rather than using locally raised silk, the factory imports it from Uzbekistan and, increasingly, from China.

Mulberries are called *tut,* or *tuta,* in Persian, Kurdish, Armenian, Georgian, and Azeri. They are black, shaped a little like long raspberries, but with a much firmer texture. They are tart-sweet and delicious, and can be eaten fresh, but they are most often dried. They are used in savory dishes in the same way dried barberries are, to add a tart note, but their primary use is for liquor. They are fermented and distilled in village homes to make *tutovka* (mulberry vodka), a clear spirit that can be delicious. People in the Caucasus drink it as they do vodka, chased by a glass of fruit juice.

Which came first in the region, mulberry fruit for distilling or the mulberry leaves as food for silkworms? The *Encyclopedia Iranica* says that in Aramaic, the ancient language spoken in Darius's Persian Empire, and still by modern-day Assyrians, the word for mulberry is *twt*. That's persuasive evidence that mulberries have been in the region for millennia, and that people have likely been making drinks from mulberries since before the time of the Persian Empire. The silkworms came later.

A CLOSER LOOK

IRAN AND KURDISTAN

As I set out to explore the Persian-influenced cuisines in the region, it seemed right to me to include Kurdistan, the autonomous part of Iraq that is predominantly Kurdish and lies along Iran's western border. Though the Kurds of Kurdistan are citizens of Iraq, they are not Arab and they share more culture with Persians than with their Arab fellow citizens: Kurds and Persians speak languages that are closely related (they're all in the Iranic language family). And there's a large Kurdish population on the Iranian side of the border with Kurdistan.

IRAN

As I mentioned in the Introduction, Iran is a kind of bridge between East and West. It is neither Arab nor Turkish, and it lies between the worlds of largely Turkic central Asia and the predominantly Arab Middle East. For centuries, until it was conquered by the Arabs in the seventh century, the country was the center of an empire that fought with the Greeks, Romans, and Byzantines for control of Turkey and the Eastern Mediterranean.

Geography

The Caspian Sea coast, which marks part of the country's northern border in a curve, is very humid, with hot summers and cool, damp winters. It's an ideal climate for growing tea, rice, and fruits. West of the Caspian Sea, Iran has borders with Azerbaijan and with Armenia, as well as a short border with Turkey. That part of Iran is also the most culturally diverse, as large populations of Azeris, Assyrians, and Kurds, often subject to persecution of various kinds, have lived there since time immemorial. The major cities are Tabriz, a predominantly Azeri town, and Urumiyah.

In the hills that border western Iran, the majority population is Kurdish, close cousins of the Kurds

SIGHNAGHI, GEORGIA—*The Kakheti region in eastern Georgia is famous for its wine and for its beautiful small towns and villages. The towns date back many centuries and were built on hillsides in what would have been, in earlier times, easily defensible locations. Like Sighnaghi, most have spectacular views of the snowy peaks of the Caucasus.*

EAST OF SHIRAZ, IRAN—*My hosts at this farm east of Shiraz were Afsar, pictured here, and her husband, Abbas. Afsar taught me how to make Farmstead Winter Soup (page 110) and Date-Nut Halvah (page 293). She bakes bread twice a week, milks the cow every day, and does all the cooking for her guests and for her family.*

who live across the border in Iraqi Kurdistan. The climate is harsh, with long winters, but in summer, flocks of sheep and goats and crops of wheat and vegetables flourish in the fertile valleys and hills. Farther south along the border with southern Iraq, the population gives way to a mix of various Arab populations and Lurs, some of them nomadic, some settled. (This is the region that was most damaged, and from which many Iranian families fled, during the Iran-Iraq War from 1980 to 1988.)

Southern Iran has a long Indian Ocean coast with a number of ports, the best known being Bandar Abbas. Fishing is an important industry. Near the rather wild and mountainous border with Pakistan to the southeast lives a mixed population that includes many Balochis. The long eastern frontier with Afghanistan is also mountainous and rugged. North of that, there's a short but important border with present-day Turkmenistan. Historically, that area, with its easy terrain of low hills, has been the invasion route for peoples coming into Iran and the Caspian basin from the east: Scythians, Seljuk Turks, Kurds, and Mongols, among others.

As to the interior of the country: South of the Caspian coast rise the high snow-topped Alborz Mountains, which run east to west and separate the coastal region from the rest of the country. The massif blocks the moisture from the Caspian, and as a result, the vast central area of Iran is high, dry plateau, broken only by rivers that drain melting snow from the mountains that border it on all sides. It is here, in what looks to the untutored eye like a vast sheet of sand and gravel, that most of the important cities of Iran are located, from Tehran, the capital, to Isfahan, Shiraz, Kerman, and Yazd. And it is here, in the fertile river valleys that vein the dry plateau, that the rich agricultural traditions and extraordinary culinary culture of Persia developed.

People

Over 60 percent of the population of Iran is Persian, most of them Shia Muslims of the Twelver sect. Some of the Persian population are not Muslim but followers of Zoroastrianism, the religion that was dominant in Iran at the time of the early Persian Empire 2,500 years ago (see Zoroaster's Legacy, page 36).

The population also reflects peoples who lie outside its borders, for in the course of conquest, various Persian rulers, most notably Shah Abbas in the early 1600s, forcibly brought populations from elsewhere and settled them inside Iran. These included a large number of Armenians, who were settled in Isfahan, and a sizable Georgian population brought to Iran from eastern Georgia. But also over the centuries, a number of Georgians, Armenians, and others moved to Iran for trade or other reasons. Many of the Armenians have left Iran since the Islamic Revolution in 1979. And most of the Georgians have assimilated into the majority Iranian culture, although some still speak a Georgian dialect.

About 16 percent of the population is Azeri (there are disputes about the exact figure, but it's more than twice the population of Azerbaijan). The northwest of the country, in and around the city of Tabriz, near the border with Azerbaijan, has an Azeri majority population. In roughly the same area live the remaining Assyrians of Iran, the descendants of the Assyrians who once ruled an empire centered in Nineveh before they were defeated by the Persians under Cyrus the Great. The Assyrians are Aramaic-speaking Christians. Other minority populations include the Kurds, who speak several Kurdish languages, all distantly related to Persian; the Lurs, who also speak an Iranic language and live near the southern Iraqi border; Arabs and Turkic peoples who live in the mountains of southern Iran; Balochis, who live in the southeast near the Pakistan and Afghanistan borders; and Turcomans, who live near the border with Turkmenistan.

Food and Agriculture

Long ago, the Persians figured out how to bring water from the snowy mountains down into the desert

TBILISI, GEORGIA—*This woman is Azeri, as are many of the women who work in the markets of Tbilisi. Like other market women in Georgia, Armenia, and Azerbaijan, she found my interest in photographing ordinary things, such as cabbages, pumpkins, and herbs, very entertaining.*

without losing too much of it to evaporation. The technique, later adopted across central Asia, was to build underground canals, called *qanats*, to transport the water. The *qanats* enabled agriculture to flourish even in places with low rainfall. Around Kerman, in the south, there are enormous orchards of pistachio trees; in and near Yazd, in the central desert, pomegranates and other fruits grow; in the river valleys near Shiraz, there's rice and wheat, as well as an abundance of fruits, vegetables, and herbs. To the west of Tehran, in a countryside that looks dry and rocky, people are now growing olives, a relatively new crop in Iran, on a vast scale for olive oil.

Early cookbooks written for the court of the Caliphs after the conquest of the Persian Empire by the Arabs contain detailed recipes

for rice and meat and vegetable dishes, as well as desserts. Because the Arabs took on many aspects of Persian culture, including cuisine, it is remarkable how many of the elements of those early recipes are still present in modern-day Iranian dishes. At the same time, the arrival of vegetables and fruits from the New World, such as tomatoes, potatoes, and various legumes, has expanded the range of ingredients available to home cooks.

KURDISTAN

The area I call Kurdistan in this book is formally part of Iraq and is often known as Iraqi Kurdistan. It lies in part of what was, for centuries, called Mesopotamia—the land between and near the Tigris and Euphrates Rivers—and has long been invaded and fought over. Kurdistan's capital, Arbil (its Kurdish name is Hawler), is one of the oldest continuously inhabited cities in the world. These days it is Kurdistan's oil that has given it some autonomy and power. In earlier times, it was the fertile soil, with water from nearby rivers to make the land productive, that made the region so attractive to invaders.

The majority population is Kurdish, part of the large population of Kurds who live in what is known

AINKAWA, KURDISTAN—*A baker in the Assyrian suburb of Kurdistan's capital, Arbil, about to place stretched dough onto a baker's pillow. He'll slap the dough from the pillow onto the hot wall of the tandoor oven. Each flatbread bakes in about four minutes.*

SULAYMANIYAH, KURDISTAN—*I love photographing barbershops with their mirrors and interesting reflections.*

distinct group in Kurdistan, also much persecuted over the centuries. Their home church is in Lalish, in Kurdistan, and large populations lived in other parts of northern Iraq, including Sinjar, until the invasion by ISIL. There are also significant populations of Yazidis in Turkey, Syria, and Armenia. (For more about the Yazidis, see Glossary.)

For years, from the early 1970s on, the Kurds, along with the Assyrians, Yazidis, and other minorities in Iraq, faced persecution and attacks by Saddam Hussein. He fought a brutal war against the Kurds and used weapons of every kind, including chemical weapons, against the civilian population.

Things changed after the First Gulf War: Kurdistan gained autonomy when the Allies created a safe haven there in 1992. That enabled the Kurdish majority to take control of oil production and to develop a local economy largely independent of the rest of Iraq. Goods and food are traded across the border with Turkey and with Iran. And a still-corrupt but functional democracy has taken root. Although the majority population is Sunni Muslim and fairly conservative, modern Kurdistan is determinedly secular.

as Greater Kurdistan, an area that includes part of many neighboring countries: Turkey, Iran, Armenia, and Syria, as well as Iraqi Kurdistan. Iraqi Kurdistan is the closest the Kurds have ever come to having an independent country. There are three different but related Kurdish languages spoken in Iraqi Kurdistan; Kurdish is an Indo-European language in the same family as Persian.

Traces of earlier populations and eras remain in Kurdistan: Many Assyrians live there, some in small villages and some in and near the capital, Arbil. There are also Assyrians living in neighboring Iran and in Turkey. The Assyrians were early converts to Christianity and have been persecuted over the centuries by many rulers and conquerors, from the Mongols to the Ottomans. The Yazidis are another

Because Kurdistan is landlocked and the Kurds there, as in Iran and Turkey, have long had second-class status and faced persecution, much of village and rural Kurdistan remains fairly traditional and socially conservative. Most women wear long dresses over pants and cover their heads with light scarves. Religious observance, such as regular prayer and abstention from alcohol, is still the norm for most Kurds.

Until recently, life was so unstable that many had no opportunity for higher education and little contact with the outside world. That is now changing, as oil wealth and local autonomy have enabled villagers to send their children to college and as social media and increased education have had an impact on people's awareness of the rest of the world.

NOTE: Recent events in Iraq and Syria have meant that Kurdistan's army, the Pesh Murga, has been engaged in fierce warfare with the invading forces of ISIL since June 2014. Even before that, a large number of Kurdish refugees from the civil war in Syria had fled to Kurdistan, and since then, thousands of refugees from the rest of Iraq have sought safety in Kurdistan.

CAUCASIA

As with many neighbors, there's mistrust among the three Caucasus nations. The Azeris and Armenians fought a war over the mountainous territory of Nagorno-Karabakh in the 1990s; they are now in a cease-fire but still actively hostile. And as small countries surrounded by larger powerful neighbors—Russia, Iran, and Turkey—they are all understandably concerned about their security. The Caucasus countries have a long, painful history of being invaded or ruled over by everyone from the Byzantines and the Persians to the Russians and the Ottomans.

At the same time, there's a vibrancy. Armenians and Georgians each speak a distinctive language that has survived invaders and conquerors for several thousand years, including the oppressions of the Soviet Union. The fall of that empire in the early '90s—the destruction of one pattern and the emergence of the individual nation-states of Armenia, Azerbaijan, and Georgia—was both painful and exciting. People lost jobs and security as Soviet industries crumbled or were sold off to enrich the oligarchs, yet that first feeling of having their own country, rather than being ruled from Moscow, was exhilarating for many.

More than twenty-five years later, after various traumas—not just the Nagorno-Karabakh war but also Georgia's two conflicts with Russia (Abkhazia and South Ossetia), and massive and growing inequality of income in all three countries—the future is a little murky.

But what people do know will endure and what they are proud of are their cultural traditions, among them, having a place of honor, their food traditions.

ARMENIA

Like the rest of the region, Armenia, called Hayastan in Armenian, has a long history (and prehistory), evidence of which, including sophisticated Urartian metalwork from over 2,600 years ago, is on display in the National Museum in Yerevan.

The majority of Armenia's 3 million people are ethnically Armenian and Christian, following the Armenian Apostolic Church. Since the country became independent from the USSR, the church has become a force for nationalistic expression. The Armenian language is an ancient one, Indo-European, with an alphabet that was created by the much-revered Mesrop Mashtots in AD 405, around the time that Christianity displaced Zoroastrianism and animism and became the national religion of Armenia. Literacy and libraries and education are still a vital part of Armenian culture.

There are other peoples in Armenia too: small populations of Russians and Kurds, as well as Yazidis (see Glossary). The Kurds and Yazidis live in villages on the high plateau. They are the descendants of villagers who fled to Armenia from eastern Turkey during the genocidal attacks by Turks on populations of Armenians, Yazidis, Kurds, Assyrians, and others, in the nineteenth and early twentieth centuries.

Since the breakup of the Soviet Union, Armenia has been an independent democratic country, and one with severe economic challenges. The economic situation is not helped by Armenia's long-running dispute with neighboring Azerbaijan over the mountainous area called Nagorno-Karabakh. The dispute, which erupted into war in the nineties and is now holding as a cease-fire, resulted in the killing of civilians on both sides and the disentangling of populations who had once been intermingled: The many Armenians who had lived for generations in the Azeri capital, Baku, and in other towns fled to Armenia, and the Azeris who had been living in Nagorno-Karabakh, and in Yerevan and other Armenian towns, fled to Azerbaijan. Nagorno-Karabakh is now controlled by Armenia (though the

RAYA TAZA, ARMENIA—*Snow-covered peaks rim the horizon that frames this small scattered farm village about two and a half hours' drive from Yerevan. The people here are Yazidi (see Glossary). Other hamlets in the area are Kurdish or Armenian.*

international community considers it still legally part of Azerbaijan); all border crossings between the two countries are closed.

Because Armenia is landlocked and has open borders with only Georgia and Iran, opportunities for trade and economic development are very limited. Recently small IT companies have started up in the Gyumri area, but apart from that, and the remittances that some Armenian expats send to Armenia, the economic picture is gloomy. As a result, many young and middle-aged Armenians, especially those living in villages, move either to Yerevan in search of work and the chance of advancement or to Russia to start afresh.

Most of Armenia is high plateau, overlooked by beautiful snowcapped mountain peaks. (Mount Ararat, the symbol of Armenia, and known as Massis in Armenian, is over 16,000 feet high. Its snow-covered peak floats on the horizon south of the capital, Yerevan, but it has been entirely inside the border of Turkey since the Turkish-Armenian War of 1920.) In and near the fertile river valleys, especially that of the Arax (sometimes written Aras) River, which marks Armenia's border with Iran and Turkey, tender fruits including apricots, grapes, peaches, quinces, pomegranates, and mulberries grow well, but in the upland areas, with their harsher climate, grazing of sheep and cattle and cultivation of hardy vegetables and fruits are the main agriculture.

AZERBAIJAN

A large proportion of Azerbaijan's nine and a half million people lives in and near Baku, the capital, which is located on the shore of the Caspian Sea. This is where the oil is, both in the area around Baku and deep under the Caspian Sea. (Oil still seeps out of the ground in the Baku area and burns with a flickering blue flame, as it has done for millennia, since before the time of Alexander the Great.)

Starting at the Caspian coast, Azerbaijan's southern borders are with Iran and, farther west, with Armenia and Turkey. But those

BAKU, AZERBAIJAN—*These university students were hanging out in a park that lies just outside one of the gates of the walled old city.*

borders are complicated: If you look at the map on page 8, you'll see the exclave called Nakhchivan, a separate part of Azerbaijan that lies between Armenia and Iran. It is a remnant of the balkanization of borders in the Caucasus that is a legacy of the Russian and Soviet eras, and a continuing cause of friction.

Because most of its territory is low-lying, Azerbaijan has been on the route taken by conquerors arriving from central Asia from the time of the early Medes and Scythians to the Mongols and Seljuk Turks. They would travel across the south of what is present-day Turkmenistan, come into Iran, move along the southern edge of the Caspian Sea, and then go north and west into Azerbaijan. We know from archaeological sites that humans lived along the Caspian coast well before those invaders of the last three thousand years. The petroglyphs in Gobustan, near Baku, which depict people hunting, herding goats, and paddling large boats, are Mesolithic; other sites date from even earlier.

Russia defeated Persia and took full control of the three Caucasus countries—Azerbaijan, Armenia, and Georgia—in 1828. Nearly a century later, as the Russian Empire fell apart during the Russian Revolution in 1917-18, Azerbaijan, together with the Azeri part of northwest Iran, declared itself an independent republic. But by 1920, Soviet Russia had taken military control of present-day Azerbaijan (and Iran had reasserted control over the rest of the Azeris). From then until the breakup of the Soviet Union in the early 1990s, Azerbaijan was part of the USSR. Since then it has established itself as an independent country. Azerbaijan is staunchly secular and ruled by an authoritarian regime that is famous for its corruption.

Azerbaijan's ongoing dispute with Armenia over the territory of Nagorno-Karabakh (see Armenia, page 347, for details) means that the country has closed its borders with Armenia and that the Armenians who used to live in Baku and other towns have left. The mirror to this is that Azerbaijan has had to absorb Azeri refugees who fled Armenia and Nagorno-Karabakh during and after the war.

Most Azeris' mother tongue is Azeri, a Turkic language that is laced with words of Persian origin. The alphabet is Roman, but with more letters, rather like the alphabet used in Turkey. Because of the country's long domination by Russia, many older Azeris speak Russian, and it is still widely taught in the schools. There are also populations whose first language is not Azeri but one of the Tat languages. Tat is a family of Iranic languages, a remnant of the languages spoken in the region before the invasion of Turkic peoples from the eleventh century onward. Tat languages are spoken by the people of Lahich and several other villages in the foothills of the Caucasus.

Azerbaijan's enormous oil wealth is largely concentrated in Baku and among the few who form the Azeri elite. The result is that in the towns and villages outside Baku, people are educated but live frugally on relatively low incomes, and with inadequate infrastructure.

Azerbaijan is rich in agricultural produce: rice and tea, fruits and vegetables. Herds of dairy and beef cattle, as well as sheep and goats, graze on the slopes of the Caucasus foothills.

GEORGIA

In Georgian, the name for the country is Sakartvelo. The population is majority Georgian, but with strong regional differences in language and culinary traditions. Sizable Armenian and Azeri populations live in the capital, Tbilisi, and in other cities.

The Black Sea coast is lush and fertile. Its principal city is the port of Batumi. (Abkhazia, on the Black Sea coast, separated from Georgia in the 1992-93 war. Georgia's remaining coastline is less than a hundred miles long.) Most of Georgia's northern border is with Russia, at the Caucasus Mountains. On the south, it borders Turkey and Armenia, and to the east lies Azerbaijan. For sixty years, the southern border with Turkey was the border between the West and the USSR and thus was a heavily fortified military zone.

The area is still populated by a mix of Russians and Armenians, with Georgians a minority.

Georgians speak a language that is non-Indo-European and is related to only a few other Caucasus languages. The earliest Georgian alphabet dates back at least to the fourth century, and possibly before. As in Armenia, literacy and education are important elements of Georgian culture. Since independence, the Georgian Orthodox Church has become a vehicle for the expression of nationalism, often of a narrow and intolerant kind.

Like Armenia and Azerbaijan, Georgia had its own local kings and rulers but was also under Persian rule intermittently for centuries, until it came under Russian control in the early nineteenth century. In 1921, the country was forcibly incorporated into the USSR; it gained independence when the Soviet Union broke up in the early '90s. Since then, there have been two wars along Georgia's northern border. Georgians view both—the breakaway of the region called Abkhazia and the secession of South Ossetia— as troubles instigated by Russia, the Goliath that lies across the Caucasus Mountains. Georgia is now a relatively stable, if economically vulnerable, democracy.

The country has a long history (and prehistory), with archaeological sites yielding evidence that the Georgians may well have been the

KAZBEGI, GEORGIA—*Gergeti Holy Trinity Church is perched high on a mountain shoulder below Mount Kazbek, at 16,512 feet the third-highest mountain in Georgia. A few miles further up the road, called Russian Military Highway, lies the border with Russia.*

first people to know winemaking. Like the Armenians and the early inhabitants of Azerbaijan, the early people of Georgia cultivated wheat and other grains and legumes.

Because the country has many distinct climatic zones and regions isolated by rough terrain (rather like Switzerland), the food has a strong regional identity. Most Georgian dishes have very specific regional origins. Rather like in parts of Italy even now, people identify with their home region and local cuisine and speak a regional dialect.

Georgia's culinary regions can be divided roughly between the west,

with its abundance of fruit of every kind, a greater reliance on corn, and more intense seasonings, especially in the mountainous regions of Svaneti and Racha (more raw garlic and a liking for black pepper and chiles, for example) and the east, with its vineyards, preference for wheat breads, and milder, more subtle layering of flavors. That division mirrors a period long ago, when control of what is now Georgia was split between the Byzantine Empire, which held western Georgia, and the Persians, who ruled the rest (along with the territories of present-day Azerbaijan and Armenia).

TRAVEL NOTES

BECAUSE THE POLITICS OF THE REGION ARE CHANGING RAPIDLY—IRAN, for example, cut off for so long from open trade, recently signed a nuclear agreement with the world powers, so sanctions have eased dramatically—travel advice should be checked against the current situation, and then double-checked. If you would like to visit any part of the region, look online for visa requirements and be sure the information is up to date.

As of 2016, Georgia and Armenia are both easy to access; visas are issued at the border whether you arrive by land or by air. Azerbaijan and Iran are more difficult for most travelers in that visas for most nationalities are relatively expensive and require a longer lead time. The Azeri visa can now be applied for online, but it requires an invitation. As sanctions ease and Iran is welcomed back into full engagement with the rest of the world, visa requirements and delays should be less onerous. As for Kurdistan, when I went in 2014, I was stamped into Iraq at the airport in Kurdistan's capital, Arbil, with no fuss. Since then there have been attacks by ISIL; Kurdistan is now overwhelmed with refugees from Syria and from other parts of Iraq. I am assured by Kurdish friends that most of the country is still easily accessible and is safe behind the protective wall of the Kurdish military (the Pesh Murga), but the situation is changing all the time, so do get updated information from a source you trust.

When you go, keep in mind that each country and culture has its own sense of propriety, and rules of social engagement. In Iran there are specific clothing rules for women: at a minimum, wear a long-sleeved top that covers you from the neck to almost the knees, over trousers, and a scarf on your head. You'll want to dress with decorum in Kurdistan and Azerbaijan too, though there are no rules and people are fairly relaxed about foreigners' attire. In the Muslim countries and in Kurdistan, don't expect to find much alcohol (none legally in Iran; some in restaurants in Kurdistan and Azerbaijan, but little in private homes). Everywhere there's a code of hospitality, and it's important to be graceful about accepting generosity. It's also a good idea to figure out ahead of time ways of reciprocating, even on a small scale. I like to carry presents with me to offer to people, small pieces of jewelry, for example. Good lipsticks and other makeup are another possibility, except in Iran, where all women are more knowledgeable about makeup than I could ever be.

ISFAHAN, IRAN—*A man taking a mouthful of* havij bastani, *a kind of ice cream float, made with Persian ice cream and carrot juice. The ice cream,* bastani, *is very sweet, made with eggs, milk, and sugar; flavored with pistachios, saffron, and rosewater; and thickened with salep (powdered orchid root), which gives it a firm, mouth-satisfying texture.*

There are hotels in Armenia, Azerbaijan, and Georgia, but if you are interested in local food culture, I recommend homestays. You can find sites online, or even wait until you arrive in the country to figure out your homestay bookings. In Kurdistan, though, it's best to book ahead, for there are often shortages of hotel rooms in the main towns.

As for Iran, it can take time to arrange a visa (depending on which passport you hold), but otherwise travel is quite easy. (Note that your visa will be denied if you hold an Israeli passport or have an Israeli entry stamp in your passport.) As tourism has started to boom, there is a shortage of hotel rooms, so accommodations can be tight. You'll want to make reservations in the larger cities, especially if you are traveling in high season (spring or fall). There are also now a few guesthouses in smaller towns. For those, check online or with an Iranian travel agency. If you have only a short time, you might want to go with a tour. Remember that distances are huge. Don't hesitate to fly or take a train between cities. And take your time. Try to resist the urge to rush around and "see it all." When you stop and hang around, especially if you have the luxury of traveling on your own, you open the possibility of meeting people and having interesting conversations. There's nothing better.

GLOSSARY

ACHAEMENIDS, ACHAEMENID EMPIRE: The Achaemenid empire and dynasty founded by Cyrus the Great lasted from about 550 BC to 330 BC and stretched from present-day Turkey, Egypt, and Libya into central Asia and southeast to India. It was the first great Persian empire, with an estimated 40 percent of the world's population at the time living within its boundaries. From the capital at Persepolis, the rulers of the empire waged war against the Greeks, who sought the same supremacy over the eastern Mediterranean.

The Achaemenids, who were conquered by Alexander the Great in 330 BC, had an enormous impact on Western civilization: They established a bureaucratic administration for the empire that included a postal system; a common language; a system of local administrators, called *satraps*; and laws that applied across the empire. They also emancipated slaves, including the Jews of Babylon.

ADVIEH: This Persian spice blend varies from household to household. The classic one, widely sold in Persian groceries, is a blend of ground cardamom, cassia, and cumin and dried rose petals, in a proportion of one part cumin to two parts of each of the others. I find both cardamom and cassia quite penetrating and so my preferred proportion is two parts dried rose petals to one and a half parts of each of the others. Mix them together and store

the *advieh* in a clean, dry glass jar; shake it before you use the mixture.

ALBANIA, CAUCASIAN ALBANIA: From the first century BC until the second century AD, a kingdom called Albania lay between the greater and lesser Caucasus mountain ranges, roughly in the location of present-day Azerbaijan, bounded by Armenia to the west and the Caspian Sea to the east. It should not be confused with the present-day country called Albania, on the Adriatic Sea. There are a few written fragments of the original Albanian language, which seems to have been erased first by the Parthians and then the Persians, both of whom conquered the kingdom in the third century AD.

ALEXANDER THE GREAT: At a young age, the storied Macedonian began to conquer territory east of Greece. He and his armies vanquished Persia, defeating Darius III in 330 BC, and eventually reached the Indus River. When Alexander died, the empire was divided among his generals.

ALMONDS, GREEN ALMONDS: Almonds, like walnuts, are the drupaceous fruit of a tree in the *Prunus* genus—*Prunus dulcis*, also known as *Prunus amygdalis*. The tree is native to western Asia and to Europe and is closely related to the peach. The husk of the fruit contains the almond, which when ripe has a hard outer shell

that protects the kernel, or nut, inside. Green (unripe) almonds (*chaghaleh badoom* in Persian) are pale to medium green, with velvety skins that have not yet hardened into a shell: You eat the whole thing, nut and skin. Green almonds are a springtime treat for Persians and others who live where almonds grow. Look for them in Persian, Turkish, and Arab groceries in the spring.

ANGELICA (GOLPAR): *Heracleum persicum*, commonly mislabeled "angelica" and called *golpar* in Persian, is a plant native to Iran with seeds that are used as a flavoring and a spice. The plant, also known as Persian hogweed, is in the *Apiaceae* (formerly *Umbelliferae*) family, which also includes coriander, celery seed, true angelica, parsley, and lovage. Golpar is aromatic and slightly bitter, and it is often mixed with salt (it is then called *golpar namak*; see the recipe on page 30). On its own or mixed with salt, it's sprinkled on cucumbers, pomegranate seeds, cooked potatoes, and other vegetables to add another layer of flavor.

APRICOTS, DRIED APRICOTS, APRICOT LEATHER: Apricots are the fruit of several closely related species in the *Prunus* (stone fruit) family. The most common are *Prunus armenica*. As the name indicates, botanists long believed that apricots originated in the Persian culinary region, but these days there is some dispute. We do know that they have been

LAHICH, AZERBAIJAN—*Fancy versions of the traditional hat worn by Azeri women displayed in a small shop.*

cultivated there for more than three thousand years. The orange fruits are fragile when ripe. Some are very sweet while others are tart. They are commonly preserved by being split and dried; they are also cooked, mashed, and spread flat to dry as fruit leather (see Fruit Leather, page 314, and photo, page 315). The dried fruits are widely used in both sweets and savory dishes. Look for tart-tasting dried apricots, preferably those that have not been treated with sulfur; the unsulfured dried apricots are darker in color rather than brilliant orange.

ARAB CONQUEST: After the death of Mohammed and the struggles for succession, the Caliphate form of government was established to rule the Arabian Peninsula. Attacks on the Persians began around AD 630 and ended with the conquest of Persia in AD 651. Following the conquest, many Persians converted to Islam; others fled.

ARAB NOMADS: The Khamseh federation in Iran's eastern Fars Province (in the hills east of Shiraz) is a grouping of five nomadic tribes: Arab, Nafar, Baharlu, Inalu, and Basseri. The family I spent time with (see Nomad Encounter, page 190) were Arabic speakers and part of the Khamseh.

ARABIC: Arabic is a Semitic language with many dialects. Following the Arab conquest of

Persia in the seventh century, the official language became Arabic and the alphabet used to write Persian shifted from Pahlavi script to the Arabic alphabet. In the following centuries, efforts by Persians to preserve Persian culture resulted in the revival of Persian language and its resurgence in poetry and daily life. Persian is still written using a version of the Arabic alphabet, and numbers in Iran are also written in Arabic.

ARAMAIC: Versions of the family of ancient languages referred to as Aramaic are still spoken by Assyrians in Iran, Turkey, Syria, and the diaspora. Aramaic is also used in the rituals of Assyrian churches (see Chaldeans and Orthodox Churches). It is a Semitic language and is written in an alphabet that was the precursor of the Hebrew and Pahlavi alphabets.

ARMENIA, ARMENIAN: Armenia today is a small part of what is often referred to as Greater Armenia, which extended east from the Mediterranean coast of Turkey and Syria to present-day Armenia. (In Armenia, the country is called Hayastan.) The precursor civilization in Armenia was called Urartu, and lasted from the eighth century BC until about 585 BC, when it was succeeded by an Armenian kingdom. The Urartians traded actively with the Phoenicians and others in the Mediterranean. At its largest extent, the Armenian kingdom

included parts of present-day Turkey, Iran, and Syria. The kingdom's fortunes waxed and waned over the centuries, as it was conquered successively by the Romans (under Pompey the Great), the Persians, and others. Armenia was the first country to declare itself Christian, around AD 300. The Armenian language is an old Indo-European one, with an alphabet that was developed in the early fifth century by Mesrop Mashtots, a man who is still revered by Armenians.

BAHARAT: In Iraqi Kurdistan the word for "spice blend" is *baharat*; its name derives from the Arabic word *bhara*, meaning spice. The classic Kurdish *baharat* used with meat dishes includes cassia (*dachini*), coriander, cumin (*zeera*), cloves (*mexakh*), cardamom (*he*), black pepper (*allat*), and turmeric (*curcuma*), and often nutmeg and some kind of paprika or cayenne (*biber*). The *baharat* for breads in Kurdistan is usually powdered fenugreek (*shemli*) and nigella.

BARBERRIES: Barberries grow on a shrub that is part of the *Berberis*

family, native to Europe and West Asia. The small oval berries have a sharp, tart taste and a dull red color. They are used in Iran and the rest of the Persian culinary region to give a tart edge to savory dishes (see Barberry Rice, page 215; Tabriz Meatball Soup, page 100; and Onion Salad with Barberries, page 51), and to make jams and juice. Barberries are rich in vitamin C and pectin. They dry very well and are available in Persian and Arab grocery stores; the dried berries soften after a short soak in water or during cooking. Although the plant grows well in North America, the most common variety, *Berberis vulgaris*, is an alternate host to the fungus that causes rust in wheat. Consequently, its cultivation is prohibited in Canada and in parts of the United States.

BEANS AND LENTILS: The seeds of leguminous plants, often referred to as pulses, include dried beans and the smaller disk-shaped lentils. They come in all shapes and sizes and many different names are used for them, which can be confusing. They are a good source of protein and fiber and because of the former are especially appreciated by vegetarians. The seeds are

dried after harvest and can be stored for months, which makes them a low-cost (and versatile) pantry item for home cooks. Many people believe that soaking dried beans overnight before cooking them shortens the cooking time; I find it doesn't make enough difference with smaller beans that cook relatively quickly, but I do soak chickpeas (garbanzos) and kidney beans. Using a pressure cooker shortens cooking time substantially but I have never used one.

NOTE: It's important to cook all beans thoroughly, both for digestibility and to eliminate toxins. This is especially true in the case of kidney beans, because if not cooked thoroughly they can cause a kind of food poisoning. Cook them at a strong boil, rather than in a slow cooker, to make sure that the temperature in the center of the beans reaches at least 176°F, the level at which all toxins are killed.

THE LEGUMES USED IN THE RECIPES IN THIS BOOK INCLUDE THE FOLLOWING:

Black-Eyed Peas: Also called cowpeas, these are the seeds of *Vigna unguiculata* subsp. *unguiculata*. The peas are rounded and off-white, with a black dot that makes them easy to identify. They take about 1½ hours to cook in boiling water.

Chickpeas (also known as garbanzos): Chickpeas (*Cicer arietinum*) are relatively large and round, with a dented line around their equator. The

off-white beans take a long time to cook (about 2 hours of hard boiling) but are worth the time. They can be mashed to a paste (to make hummus, for example) or eaten whole, and have a sweet, appealing flavor. Smaller chickpeas, with a darker brownish color, are the ones most commonly used in India (where they're known as *channa*).

Kidney Beans: Kidney beans (also *Phaseolus vulgaris*) usually take more than 2 hours to cook (see Note above). They may be dark wine-red or a deeper, almost purple magenta color, as well as a pale or speckled pink. The meaty, rich-tasting beans are best paired with oil to smooth out their slightly mealy texture.

Lentils: The seeds of *Lens culinaris* are disk-shaped and cook more quickly than globe-shaped legumes such as chickpeas. The lentils called for in this book are brown lentils; they have a satisfying meaty, earthy flavor.

Mung Beans: These small, olive-green round beans are from the plant *Vigna radiata*, which is native to India. Common bean sprouts are made from soaking the beans in a little water. Their outer skin is olive green, but the bean inside is a golden yellow; hulled and split versions of mung beans are sold in Indian groceries as *moong dal*. Whole mung beans take about an hour of boiling to soften completely.

Navy Beans: Small, white, and oval, navy beans are another bean in the *Phaseolus vulgaris* family. I like their meatiness, and their relatively short cooking time (about 1 hour).

Split Peas: Yellow split peas are the dried fruit of *Pisum sativum* that has been hulled and split in half. The hulling and splitting means that they cook relatively quickly (in just over an hour). They are rich in protein and complex carbohydrates. When cooked and left to cool, they congeal, rather as cooked polenta does, because the starch seeps into the cooking water during cooking and then sets as it cools.

BEEF, BABY BEEF, BEEF SHANK, ETHICAL VEAL: Beef is much more common in Georgia, Kurdistan, and Armenia than in neighboring Azerbaijan or Iran. The meat, most often from young animals that are twelve to eighteen months old, is often called baby beef. The term "ethical veal" refers to the meat of young animals that have been weaned and then fed on grass and grain until slaughtered at eight to twelve months old. The meat is redder than the pale white meat of milk-fed veal, but it is not as flavorful as that of baby beef. Beef from full-grown animals can be substituted for baby beef in the recipes in this book. Beef shank, like lamb shank, has a rich flavor and needs to be slow-cooked until very tender (see Spiced Beef Shank, page 195).

BELL PEPPERS, CHILE PEPPERS: All peppers, whether sweet bells or scorching-hot Scotch bonnet chiles, are members of the *Capsicum* family. Bell peppers have no capsaicin, the substance that causes a burning sensation in the mouth and the "hotness" of hot chiles. Green bell peppers are the unripe version of the peppers, which ripen to red, yellow, orange, or purple hues. Bell peppers, also referred to as sweet peppers, may be the classic bell shape or may instead be longer, with a squared-off lower tip. For more about chile peppers, *see* Cayenne.

BITTER ORANGES: Known in Persian as *naranj* and sometimes in English as Seville oranges, bitter oranges (*Citrus x aurantium*) have a bumpy peel and their color is a duller orange than ordinary sweet oranges. The peel is used fresh or dried for intense orange flavor (dried bitter orange peel is sold in Persian and Arab groceries, and check online for mail-order sources) with no hint of sweetness. The juice is the main flavoring ingredient in an orange *sharbat* (see page 332), and the juice can also be used in salad dressings and as a souring agent in marinades or stews. The growing season in Spain and other parts of the Mediterranean traditionally runs from January to March, but the oranges are now being grown in California, where the season extends into April. Look for them at specialty shops and Mediterranean and Persian groceries. You can freeze bitter oranges whole for later use; thaw before using.

BLUE FENUGREEK: Found only in the Swiss Alps and the mountains of Georgia, blue fenugreek (*Trigonella caerulea*) is native to Europe. Although Georgians call it *utskho suneli*, meaning foreign spice, it is an essential ingredient in Georgian cooking. It's sold with the dried seeds and leaves mixed together. I hope that with the growing popularity of Georgian food, blue fenugreek will soon become available in North America. In the meantime, you can substitute a mix of dried fenugreek leaves and powdered fenugreek, as specified in the recipes.

BORAGE: Borage (*Borago officinalis*), an herb that is native to the Mediterranean, has medicinal as well as culinary uses. Its star-shaped violet-blue flowers are dried and used to make an aromatic herbal tea in Iran and elsewhere. (Its name in Persian is *gol gav zaban*, meaning cow-tongue flower.) The tea is believed to be calming as well as a diuretic. Borage leaves are cooked in soups and as a green on their own. The tea and the leaves have a number of uses in traditional and naturopathic medicine.

BULGUR: Bulgur is cooked dried wheat that has been pounded into different-sized flakes. It's widely used in both Kurdistan and Armenia, as well as throughout the eastern Mediterranean. In Kurdish it's *sauer*; in Armenian, it's *gorgot*. Bulgur is sold in Mediterranean and Arab groceries as well as many

KERMAN, IRAN—*Dried flowers for making tea, with dried safflower blossoms at left and borage flowers at right.*

mainstream markets. The packages will be marked fine, medium, or coarse. *Also see Wheat.*

BUTTER, BUTTER-GHEE: Butter is used in the Persian culinary world for baking, for cooking vegetables, and as a flavoring, especially in rice dishes. Butter-ghee, a kind of clarified butter, is more stable than regular butter and keeps well, which is why it's the most common form found in the region. You can make your own butter-ghee or buy it in Persian, Arab, or Indian shops.

To make butter-ghee: Heat butter gently in a heavy saucepan until the milk solids separate from the clear liquid. Skim off the solids and reserve them to use as a flavoring for rice or vegetables. Transfer the liquid ghee to a clean glass jar and store in a cool place. Ghee is also made from hydrogenated vegetable oil, hence the specification for butter-ghee in these recipes.

BYZANTINE EMPIRE: Also known as the Eastern Roman Empire, with its capital in Constantinople (present-day Istanbul), the Greek-speaking Byzantine Empire vied with the Persian Empire for control of the eastern Mediterranean, the Caucasus, and what is present-day

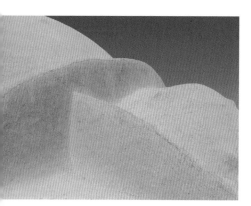

Turkey. For example, at times control of the Caucasus region was divided by treaty between the two empires, with western Georgia being allocated to the Byzantines while eastern Georgia, Armenia, and present-day Azerbaijan were under Persian rule. The Ottoman conquest in the fifteenth century ended the Byzantine Empire's reign.

CALENDARS: The Persian calendar is rooted in traditional rituals and beliefs. An Islamic calendar governs Islamic religious observances in Iran, but the official calendar of Iran (and neighboring Afghanistan) is based on the seasons and the sun's annual movement. The years have 365 or 366 days, as in the Western calendar, but the New Year is at the spring solstice, around March 21. Years are counted from that date (the year 0 is the Western year AD 622, as it is in the Islamic calendar).

Thus calendars in Iran show two versions of the year (three if you include the Western calendar). In 2016, the Persian calendar, with the new year starting around March 21, will be at year 1395. The Islamic calendar, which is lunar and has only 354 days, rotates in relation to both the Western and the Persian calendars. In 2016, the Islamic New Year falls in October, after which the Islamic year will be 1438.

Of course, various other people in Iran and Greater Persia have different calendars. The Armenians and Assyrians,

KASHAN, IRAN—A detail of the adobe roof of a traditional merchant's house, now a small museum.

being Eastern Rite Christians, have a religious calendar that is Julian, so their holy days are about twelve days later than those observed by Western Christians (Christmas falls on January 7, for example). The Chaldeans, as Roman Catholic Assyrians, base their festivals and holy days on the Western calendar. And the Jews of Iran, like Jews all over the world, use a lunar calendar to mark their holy days, a calendar in which the Western year 2016 is 5776 until the Jewish New Year in early October, when it becomes 5777.

In Georgia, Armenia, Azerbaijan, and Kurdistan, the Western calendar is used for everything but religious events and anniversaries.

CARDAMOM: The cardamom plant is a member of the ginger family (*Zingiberaceae*) and is native to India and Sri Lanka. The flavor is in the small brown-black seeds, which are contained in small pods. Cardamom is sold as both whole pods and powdered. I recommend you buy unbleached green pods (not white) and store them in a sealed container. The word for cardamom is *hel* in Kurdish and Persian, *hil* in Azeri, and *ili* in Georgian.

CARDOON: This member of the sunflower family (*Cynara cardunculus*) is a close cousin of the artichoke. The stems, harvested before the plant exhibits its tall, thistle-like flowers, are eaten as a vegetable, first blanched to remove bitterness and then simmered. Cardoons are native to the eastern Mediterranean and are still grown as a vegetable crop in France and Morocco.

CASSIA: A close relative of cinnamon and commonly labeled cinnamon in North American grocery stores, cassia has a stronger, less subtle taste than true cinnamon. Cinnamon can be substituted, but its taste is more perfumed and less punchy than that of the more familiar cassia. Cinnamon sticks are curled pieces of the inner bark from several related trees and are correctly referred to as quills. Cassia quills, from the tree *Cinnamomum cassia*, are tougher than the quills of tree cinnamon, *Cinnamomum verum*, which are more fragile and more expensive.

CAYENNE, CAYENNE POWDER, DRIED RED CHILES: Cayenne is a chile pepper that is just one of many varieties of *Capsicum annuum*. Cayennes are long and narrow, with pointed tips; they have medium chile heat (from the capsaicin in their membranes and flesh) and a slightly sweet flavor. Dried red cayenne chiles are widely sold in grocery stores as well as in Asian groceries, are dark red and a little wrinkled. Dull orange-red cayenne powder or pepper is the dried and ground form of the chile. It usually has a strong, intense chile heat, but powders vary in their intensity, so when you buy a fresh batch, start slowly with it, using a little, until you have a sense of how much heat and flavor it will give.

CELERY LEAF: *See* Leaf Celery

CHADOR: A full-length piece of cloth, most often black, that is worn by some women in Iran and elsewhere. It has no fastenings, and is draped on the head and held closed at the front with one hand.

CHALDEANS, CHALDEAN CHURCH: Rather confusingly, the Chaldean Church and its members, who call themselves Chaldeans, are not remotely related to the ancient people called Chaldeans. The Chaldean Church is aligned with the Roman Catholic Church, and most of its adherents are ethnic Assyrians living in Kurdistan and in the rest of Iraq, and in Turkey, Syria, and Iran, as well as in diaspora in the United States and elsewhere. They call themselves Chaldeans to distinguish themselves from the Assyrians who follow the Eastern Rite or Orthodox churches. The language of the church is Syriac, an Aramaic language.

CHERVIL: A delicate annual herb, *Anthriscus cerefolium*, chervil has a subtle licorice or anise flavor; fine, lacy, bright green foliage; and tender, slender stems. It is related to parsley but has none of that herb's vigor (and occasional toughness).

CINNAMON: *See* Cassia

CITRIC ACID, CITRIC ACID POWDER: Also known as sour salt, powdered citric acid is used as a preservative. It can take the place of lime or lemon juice and in this book is given as an alternative in the recipe for Apricot Moraba (page 318). That recipe comes from Azerbaijan, where limes and lemons were nearly impossible to find during periods of the country's history (particularly the Soviet era). Look for citric acid in well-stocked grocery stores near pectin and other canning supplies.

COLCHIS: Colchis was an independent kingdom in the

TBILISI, GEORGIA—*New World foods in a very Old World place.*

western part of present-day Georgia and is famous in myth as the destination of Jason and the Argonauts when they were searching for the Golden Fleece. The neighboring kingdom to the east was called Iberia. Colchis was conquered by the Greek kingdom of Pontis in 164 BC. The Colchians spoke a Khartvelian language that is related to modern Georgian. *See also* Albania *and* Iberia.

CORIANDER: Coriander (*Coriandrum sativum*) is both an herb and a spice; the herb is more often known as cilantro in the United States. The seeds are used in savory dishes and spice blends, including the Georgian spice mix called *kmeli suneli* (see page 28). The tender leaves and finer stems of the plant are used in many parts of the Persian culinary region, both as a flavoring and a garnish.

CORNELS: The oval, cherry-sized fruit of the tree *Cornus mas*, which is native to the Caucasus and Europe, is a little tart, like sour cherries. The fruits are called cornels, Carnelians, or Carnelian cherries and may be a deep red, orange-red, or pale yellow. The tender flesh surrounds a long pit. Cornels can be substituted for sour cherries or sour plums in sauces, condiments, and pies and strudels.

CUCUMBER, PERSIAN; CUCUMBER, ENGLISH; CUCUMBER: Cucumbers are the fruit of a vine (*Cucumis sativis*) that is native to South Asia and a member of the *Cucurbitaceae* family. Many different cultivars are found worldwide. Those used in Iran, Kurdistan, and the Caucasus have delicate fine skins and few seeds, and they are eaten sliced or chopped, and usually peeled. They may be short or long but are always slender, quite unlike the fat, thick-skinned cucumbers common in North America. The long, fine-skinned cucumbers known as English or European cucumbers and the shorter Persian cucumbers, sometimes called Mediterranean or Lebanese cucumbers, are the closest North American equivalents to those grown in the region.

CURRENCIES: Each of these countries has a different currency: the Azeri monat; Armenian dram; Georgian lari; Iranian rial; and Kurdish (Iraqi) dinar. Iranians often refer to money as *toman*, the word for a previous currency, and that's the word you'll often encounter in books and movies, even contemporary ones. These days a toman is worth one-tenth of a rial (like a dime to a dollar).

DAIRY PRODUCTS: *See* Butter, Butter-Ghee; Kashk; Whey; and Yogurt.

DAMSONS: *See* Sour Plums

DILL: A plant in the *Apiaceae* family (a relative of carrots and nigella), dill is both a spice and an herb. Fresh dill is much more aromatic and potent than dried. Dill seeds, the fruits of the plant, have a strong anise-like aroma and flavor. Dill is used in Georgian spice blends, and both the fresh leaves and the seeds are essential for Green Ajika (page 40), the Georgian herb paste.

DOSHAB: The word *doshab* is most commonly used in the Persian culinary world for a thick grape syrup, but it can also mean mulberry syrup. *Doshab* is like a thick *robb* (see page 335) and is an important food and flavoring in Armenia, Georgia, Iran, and Azerbaijan. It's made by pressing the fruit for its juice and cooking it down to a very thick syrup.

DRIED FRUITS: Drying fruits is a traditional way to preserve them. In the region, apricots and plums are dried whole or halved, while apples are cut into strips or chunks and strung on threads. Most dried fruits are used to give dishes tartness, but they also may be a wintertime snack. *Also see* Apricots, Barberries, and Sour Plums.

DRIED HERBS: Drying is the most common and easiest way to preserve the fragrance and flavor of fresh herbs for use through the winter. Dried herbs may be more intense in flavor than their fresh counterparts, although sometimes the reverse is true. Quantities of fresh and dried herbs are not usually interchangeable, and fresh herbs are not always a good substitute for dried. *See also* specific herbs.

DRIED LIMES, DRIED LIME POWDER, *LIMOO BASRAHI,* *LIMOO OMANI:* Dried limes are a common flavoring ingredient in Persian and Kurdish cooking. Known in Iran as *limoo omani* (meaning limes from Oman) and in Kurdistan as *limoo basrahi* (limes from Basra, a port in southern Iraq), they give a distinctive tartness and almost smoky, aromatic flavor to simmered dishes. Limes chosen for drying are soaked in saltwater and then dried in the sun until wrinkled, completely dried out, and brownish black. You can buy dried lime powder at Arab and Persian groceries or grate a whole dried lime with a Microplane or other fine grater to produce dried lime powder.

DRIED ORANGE PEEL: Available from Persian and Arab groceries, dried orange peel is used to flavor meat dishes. The peel must be boiled in several changes of water to remove bitterness.

EASTERN ORTHODOX CHURCHES: *See* Orthodox Churches

EGGPLANT: The advice that eggplants must be salted to draw out their bitterness and then rinsed before using has never applied to the long, slender pale and dark purple varieties we call Asian eggplants. It's also not necessary today for most Mediterranean or round, fat eggplants, because horticulturists have developed fruits that have fewer seeds and less bitterness than the old varieties.

EMMER: An early form of wheat with 28 chromosomes (as opposed to the 42 found in modern wheat), emmer is known as *hajor* in Armenia (see The Armenian World of Wheat, page 228).

ENGLISH CUCUMBER: *See* Cucumber

FARRO: In Italy, the whole unmilled wheat berries of emmer, einkorn, and spelt are all sold labeled as *farro*.

FARSI: The Persian language is called Farsi in Iran (as French is "français" in France and German is "Deutsch" in Germany). I use both words interchangeably in this book when referring to the national language of Iran. It is an Indo-European language, like Tajik and Kurdish, and all are members of the Iranic family of languages. It's written in Arabic script, which replaced the original Pahlavi script some time after the Arab conquest of Persia in AD 651.

FAT, RENDERED FAT: Fat gives flavor and makes most meats more tender. Rendered fat can be used as a cooking oil. To render fat, cut chunks of fat into small pieces and place in a heavy skillet with a little water over medium-low heat. As the fat starts to melt, raise the heat to medium. Pour off the fat into a dry glass container, cover, and refrigerate.

FENUGREEK, FENUGREEK POWDER, FENUGREEK LEAVES: Fenugreek is a leguminous plant (*Trigonella foenum graecum L.*) that is used as a spice and an herb in Greater Persia and beyond. Fresh fenugreek leaves are used in Indian cooking. Dried fenugreek leaves are a staple herb in the Persian pantry; see the recipes for Kerman-Bazaar

Lamb Stew, page 186, and Persian-Style Fried Fish Fillets, page 139, where they impart a maple syrup–like flavor. They are sold in Persian and Indian groceries, usually as a slightly coarse mixture of dried leaves and stems. Grind them to a powder in a mortar or crumble between your fingers before adding them to a dish. The hard, triangular, orange-yellow seeds are a legume, although when ground to a powder, they are used as a spice (*shemli* in Sorani Kurdish, *shanbalile* in Persian). Fenugreek powder is bitter on its own, but when combined with other ingredients, or toasted or cooked, it develops an enticing flavor with hints of maple syrup and an appealing nuttiness. *See* Blue Fenugreek.

FISH: A number of kinds of fish are mentioned in this book as candidates for various recipes, but please do not feel bound by my suggestions, and do substitute fish that you prefer. If you have access to a good fish store where they can tell you about the source of your fish, try to buy fish that are not on the endangered species list.

Alaskan Black Cod: The fish known in the United States, Canada, and the UK as black cod is more properly called sablefish (*Anoplopoma fimbria*). It is found in deep waters in the North Pacific (hence the frequent inclusion of the adjective "Alaskan" in its name). The fish is rich in oils and in omega-3 fatty acids (as wild salmon is). It is ideal for grilling and frying and when cooked can be flaked into large succulent pieces.

KERMAN, IRAN—*Peanuts, pistachios, sunflower seeds, and toasted, salted chickpeas, all favorite snacks, plus blocks of crude sugar, at a stall in the bazaar.*

Black Sea Bass: *Centropristis striata* is fished in the North Atlantic off the east coast of North America. It is a type of grouper (*Serranidae*). The flesh is white, firm, and mild-tasting and the fish available in shops weigh between 1½ and 3 pounds.

Branzino: *Dicentrarchis librax* is known as Mediterranean sea bass, European sea bass, spigolo, loup de mer, or sea dace. The flesh of this attractive slender fish is firm-textured. Branzino is often sold whole, but you can also find fillets. It can be grilled, baked, or fried. It is caught wild in the Mediterranean Sea and is farmed in various countries in the Mediterranean basin.

Haddock: *Melanogramus aeglefinus* is a North Atlantic species recognizable by the black stripe that runs the length of the fish. A firm-textured fish that has become increasingly expensive, haddock lends itself to grilling and frying.

Ling Cod: Although *Ophiodon elongatus* is also known as lingcod (one word) or buffalo cod, it's no relation to cod. Found off the west coast of North America, ling cod is prized for its firm flesh.

Pickerel: A freshwater fish like pike in the genus *Esox*, pickerel swims in lakes and rivers from Siberia to northern North America. Its firm, sweet flesh makes it ideal for grilling or frying, either whole or in fillets.

Snapper, Red Snapper: The name snapper is given to a number of fish, of which the most familiar— because it is so distinctive-looking and available in North America— is the red snapper (*Lutjanus campechanus*). It is a pinkish red in color and is fished in the Gulf of Mexico and in the Atlantic near the southern part of the United States. Other snappers have the same shape (a sloping profile from the nose up to the dorsal [back] fin), and some (the dog snapper and mutton snapper) have prominent canine teeth, unlike

NEAR MASSOULEH, NORTHERN IRAN—*Low, trimmed rows of tea bushes, a characteristic sight in the Caspian region, not only in Iran, but also in Azerbaijan.*

the red snapper. All have tender white flesh that is mild-tasting and a little delicate. They can be grilled or roasted or fried.

Striped Bass: Also known as rockfish or striper or Atlantic striped bass, *Morone saxatilis* is found along the Atlantic coast of North America. The fish spawn in fresh water upriver, but live as mature fish in the ocean. As the common names suggest, they have dark stripes running lengthwise along their sides. The fish can grow huge, up to thirty pounds. The flesh is white and mild-tasting and adapts to many kinds of cooking, from poaching to frying to grilling.

Sturgeon: A number of different varieties of fish in the *Acipenseridae* family are known as sturgeon. Sturgeon are native to cold and temperate waters in North America, Europe, and Asia, with the Caspian and Black Seas being most famous for sturgeon. Unfortunately, the sturgeon fishery in those waters is threatened by overfishing and pollution. Sturgeon are now being farmed in several places in North America for their roe—caviar— which commands a premium price. As a result, farmed sturgeon is now becoming increasingly available in North American fish markets. The flesh is firm and rich and slightly sweet, ideal for grilling, and a real treat.

GAZ, GAZO: The best and most famous examples of this much-loved form of nougat come from Isfahan in Iran, although the *gaz* made in Kurdistan is also prized. This is not surprising since an essential ingredient of authentic *gaz* is a sweet sap from the leaves

of tamarisk trees, which grow in the Zagros Mountains, along the border between Iran and Kurdistan. The sap is extruded by insects and left on the leaves, then gathered. Other nougat ingredients include egg whites, rose water, and pistachios.

GEORGIAN SPICE BLEND: This blend, *kmeli suneli* in Georgian, gives Georgian cooking its distinctive flavors. Homemade is usually best (see the recipe on page 28), but it is easier to buy it ready-made. Commercial versions from Georgia are becoming more available in North America. Some are salted and some not, so wait to taste before adding salt to the dish. Kalustyan's on Lexington Avenue in New York City carries it and will ship mail orders.

GHEE: *See* Butter

GOLPAR: *See* Angelica

GREEK-STYLE YOGURT: *See* Yogurt

HERBS: Fresh and dried herbs play a big role in the Persian culinary region. Fresh herbs are eaten at most meals as a kind of flavoring or salad accompaniment at the table (see Herb Plate, page 23). Both dried and fresh herbs have a role in cooking. Many of the recipes in this book give equivalents for fresh and dried herbs.

Often the dried forms of herbs are much stronger tasting per volume or weight than their fresh equivalents (dill, basil, and tarragon are among the exceptions). This means that the substitution for, say, a cup of fresh fenugreek leaves would be 2 tablespoons powdered dried fenugreek leaves.

Care of Fresh Herbs: Store fresh herbs in the refrigerator or another cool place in a tightly sealed plastic bag or wrapped in a damp paper towel inside a plastic bag. There's now better access to fresh herbs year-around, but if you have the space and the time, grow your own; many herbs thrive indoors in winter. It's always good to have the following fresh herbs on hand: mint, flat-leaf parsley, and tarragon. I also like to have dill and sorrel for an herb plate. Fresh fenugreek leaves are available in the spring from South Asian and Persian groceries. Other fresh greens that serve as both herbs and greens include scallions, watercress, and purslane.

HONEY, HONEY BEES: Honey, along with ripe fruit, is the original sweet. In this long-inhabited region, honey was used as a sweetener until sugar became more available. Thus, for example, the sweet syrup that drenches the cookies from Yazd (see Oasis Baqlava, page 295), though now made with sugar, would have originally been made from honey. Honey from the Caucasus is special, because the bees that make it are distinctive. The bees indigenous to the region are *Apis mellifera caucasia*, and beekeeping is widespread, especially in Georgia and Azerbaijan. The bees are darker colored than European and North American bees.

IBERIA (CAUCASUS): Iberia was an ancient kingdom in what is now eastern Georgia. Its first king ruled in the third century BC. from the town of Mtskheta, not far from present-day Georgia's capital, Tbilisi. The Roman general Pompey conquered Iberia, along with Armenia and Colchis, in 65 BC. The following four centuries saw control of Iberia pass back and forth between Persia and the West (first Rome and later Byzantium), as it lay on the border between their respective spheres of influence.

IRAN: The modern country of Iran has undergone enormous changes internally and in its relationship to the rest of the world over the last hundred years. Rich in oil and natural resources, with a well-educated population and a pride in its long history, Iran has been governed by a theocracy since the revolution of 1979. Before then, under the Shah, an absolute ruler, there was a push for modernization and secularization. In the early part of the twentieth century, Britain and Russia competed for control and influence there, while during the Second World War, Iran was occupied by the British. Some of that history may explain the paranoia that the current regime expresses about other powerful nations. The name Iran goes back in history, and is related to the word *aryan*. *See also* Persia.

JERUSALEM ARTICHOKES, SUNCHOKES: Now widely available in farmers' markets and large grocery stores, these hardy vegetables are the tubers of a variety of sunflower (*Helianthus tuberosus*) native to North America. The flavor is reminiscent of artichokes and the Jerusalem part of the name probably comes from *girosol*, the French word for sunflower. The plant is a perennial, and Jerusalem artichokes can survive in frozen ground, which makes them a hardy winter vegetable for people in the colder parts of North America. Scrub them thoroughly and then roast them, or slice and stir-fry them. (They can cause flatulence if not thoroughly cooked.)

JEWS, JEWISH POPULATIONS: Until recently, there were important Jewish populations living throughout the Persian culinary world. After the creation of the State of Israel in 1948, a number of Jews in the region made *aliyah*, and moved to Israel. Those in Georgia, Armenia, and Azerbaijan, like Jews in the rest of the Soviet Union, faced intermittent persecution but had great difficulty leaving until after the USSR broke up in the early 1990s. There are still small Jewish populations in each of the Caucasus countries. In Halabja, in Kurdistan, friends pointed out to me the Jewish part of town and told me that the last inhabitants had left in the 1980s, fleeing the violence of Saddam Hussein. In Iran, the Jewish population has a long history, going back to the time of Darius and the story of Queen Esther. It has faced intense persecution at times, and yet over the centuries survived and created a rich distinctive culture. Because of the intense hostility of the government toward Jews and toward Israel following the Islamic Revolution, many more Iranian Jews left in the 1980s, so that the Jewish population of Iran now numbers less than ten thousand people. Jewish versions of Persian rice dishes use oil rather than butter. For traditional Jewish versions of dishes from the Persian culinary region, consult Claudia Roden's *The Book of Jewish Food* (see Bibliography).

YEREVAN, ARMENIA—*Clay pots and wine jugs for sale at the weekly antiques market.*

KASHK: In Persian and Kurdish, it is *kashk*, while in Azeri and other Turkic languages, this is known as *qurut*; in Armenian, it's *chortan*. Whatever the language, *kashk* is a fermented-milk product, traditionally made from concentrated (cooked-down) whey, the liquid remaining after butter is made from milk. In some places, it is made from concentrated yogurt or sour milk. *Kashk* has a strong cheese-like flavor, and it adds pungent intensity to vegetable dishes and thick soups, rather in the same way that aged Parmesan does. In North America, *kashk* is most often available in the form of small dried white disks or balls with a strong cheesy aroma. Although they are designed to be kept at room temperature, I refrigerate mine on hot days. *To reconstitute dried kashk:* Soak the dried disks in warm water until softened a little. Chop them into small pieces, or transfer them, with the soaking liquid, to a food processor or blender and process to a paste.

Kashk is also available as a thick, off-white paste that, once opened, has a short shelf life and must be refrigerated. Unless you use it a lot, I recommend dried *kashk*.

KHACHAPURI: The Georgian word for a whole array of filled breads is *khachapuri*, with *puri* meaning bread; the best known are filled with cheese. The breads may be leavened by baking powder (see Cheese-Filled Quick Breads, page 251) or yeast (see page 253). The fillings are most commonly a mix of a fresh cheese with yogurt and perhaps herbs. The breads can also be filled with cooked kidney beans or other beans. The filling is usually enclosed in the bread but can also top it, as it does in traditional *adjaruli khachapuri*, which is boat shaped and filled with cheese, topped with an egg, and eaten drizzled with melted butter.

KURDISH, KURDISTAN, KURDS: The Kurdish people, who speak a number of different but related northwest Iranic languages, live in a large area that spreads over five countries: Iraqi Kurdistan, Iran, Armenia, northern Syria, and Turkey. Having arrived in the region from the east millennia ago, they are one of the largest groups in the world to be without a country. The main Kurdish peoples and languages are Sorani, sometimes called Gorani (in southern Kurdistan), Hawrami (in Iran and also in the Halabja area of Kurdistan), and Kurmanji (in northern Kurdistan, Turkey, and Armenia). Most Kurds are Sunni Muslims; some converted long ago to Yazidism (see Yazidis) and now consider themselves a separate people. A Kurdish nationalist movement has been active for years. The government of Turkey has waged war on the Kurds, occasionally negotiating settlements and then resuming hostilities. The Kurdish population in Armenia is small and still raises sheep and goats in a seminomadic style of life. In Iraqi Kurdistan, the Kurds are the majority, while in Iran, they have often been persecuted by the central government.

LEAF CELERY: Also known as celery leaf, herb celery, cutting celery, or Chinese celery, *Apium graveolens* var. *secalinum* is related to the familiar stalk celery we eat (*Apium graveolens* var. *dolce*), but is closer in both appearance and taste to wild celery, or smallage. The dark-green leaves resemble those of flat-leaf parsley and have a pungent celery flavor, and so should be cooked in dishes rather than eaten raw. The stems are narrow and hollow and are used as a flavoring for stock. Look for leaf celery in Chinese and eastern Mediterranean groceries.

LEEKS: Like garlic and onions, leeks, members of the *Allium* family, are a much-loved and useful vegetable in the Persian culinary region, especially in Iran. Their white and tender green parts are eaten, while the tougher tops of the leaves are best used as flavoring, in stocks or soups, for example. Leeks are cold-tolerant and easy to grow in temperate climates. To use them, first trim off the root ends, then slice the white and tender green parts and submerge them in cool water to remove sand and grit that might be caught between the layers of leaves. Drain the leeks and wash a second time to make sure they are free of sand. Leeks keep well in a cool place or the refrigerator.

LIMOO BASAHI, LIMOO OMANI: *See* Dried Limes

LOVAGE: *Levisticum officinale* is a tall perennial herb in the *Apiaceae* family that is native to Iran and the eastern Mediterranean. Its yellow-green leaves look a little like celery leaves and have a strong, almost hot, celery-like taste. The plant grows well in temperate climates and is widely used in Europe as well as in West Asia. The seeds are a spice and the leaves an herb.

MANTEAU: The word used in Iran for the basic outer garment worn by women, *manteau* is French for coat. In Iran it is generally knee-length and long-sleeved, with a front closing up to the neck. It's worn over long trousers or leggings, and with a head scarf. In urban environments, many women wear fashionable, very fitted manteaus with sleeves that are less than full-length, and they pair them with eye-catching shoes and head scarves. Women in more conservative environments wear a black manteau, a dark head covering, and, over that, a black chador, the full-length piece of cloth that hangs from the top of the head to the ground and is held closed in front with one hand.

MARIGOLD FLOWERS, POWDERED MARIGOLDS, MARIGOLD PETALS: In Georgia, the yellow tint that is so prized in the region comes from dried marigold flowers, not saffron. They give yellow color and a faint aroma to various dishes. The powder, known as *zaffran*, is an ingredient in the Georgian spice blend *kmeli suneli* (see page 28). In Azerbaijan, the same color is obtained from safflower blossoms, while in Kurdistan, turmeric gives a yellow hue to rice and other dishes. Dried marigold flowers are sold in Middle Eastern and Turkish groceries. Grind the petals to a powder in a mortar or crumble with your fingers.

MINT, DRIED MINT: The leaves of *Menthe piperita*, common peppermint, are well known in Europe and North America. In the Persian culinary world, mint is often used in its dried form, either as desiccated leaves or as a fine green powder. The Persian word for mint is *poonga*, which is also used in Kurdish. Mint is a perennial that grows well in most climates, even those with cold winters.

MONGOLS, MONGOL INVASIONS: The Mongols, an army on horseback, swept west from central Asia in the thirteenth century, first under Genghis Khan and then under the leadership of his sons and descendants. Genghis Khan had reached Persia and the Caucasus by the time he died in 1227. Subsequent invasions in the middle of the thirteenth century by later Mongol armies devastated parts of northern Iran, Kurdistan, Mesopotamia, and the Caucasus. The invaders laid waste to libraries, villages, monasteries, churches, and cities all across the region.

MORABA: The word *moraba* refers to a kind of thick jam, or fruit confit, throughout the region, no matter what language is spoken (see recipes on pages 318 and 321).

MULBERRIES: Known as *tut* in most of the languages of the Persian culinary world, mulberries grow on a flowering tree (*Morus*). They look a little like elongated raspberries or blackberries but have a firmer texture than either. The fruit may be red, white, or black: Red mulberries are native to North America, white mulberries to China, and black mulberries to Persia and the Caucasus. Both black and red mulberries have an intense, sweet-tart flavor, while the white ones are milder. Dried mulberries are sold in Persian grocery stores. The leaves of mulberry trees are food for silkworms. Local production of silk, formerly a household craft in the Caucasus, has pretty much disappeared (see Mulberry Country, page 339).

NAGORNO-KARABAKH: A mountainous region situated between Azerbaijan and Armenia, Nagorno-Karabakh was majority Armenian in population but lay within the Azerbaijan SSR in Soviet times. Before the Soviet Union broke up, there was a pro-Armenia vote, but after the breakup, a vicious war resulted in the exodus of Azeris from the territory. It is now controlled by Armenia, and there is a poorly observed cease-fire that results in soldiers being killed every year along the border. The cost of this "hot" cease-fire is huge for both Azerbaijan and Armenia in terms of manpower and money. It also means that the border crossings between them are closed.

NETTLES: The tender leaves and tips of young nettles (*Urtica dioica*) are used as a green vegetable in the spring, typically in soups and in *kuku'ye sabzi* (see Persian Greens Frittata, page 80). Once cooked, nettles lose their sting and have a flavor somewhat like spinach. They are rich in vitamins A and C, calcium, and iron.

NIGELLA: A spice with a slightly oniony flavor, nigella is the seed of an annual, *Nigella sativa*. The plant is related to carrots and Queen Anne's lace, with tiny teardrop-shaped seeds. Nigella seeds are sometimes mislabeled black cumin, although they are no relation to cumin. In South Asian stores, they are usually labeled *kalonji*.

NOU-ROZ: Nou-Roz is the Persian name for the New Year that is celebrated at the spring equinox by the people and countries of the Persian culinary region and beyond. It's now a secular public holiday in Azerbaijan, Iran, Iraqi Kurdistan, and Uzbekistan. In Zoroastrian tradition, the origin of the holiday, it marks the moment when the sun crosses into the north at the equinox, and it is a holy or religious celebration. In Iran, the festivities last for thirteen days.

OIL: The main cooking oil in the region these days is sunflower oil, extracted from the seeds of sunflowers grown for the purpose. And butter and butter-ghee are used in many dishes, such as Persian rices, as well as in sweet baking. Rendered lamb fat is used in some stews. Olive oil production is still small in Iran and smaller yet in Azerbaijan and Armenia, but olive oil is gaining in popularity, especially in Iran. *See also* Butter, Butter-Ghee; Fat, Rendered Fat; Olives; *and* Sunflower Oil.

OLIVES: Ancient records indicate that olive trees grew in Persia three thousand years ago, yet only recently have olives been eaten and olive oil used for cooking. Instead, the oil was used for soap and oil lamps. An article in the *Encyclopedia Iranica* (see Bibliography) traces olives and olive trees from earlier times, noting that the trees grew in southern Iran, in Khuzestan Province. But most olive groves are in Gilan Province, in the Caspian region, on the north slope of the Alborz Mountains. These days olives are big business: Iranian producers are selling olive oil as well as cured olives. Olive oil is also beginning to be used in Azerbaijan and in Armenia. In Armenia there is at least one plantation, begun by a Western Armenian from Syria who moved to Armenia, that is now producing oil and olives. Georgia and Georgians seem to have no history of olive production, despite the history of Greek colonization of the Black Sea coast over the millennia.

The other people who use olive oil are the Yazidis, for whom it is important in their religious ceremonies (see Yazidis). Consequently, at Yazidi temples there are large earthenware barrels of oil stored underground, to keep the oil cool. The Yazidis cultivate olive trees in Kurdistan and elsewhere to ensure a supply.

ORTHODOX CHURCHES: The Christians of Greater Persia speak many languages and are members of a number of different churches. Most are Orthodox, with the exception being the Chaldean Church (*see* Chaldeans). The Orthodox or Eastern Rite churches include the Armenian Apostolic Church (which is Oriental Orthodox), headquartered in Etchmiadzin, near Yerevan, and the Georgian Apostolic Autocephalous Orthodox Church (which is Eastern Orthodox), headquartered in Tbilisi. There are, as well, a number of Eastern Orthodox Assyrian churches, including the Assyrian Church of the East, now headquartered in the United States, and the Syrian Orthodox Church, headquartered in Damascus.

PAHLAVI: The ancient alphabet called Pahlavi was used to write Persian until the Arab conquest, when it was replaced by Arabic script. Pahlavi is also the family name of the Shah of Iran, who ruled from 1941 until he was deposed in the revolution of 1979.

PASTRY FLOUR: Sold as white or whole wheat flour, pastry flour has a low protein content (usually less than 9 percent), which results in a tender crust when used for pies and pastries.

PEPPERS: *See* Bell Peppers *and* Cayenne

PERSIA, PERSIAN, PERSIANS, PERSIAN EMPIRE: *Persia* is the name that the country now called Iran was known by for millennia. The name comes from the region called Fars, or Pars, which is the place of origin of the first Persian Empire. (The city of Shiraz is the capital of Fars Province in modern Iran.) Similarly, the language spoken in Iran is Persian. (In Persian, the word for the language is "Farsi.") Persian (and its predecessors, Middle Persian and Old Persian) is the language of poetry and literature. The great epic poem *Shahnameh*, written in Persian by the poet Ferdowsi between circa AD 977 and 1010, is credited with reviving and strengthening the Persian language when it had been weakened by the imposition of Arabic in public life following the Arab conquest. Most people in Iran speak of themselves as Persians when speaking English. They may say they are Iranian in terms of nationality, but their identity and their culture is Persian (unless they happen to be Assyrian, Kurdish, Armenian, or Azeri).

The first great Persian Empire, the Achaemenid Empire, was created by Cyrus the Great and lasted from 550 BC to 330 BC, when it fell to Alexander the Great. Rulers after that included the Seleucids and the Parthians. Another Persian Empire, the Sassanian Empire, lasted from AD 224 to AD 651, when it was defeated by the Arabs. *See* Arab Conquest.

PERSIAN CUCUMBER: *See* Cucumber

PERSIAN POETS: The list of Persian poets is long. Here are a few of the best known: Ferdowsi (935–1025) is famous for his epic poem *Shahnameh*, which describes the origins of Persia and is written in Persian, with a marked avoidance of words with Arab origins. This is significant, as it marks the start of a revival of Persian language after the Arab conquest of Persia. Ferdowsi's tomb is in Tus, outside Mashad in northeastern Iran. Omar Khayyam (1048–1131), who was born in the same region, is more famous among Persian and Arab scholars as a scientist and

mathematician than as a poet. Yet he is perhaps the best-known Persian poet among English speakers because of the famous nineteenth-century translation of his poetry by Edward FitzGerald, titled *The Rubaiyat of Omar Khayyam*. The poet Hafez (circa 1325–1389) lived and worked in Shiraz, now the site of his tomb. His poetry, well known and beloved by Persians, both celebrates the pleasures of love and wine and attacks hypocrisy. Saadi (circa 1210–1290), another poet from Shiraz, was widely traveled. He lived through the upheavals caused by the Mongol invasions and wrote about the people he met on his travels through India, central Asia, and Anatolia. Rumi (1207–1273), known as a Sufi mystic as well as a poet, wrote in Persian. His most famous work, composed in Konya (now in Turkish Anatolia), is *Mathnawi*.

PICKLES: Throughout Persia and the Caucasus, pickles—*torshi* in Persian—are a part of the herb plate that accompanies most meals and are eaten in the winter in place of fresh vegetables. White radishes are the most common pickled vegetable; they often are tinted pink with a little beet juice. In Georgia and Armenia, pickles tend to be made with salt brine rather than vinegar. Mild or slightly hot peppers, garlic, and onions are often pickled too. Persian-style pickles are widely available in specialty stores and some large groceries, as are pickled peppers, garlic, and onions.

POMEGRANATE JUICE: Unsweetened pomegranate juice is now available in North

MASSOULEH, NORTHERN IRAN— *Green olives from Iran.*

America. It's a good fallback when you don't have the time or inclination to squeeze your own, although I prefer to do so. If you buy pomegranate juice to cook down to molasses, check that the juice is pure, not sweetened or from concentrate.

POMEGRANATE MOLASSES: The cooked-down juice of tart (nonsweet) pomegranates is called pomegranate molasses or pomegranate concentrate in English. In this book, I use the term pomegranate molasses. It's an indispensable ingredient in the region, tart with a sweet edge that enlivens everything from salads (see page 48) to Persian *fesanjun* (see page 204) to marinades (see page 165). The name for the molasses in Persian is *robb-e-anar*, or pomegranate *robb* (*robb* meaning a thick or reduced syrup made of fruit juice). You can make your own (see page 335), but it's much easier to buy it. My favorite brand is Cortas, made in Lebanon.

POMEGRANATES: The fruit of a small tree, *Punica granatum*, pomegranates are native to Persia, where they are called *anar*. From late September until February, the trees bear fruit, which may be tart/sour or sweet. Pomegranates have a thick, leathery skin that prevents them from losing moisture in the dry climates in which they thrive. Inside, in chambers separated by bitter white pith, are bundles of seeds coated with juicy red pulp. Choose firm, heavy fruit, an indication that they are fresh and juicy. For eating and seed-collecting instructions, see page 333.

PULSES: *See* Beans and Lentils

PURSLANE: An annual plant (*Portulaca oleracea*) that is usually treated as a weed in North America, purslane is a valued green in the Persian culinary region and beyond. It is a succulent with thick reddish stems and leaves that have a slightly mucilaginous texture. It is cooked in soups (see Purslane

YEREVAN, ARMENIA—*Persian-style rice cooking pots, including copper ones. The shape, wider at the bottom and tapered inward toward the top, ensures a generous amount of bottom crust. It also helps funnel the steam and heat up into the piled rice at the last stage of cooking (see Basic Persian Rice, page 211).*

Soup, page 99) and eaten raw in salads. In North America, it's sold at some farmers' markets; once you recognize it, you may discover it growing wild by the roadside or in your own garden.

QANAT: *Qanat* is the Persian name for the underground water channels that for millennia have been used to bring water from the mountains to the desert while keeping it cool and preventing loss through evaporation. The system was developed in Persia and later spread into central Asia, including China's Xinjiang Province.

RENDERED FAT: *See* Fat, Rendered Fat

RICE, BROKEN RICE, RICE BROKENS, RICE FLOUR: Different types of rice have widely different characteristics. The most noticeable are the size of the grains (long, medium, or short) and the texture of the cooked rice (separate and almost dry grains or clinging/sticky grains). Basmati is long-grain and high in amylose, which means that it can absorb a lot of water as it cooks to a tender but firm texture, with grains that remain separate. (In contrast, lower amylose rices such as jasmine, or Japanese, rice have soft clinging grains.) When buying basmati rice, look for rice from India or Pakistan (Persian rice is unavailable in the West; if you find some, do buy it!). Make sure to wash it well, as directed in the recipes.

"Rice brokens," or "broken rice," refers to a low grade of rice that has, as the name indicates, a large proportion of broken grains (this happens during the

milling process). Brokens are used in dishes such as rice pudding, where their loose starches are desirable. You will find rice brokens in Asian grocery stores. You can substitute whole jasmine or other rices by breaking them a little in a food processor, or instead placing them on a cloth on a work surface, topping with another fine cloth, and rolling a heavy rolling pin over them to break them a little. The rice flour called for in this book is always the flour of regular rice (*not* glutinous rice). Please read the package carefully, since the two types of rice flour are *not* interchangeable.

ROSE HIPS: The fruits of roses are a familiar sight in the autumn when the flowers have faded; in their place are swollen rounds that look like berries and turn to red-orange, or sometimes a dark purple, as they ripen. These are rose hips, also known as rose haws. Rose hips are loaded with vitamin C and have a pleasing clean tartness, with a hint of sweet. They keep well if stored in a cool place. To use, boil them whole in a little water until soft, then press through a strainer and discard the debris. Use the thick juice extract to make jam or soup (see Rose Hip Soup, page 98).

ROSE PETALS: Dried rose petals are sold in Persian and Arab groceries and in gourmet shops. Crushed to a powder, they add a lightly perfumed flavor to dishes. Fresh rose petals are used in the production of rose water (see below).

ROSE WATER: Water scented by flowers, including roses, is produced by steam distillation. The city of Kashan in central Iran, not far from Qom, is a famous source of distilled scented waters (see photo, page 279). Rose water has an intense flavor and should be used with a light hand. It flavors many Persian sweets and can also add a distinctive, pleasing layer of flavor to savory dishes such as the soups called *ash*.

SAFFRON: Saffron threads are the stigmas of a crocus flower, *Crocus sativus*. Iran is the largest producer of saffron in the world. (For more on saffron production, see Seeking Saffron, page 25.) Saffron is available in spice shops and well-stocked grocery stores. The yellow color given by saffron is very much desired in the whole Persian-influenced world and beyond. True saffron is very expensive, but just a few threads are enough to dye a cup of warm water to use in rice and other dishes. (Less-reputable sellers may substitute safflower stigmas or other plant material for saffron and offer it at a lower cost; it will color the water but won't have the same aroma and flavor.)

SAFFRON WATER: The best way to transform saffron into a usable spice, flavoring, and coloring is to make saffron water (see page 27). The stigmas can be used whole or ground to a powder, then dissolved in a little hot water.

SAJ, SAJJ, SAAJ: A *saj* is a shallow round pan looks like a shallow wok and is used dome side up as a cooking surface for breads (see photo, page 246). They are used primarily by Kurds and other peoples in the Persian world and Turkey whose backgrounds are nomadic, as well as by the Bedouin and other Arab nomads.

SALEP: A powder that is used as a thickener in Persian ice cream (*bastani*) and in desserts, *salep* (*salaab* in Persian) is ground from the root of several plants in the *Orchis* family. When it traveled to England, it became the basis for a thickened drink known as *saloop*.

SAMANU, SAMANOO: In the days leading up to the Zoroastrian New Year, Nou-Roz, home cooks prepare *samanu*—a slightly sweet paste made of sprouted wheat that is mixed with water and cooked very slowly until thickened (see Zoroaster's Legacy, page 36).

SASSANIAN EMPIRE: The Sassanian dynasty ruled the Persian Empire from AD 224 until the time of the Arab conquest in AD 651.

SCALLIONS: A member of the *Allium* family, like onions, scallions are also known as green onions. They are immature; that is, they have tender green stems and a slender white bulb. The whites and tender greens are eaten raw or used in cooking.

SEA BUCKTHORN: A thorny shrub-tree (*Hippophae rhamnoides*) with clusters of intensely gold-orange berries (see photo, above), sea buckthorn is native to central Asia and Europe. The name probably derives from the fact that the bush thrives in salty soil near the seashore. It also does well in dry sunny

YEREVAN, ARMENIA—*Fresh barberries, left, and sea buckthorn berries, right, at the market.*

conditions, such as those in parts of the Caucasus and Iran. The tart, astringent berries, which are rich in oils, are pressed for juice and baked in pies. Because of its oil, sea buckthorn has recently become popular as an ingredient in skin creams and other cosmetics.

SHARBAT: *Sharbat* is a type of drink popular in Iran and Azerbaijan, made by mixing water and a fruit syrup and pouring it over ice. The fruit syrups are often aromatic with rose water or other flavorings.

SHIA ISLAM, TWELVERS: Ali and his sons Hassan and Husseyn (also spelled Hussein) were the first three imams in Shia Islam— that is, successors of the Prophet Mohammed.

The Shia believe that truth from God is transmitted by the imams, that the imams are infallible, and that the imams must be male descendants of Ali (whose wife was the Prophet's daughter Fatemah). As various Shia sects diverged, each developed a different interpretation of the

YAZD, IRAN—*Rock sugar made by hand in a shop in the Yazd bazaar, where liquid sugar is cooked down until crystallized. The crystals are sold in blocks like these or in sticks that can be dipped into tea.*

lineage. The Ismailis and the Twelvers are the largest groups of Shia. The Twelvers practice the version of Shia that is the dominant religion in Iran and has the most believers worldwide. They believe in a lineage of twelve imams, nine more after Husseyn, eight of them historic and the final twelfth, called Mahdi, being the imam still to come. The shrine in Mashad of the seventh imam, Imam Reza, who was martyred nearby, is the most holy shrine in Iran for Twelvers.

SKEWERS: Metal skewers are the traditional tool for cooking *shashlik*/kebabs; they can be found in Persian, Arab, and Turkish grocery stores and some housewares shops. The metal transmits heat to the center of the meat or vegetable for even cooking. Look for wide, flat skewers for kebabs made of ground meat (such as Iranian *koobideh kebab*; see page 161), and narrower ones for chunks of meat and vegetables, and for cooking fish *shashlik* (see page 156). When assembling skewers for grilling, be sure not to cram too much onto them, or the pieces of food may burn before the center is cooked.

SORANI, SORANI KURDS: There are several distinct populations of Kurds living in Kurdistan, Iran, Armenia, and Turkey who speak related but different languages. The Sorani Kurdish are the majority population in Kurdistan, notably in the southern half that includes the capital, Arbil, and the cities of Halabja and Sulaymaniyah. *See also* Kurdish, Kurdistan, Kurds.

SORREL: Common sorrel (*Rumex acetosa*) is a large-leafed perennial herb that grows well in temperate climates, especially if there is plenty of water. Sorrel leaves are tender and bright green, with a lemony citrusy flavor.

SOUR PLUMS, DAMSONS, TKEMALI PLUMS: There are a number of plums (fruits of the family *Prunus*) that are treasured for their tartness rather than their sweetness. They may be used fresh for sauces and condiments or dried whole or processed into fruit leather for longer keeping. Some sour plums are sour because they are picked before they have ripened, while others, which may be green, dark purple, or red, are distinctly sour when fully ripe. The unripe bright green plums, called *gojeh sabz* in Persian and *tkemali* in Georgian, are a springtime treat. Ripe dark sour or tart plums include damsons (*Prunus insititia*), which

are purple and slightly elongated, and the Georgian plum *tkemali* (*Prunus ceracifera*), a small red plum known in English as a cherry plum.

SPELT: A variety of wheat, spelt (*Triticum spelta*) grows well in tough terrains and can be used for bread making, as well as eaten as whole wheat berries. In Italy, it's one of the three varieties of wheat that are eaten as unmilled whole berries and known as *farro*; the other two are emmer and einkorn. *See also* Emmer.

SPOON JAM: From Serbia and Romania to Greece, Turkey, and the Caucasus, there is a tradition of serving thick, jam-like sweets on a spoon as a hit of sweet to eat with a glass of cold water or hot tea. Apricot Moraba (page 318) and Carrot Moraba (page 321) are made in the style of spoon jam.

SUFISM, SUFI ISLAM: A branch of Islam that is focused on the mystic, the ecstatic, and the interior, or spiritual, Sufism is shunned and despised by some Sunnis and Shia. Others accept it as a legitimate and rich school of Islam.

SUGAR, CONFECTIONERS' SUGAR, FINE SUGAR, ICING SUGAR, PEARL SUGAR, ROCK SUGAR: The recipes in this book call for familiar refined white sugar, the same sugar that is used to sweeten tea and coffee in the regions. Rock sugar, made of sugar syrup that has been heated to boiling and then cooked slower so it forms large golden crystals (see photo, above), is dipped into tea to sweeten it by some people in Iran. Specialized sugars called for include icing sugar, also known as powdered sugar, which is finely ground granulated sugar mixed with a little cornstarch (to prevent caking). Fine or superfine sugar, also called castor sugar or baker's sugar, is a finer version of granulated sugar and is valued for its quick-dissolving properties. Large crystal sugars include pearl sugar, which is used as a decorative topping because it doesn't melt in the oven's heat.

SULUGUNI: A traditional cheese of Georgia, originally from the Samegrelo region and now found in markets throughout the country, suluguni is, like mozzarella, a pulled-curd cheese, but it has a firmer texture and a slightly stronger flavor. It may be made from cow, goat, or buffalo milk and melts beautifully when heated. Mozzarella is a good substitute.

SUMAC: Sumac is a dark red spice from the drupes of a bush in the *Rhus* family. Ground sumac has a sparkling lemony taste. It's sprinkled on kebabs in Kurdistan, Iran, and Azerbaijan and used as a table condiment in Azerbaijan. It is also an essential ingredient in the eastern Mediterranean spice blend called zatar. The word *sumac* comes from the Aramaic word for red.

SUMMER SAVORY: An annual herb (*Satureja hortensis*), summer savory has small leaves and lilac-colored flowers. It is used in some Georgian dishes. In Europe it is usually part of the classic blend known as herbes de Provence. The less-common winter savory is a perennial.

SUNFLOWER OIL: The major cooking oil in the Persian culinary world, and produced throughout the region, sunflower oil comes from locally grown sunflowers (*Helianthus annuus*). Georgia produces about 50,600 tons, while Iran's production is about 96,000 tons. Sunflower oil is also produced in Armenia, Azerbaijan, and Iraq.

The oil is a mixture of linoleic and oleic acids (mono- and polyunsaturated fats). It may be pressed from the seeds or extracted from them using chemical solvents (refined). Pressed oil (called expressed) has a pleasant taste and a pale golden-yellow color, but it is less stable than refined oil and has a lower smoke point (about 220°F). Refined oil has a high smoke point, comparable to peanut oil (about 435°F), and it is more stable, but its flavor is less interesting. Sunflower oil is now widely available in North America. Use the refined oil for frying and try to find organic cold-pressed oil for use in salads and other dishes that are raw or cooked at low temperatures. If you wish, substitute a mild-tasting extra-virgin olive oil for sunflower oil, as indicated in the recipes.

SUNNI ISLAM: More Muslims are Sunni than Shia. The fundamental split between the two came soon after the death of Mohammed, when there was a dispute over the governance of the faithful. As with other faiths, there are many styles of Sunni Islam, some very moderate and others more extreme. Most Kurds in Kurdistan are Sunnis; about 15 percent of Azeris are Sunnis.

TAMARIND: The fruit of the tamarind tree (*Tamarindus indica*, native to Africa) has tart pulp that is used as a souring ingredient in cuisines from Iran to India and Southeast Asia. Tamarind trees grow well in tropical and subtropical climates and give generous shade. The name derives from the Arabic *tamar hindi*, meaning Indian date. Tamarind is believed to have powerful medicinal properties; it's rich in iron and potassium and in B vitamins (especially B1) and is thought to aid digestion.

The long pods (tamarind is a leguminous tree) encase the pulp, which is typically sold as dark, firm blocks packed with seeds and plant debris. The pulp must be cut into pieces and soaked in warm water for about 15 minutes to soften, then strained and pressed through a sieve to produce tamarind liquid; the seeds and other solids are discarded.

TAMERLANE: Tamerlane is the name by which the Turco-Mongol

MASHAD, IRAN—At an Afghan-style bakery near the Imam Reza shrine, one baker is slapping dough onto the wall of the tandoor oven, his face covered with a cloth against the heat; another is stretching dough; and the third is shaping dough into rounds.

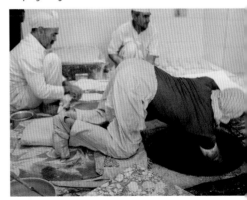

TWO HOURS WEST OF BAKU, AZERBAIJAN—*A kettle heats by the roadside. A man had parked his truck of watermelons nearby and was taking a break.*

conqueror Timur is best known. Tamerlane was born in the 1320s in what is present-day Uzbekistan. As head of an army of mixed Turkic and Mongol peoples, he used Islam as his uniting idea when he tried to reconquer and re-create the Mongol empire of Genghis Khan, which had fragmented in the late 1200s. Tamerlane successfully took control of Greater Persia and most of central Asia, as well as eastern Turkey, Iraq, and Afghanistan, murdering thousands and laying waste to cities, towns, and villages. His empire crumbled after his death in 1405.

TANDOOR: *Tandoor* is the most common name in English for a kind of oven that is widely used in the Caucasus, central Asia, the Middle East, and North Africa, as well as in northern India and Pakistan. Other names include *tonur, tandir, tanoor,* and the Georgian *toné.*

Tandoor ovens are barrel shaped with an inner surface of clay or cement on which breads bake. The oven is heated with a fire at the bottom, and when it is hot, shaped flatbreads (leavened or unleavened) are slapped onto the hot inner walls to bake. As the breads bake, they slowly detach from the oven walls, so that they can be lifted off when done. The ovens may be heated with wood or coal or, in more modern times, with gas. Some tandoor ovens are wide and less than three feet tall (see photo, page 371); others may be four to five feet tall with an opening that is no more than a narrow ten-inch slit in the front to give the baker access.

TARRAGON: The fragrant, fine-leafed perennial herb called tarragon (*Artemisia dracunculus* var. *sativa*) is a member of the sunflower family and is an essential herb in most of the Persian culinary world. Known as *tarhuna* in Georgian, *tarhun* in Persian, and *terhun* in Azeri, tarragon is best used fresh, since dried tarragon can be bitter and lack fragrance. Both French and Russian tarragon are available as garden plants; French tarragon has much more aroma and a brighter, sweeter taste, in the anise-licorice style.

TEA: Tea (*Camellia sinensis*) has been cultivated in Persia since the late nineteenth century. It's grown in the Caspian coastal areas of both Iran and Azerbaijan, and near the Black Sea coast of Georgia. Most is of the Assamese variety (*Camellia sinensis* var. *assamica*)—also known as Assam tea. The tea leaves are plucked in spring and summer, dried, and fermented to make black tea. Some are infused with herbal flavors. The word for tea all through the region is some version of the word *chai.* Tea is drunk clear and usually sweetened with plenty of sugar (see Tea with Sugar in Iran, page 300).

THYME: The wild thyme (*Thymus serpyllum*) that grows low to the ground in the mountains and uplands of Armenia is known as *urtz* in Armenian. The aroma emanating from its small mauve flowers is intense. The closest substitute for it is the Mediterranean thyme known as zatar, which is available at Middle Eastern groceries.

TOMATOES, FLESHY TOMATOES, ROMA TOMATOES: In the hot temperatures of the region, fleshy, thick-skinned tomatoes do best. Most of the recipes that call for tomatoes in this book specify fleshy or Roma tomatoes, which hold their shape when grilled.

TURMERIC: Turmeric comes from the rhizome of an ancient plant, *Curcuma longa*, native to India. The powder made from the dried rhizome is used in the cooking of southern Iran and Kurdistan, as well as in many other parts of the world. It is often rubbed on fish before cooking. Turmeric has antibacterial and anti-inflammatory properties.

TWELVERS, TWELVER ISLAM: *See* Shia Islam

URARTU: Urartu is the name of a kingdom dating back to the

Iron Age that was situated in the Armenian highlands near Lake Van (currently part of eastern Turkey). In the Bible, the same kingdom is called Ararat. Urartu is the precursor of present-day Armenia. *See* Armenia.

URTZ: *See* Thyme

VANILLA SUGAR: To make vanilla sugar, bury a vanilla bean in a jar of sugar for several weeks; its aroma will perfume the sugar.

VERJUICE, VERJUS: The flavoring made from the sour juice of unripe (green) grapes is called verjuice or *verjus*. It is produced wherever grapes are grown, whether the grapes are used for winemaking or for something else. Verjuice is used as a souring agent in savory dishes in Armenia, Azerbaijan, Iran, and Georgia.

WALNUTS, GREEN WALNUTS: A number of trees in the genus *Juglans* produce a husked drupe (technically a fruit, not a nut), inside of which is a tough-shelled pit that protects a symmetrical kernel. The whole fruit is a walnut, but most of us use the

TBILISI, GEORGIA—*Aged farm cheeses made of cow's milk are a familiar sight at Georgian markets.*

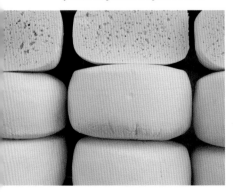

term *walnut* for the kernel that lies at its center. The best known walnut is *Juglans regia*, which is called both the Persian and English walnut. Others include the black walnut, which is native to North America, and the butternut. Walnuts are rich in oil and so once out of their shell should be kept in a cool place or in the refrigerator. In the Caucasus and elsewhere, immature, or green, walnuts are preserved in syrup (walnut *moraba*) or pickled.

WATERCRESS: A semiaquatic plant native to Europe and Asia, watercress (*Nasturtium officinale*) is rich in minerals, including iron, calcium, and magnesium, and vitamins. (Despite the Latin name, it is not related to nasturtiums, the flowering annuals.) With its refreshing, peppery taste and intensely green leaves, it's eaten as a leafy green and used as an herb. Keep it loosely wrapped in a plastic bag in the refrigerator and use it as soon as possible.

WHEAT, WHEAT BRAN, WHOLE WHEAT, WHEAT BERRIES: The common wheat grown today is *Triticum aestivum*. It's most often milled into all-purpose or whole wheat flour. Because the bran and germ have been removed from it, all-purpose flour keeps better than whole wheat flour (which still includes the bran and germ), but it has a less distinctive flavor. Wheat bran is sold at health food stores and should be refrigerated. The whole (unmilled) wheat grains are called wheat berries. Hard wheat berries take much longer to cook than soft wheat berries.

Wheats are categorized according to their protein content, often described as

hardness. Hard wheats are those with 11 to 14 percent protein. The flour made from them is often used for breads and stretched doughs. Soft wheats, with 9 percent or lower protein, yield flours more suitable for cake or pastry. In North America, all-purpose flour can be used for both bread and cakes because it has about 12 percent protein.

WHEY: Whey is the liquid that is left when milk is churned into butter. It is also the term for other nearly clear liquids drained from other milk products (for example, the liquid that is released when yogurt is drained to thicken it; *see* Yogurt). Whey makes a tart, refreshing drink. It can also be dried and the solids cultured to make *kashk* (see Kashk).

YAKHCHAL: The ice-storage houses in Iran called *yakhchal* were part of the *qanat* system of underground water channels (see Qanat). Water flowed down from the mountains and under the desert in *qanat* tunnels and in the winter was left to freeze in channels on the north (cold) side of the storage houses, even in cities as far south as Kerman. It was then broken up and stored in pits.

YAZIDIS, YEZIDIS, EZIDIS: An ethno-religious community based originally in northern Iraq, with populations in northern Syria, Turkey, Armenia, and Georgia, Yazidis number in total fewer than 1,000,000 and perhaps closer to 500,000. They seem to be ethnically Kurdish but have existed as a distinct group since the eleventh century. Their beliefs derive in part from

Zoroastriansim (fire and the sun are all-powerful) and other early Iranic religions, as well as from elements of Christianity and Sufi Islam. The revered founder of the Yazidi faith, Sheik Adi, who died in the early twelfth century, was a Sufi. His tomb and shrine, in Lalish in northern Iraqi Kurdistan, not far from Mosul, are a place of pilgrimage for Yazidis.

The Yazidis' supreme being is Melek Tawus, an archangel (one of seven created by God to run the world) who sinned but was forgiven by God. His symbol is a peacock. Several other symbols are distinctively Yazidi: the twenty-one-pointed sun, which appears on the Kurdistan flag and on Yazidi churches; and a conical, sharp-pointed roof, shaped like the top of a steeple, that has ridges and represents the rays of the sun. Olive oil is important to worshippers, being used as the oil for lamps and for other ritual purposes. Consequently, the Yazidis in Kurdistan grow olives and also import olive oil from Turkey for use in worship. In Lalish, I saw huge quantities of stored oil and oil lamps in the mother temple.

The sun, water, earth, and the seasons are all central to the religion. The principal festivals are in November, toward the end of the solar year, and at the full moon after the spring equinox, when flowers and other offerings are hung on buildings and placed by springs and waterways.

Because the Yazidis' principal deity is a fallen angel, extremist outsiders, both Muslim and Christian, have in times of strife labeled them devil-worshippers and conducted murderous campaigns against them.

YOGURT, THICK YOGURT: Yogurt is made from milk, whether cow, sheep, water buffalo, or goat, that is cultured with bacteria. In North America, it is often sold as a reduced-fat product, but in the Persian culinary world, full-fat plain yogurt is prized, used to make cooling drinks (see page 309), as a condiment, and as an ingredient in soups (see page 94). The word for yogurt in Persian is *mast*; in Georgian, it's *matsoni*. When used as a sauce or as part of a vegetable dish such as a *borani* (see page 55), yogurt is usually drained (see below) so that it becomes thicker. When thick yogurt is called for, you can substitute what is sometimes labeled Greek-style yogurt in North America.

To make thick yogurt, you need to drain it. I set a sieve over a bowl, line the sieve with a thin tea towel or cotton cloth, add the yogurt, and let it drain. I have friends who spoon the yogurt into a conical coffee filter, in its holder, placed over a bowl. Whatever method you use, let it drain for 30 minutes or longer. Once the whey is drained, the thickened yogurt tastes sweeter. Serve it lightly salted (less than ½ teaspoon salt for a cup of thick yogurt) if you like, and if serving it as a side condiment, stir in a little dried mint or some finely chopped fresh mint. You can also serve it as an accompaniment to pastries or fruit, in which case you might want to sweeten it with a little honey.

ZATAR: *See Thyme*

ZOROASTRIANS, ZOROASTRIANISM: Zoroastrianism is a religion that dates back to the writings of Zoroaster, who was born sometime before 600 BC (scholars cannot agree on his dates) in what is present-day Uzbekistan. In his scriptures, the Avesta, Zoroaster described a founder god, Ahura Mazda, composed of being and mind, who created order and wisdom out of chaos (the religion is sometimes referred to as Mazdaism). Scholars trace some of the thinking to Indian Brahmanic Hindu scriptures and some to earlier religions whose gods included Mithra and Anahita. Zoroastrianism was the official religion of the Persian Empire under the Achaemenids and the Parthian and Sassanian empires. It thus had a widespread influence on Jewish, Christian, and Islamic theology.

In this religion, the sun's cycle and the seasons give their names to the months, and the New Year, Nou-Roz, comes at the spring equinox. Nou-Roz (in various transcriptions) is celebrated in many countries in central Asia and Greater Persia. Water and fire are both considered purifying elements. A fire is kept burning continuously at all Zoroastrian temples (hence the term "fire temple"). There are active Zoroastrian temples in Iran in Tehran and Yazd, and inactive but restored temples, now museums, in Baku, Azerbaijan, and Tbilisi, Georgia. After the Arab conquest of Iran, many Zoroastrians left and eventually settled in India, where they are known as Parsis.

ANNOTATED BIBLIOGRAPHY

I'VE ENJOYED THE PROCESS OF IMMERSING MYSELF IN THE CULTURE, history, and geography of Iran, Kurdistan, and the Caucasus. Below is a list of books and articles I have found interesting and illuminating. Some are online resources, including articles and various websites. I also consulted several of the books that I coauthored with Jeffrey Alford: *Flatbreads & Flavors: A Baker's Atlas* (Morrow, 1995), *Seductions of Rice* (Artisan, 1998), and *Home Baking* (Artisan, 2003).

I've picked out a few of the many Persian food blogs I especially like. I used Lonely Planet guidebooks and a number of different maps and phrase books on my travels in the region. And I've listed a few recent films from Iran. Each of them gives a sense of daily life and of the way people interact with one another these days, both at home and out in public.

BOOKS

Abercromby, John. *A Trip Through the Eastern Caucasus*. London: Edward Stanford, 1889.
Travels of a Finno-Ugrian scholar from Tbilisi, Georgia, to Sheki, Azerbaijan; available online at Google Books.

Amiraslanov, Tahir, and Leyla Rahmanova. *The Azerbaijani Kitchen: A Cookbook*. London: SAQI, 2014.
Recipes with photos; classic Azeri dishes.

Batmanglij, Najmieh. *Food of Life: Ancient Persian and Modern Iranian Food and Ceremonies*. Washington, DC: Mage Publishers, 2011.
Many classic Persian recipes; photos and clear instructions.

Dijan, Donna. *Maman's Homesick Pie: A Persian Heart in an American Kitchen*. Chapel Hill, NC: Algonquin, 2011.
A memoir with recipes, by an American chef whose home culture is Persian; a nice blend.

Brailashvili, Nino. *Georgia as I Saw It: Ethnographic Sketches*. Tbilisi: Khelnovneba, 1990.
Sketches and watercolors of houses and people all over Georgia, by an artist-ethnographer who lived and worked in Georgia from about 1920 onward; with notes in English, Russian, and Georgian.

Buchan, James. *The Persian Bride*. New York: Mariner, 2002.
A novel that is part romance, part thriller, and a lovely appreciation of Persian culture.

Bullough, Oliver. *Let Our Fame Be Great: Journeys Among the Defiant People of the Caucasus*. New York: Basic, 2010.
More than a travel book, this is an exploration through the writings of early travelers of the peoples and history of the Caucasus; very rewarding.

Crowther, Yasmin. *The Saffron Kitchen*. New York: Viking, 2006.
A novel set in England and Iran about memory and tradition; very moving.

Dalrymple, William. *From the Holy Mountain*. London: Flamingo, 1998.
A beautifully written travel book that weaves in much history, as the author visits and meditates on the long history of the Orthodox/Eastern churches and monasteries, starting in Mount Athos and ending at Mount Sinai.

Elkana. *Forgotten Crops*. Tbilisi: Elkana, 2008.
An illustrated guide to lesser-known traditional crops with recipes; Elkana is an NGO dedicated to preserving landrace and traditional crops of Georgia.

———. *Making Wine in Kvevri: A Unique Georgian Tradition*. Tbilisi: Elkana, 2011.

Feiring, Alice. *For the Love of Wine: My Odyssey Through the World's Most Ancient Wine Culture.* Lincoln, NE: Potomac, 2016.
A thorough look at winemaking in Georgia.

Floor, Willem. *History of Bread in Iran.* Washington, DC: Mage, 2015.
Anthropology, history, and bread making in Iran, with photographs, by an economist and a scholar of the region who is also a baker; a valuable book.

Ghanoonparvar, M. R. *Persian Cuisine, Book 1: Traditional Foods.* Costa Mesa, CA: Mazda, 1982.
One of the earliest Persian cookbooks published in the United States, with practical and clear recipes.

——. *Persian Cuisine, Book 2: Regional and Modern Foods.* Costa Mesa, CA: Mazda, 1984.
This follow-up offers recipes adapted by Iranian-Americans to the ingredients and style of life they found in the United States.

Goldstein, Darra. *The Georgian Feast: The Vibrant Culture and Savory Food of the Republic of Georgia.* rev. ed. Berkeley: University of California Press, 1999.
A breakthrough book that introduced Georgian food to the West; first published in 1993.

Grigson, Jane. *Jane Grigson's Fruit Book.* New York: Atheneum, 1982.
A wonderful reference, indispensable whenever fruit is in the kitchen.

Holland, Tom. *Persian Fire: The First World Empire and the Battle for the West.* London: Little Brown, 2005.
Sets Persian history in perspective and relates it to European history.

Housden, Roger. *Saved by Beauty.* New York: Broadway, 2011.
A travel memoir of Iran by an American poet and romantic; a fine read.

Kacharava, Darejan, and Guram Kvirkvelia. *Wine, Worship, and Sacrifice: The Golden Graves of Ancient Varni.* New York: Institute for the Study of the Ancient World at NYU, 2008.
Archaeologists' view of a dig in Georgia and its significance; fascinating.

Kaplan, Robert D. *The Revenge of Geography: What the Map Tells Us About Coming Conflicts and the Battle Against Fate.* New York: Random House, 2012.
Kaplan is a longtime staff writer at *The Atlantic.* He has an interesting take on the connections between geography and power, very relevant when thinking about Iran and the Caucasus region.

Karny, Yo'av. *Highlanders: A Journey to the Caucasus.* New York: Farrar, Straus and Giroux, 2000.
A remarkable book of travel and ethnography that explores the patchwork of peoples of the Caucasus Mountains, neighbors of Georgia and Azerbaijan, with loving care.

Klinec, Jennifer. *The Temporary Bride: A Memoir of Love and Food in Iran.* London: Virago, 2014.
A gracefully written memoir with recipes about a young woman's travel in Iran, which brought her love and a husband.

Kordy, Gohar. *An Iranian Odyssey.* London: Serpent's Tail, 1991.
A memoir of growing up in Iran in the 1950s and '60s by a woman who lost her sight as a child.

Laudan, Rachel. *Cuisine and Empire: Cooking in World History.* Berkeley: University of California Press, 2013.
Food history from the beginning, tracing the cross-connections and the central importance of food supply in wars, revolutions, and the growth of empires.

Layard, Austen Henry. *Nineveh and Its Remains: With an Account of a Visit to the Chaldean Christians of Kurdistan, and the Yezidis, or Devil-Worshippers* Vol. 1. Cambridge: Cambridge Library Collection, 2013 (originally published in 1849).
A fascinating account by one of the earliest English travelers to the region.

Margvelashvili, Julianne. *The Classic Cuisine of Soviet Georgia: History, Traditions, and Recipes.* New York: Prentice Hall, 1991.
The first book I found published in English about Georgian cooking.

McLagan, Jennifer. *Odd Bits: How to Cook the Rest of the Animal.* New York: Ten Speed, 2011.

Useful book for getting comfortable with cooking the less usual "bits."

Ministry of Agriculture, Georgia. *Georgian Cheese.* Tbilisi: Anakila, 2010.
Describes cheese-making techniques and regional cheeses of Georgia, with photos; in English and Georgian.

Molavi, Ashvin. *The Soul of Iran: A Nation's Journey to Freedom.* New York: Norton, 2002.
Memoir and history, presented in the form of travels and stories from people the Iranian-born author met on his travels. Rich.

Nabhan, Gary. *Cumin, Camels, and Caravans: A Spice Odyssey.* Berkeley: University of California Press, 2014.
The spice trade and the cross-influences it initiated, told in stories of the author's travels.

Nafisi, Azar. *Reading Lolita in Tehran: A Memoir in Books.* New York: Random House, 2008.
First published in 2003, a big best seller that gives a sense of the oppressiveness of life in Iran in the years immediately after the 1979 revolution.

———. *Things I've Been Silent About: Memories of a Prodigal Daughter.* New York: Random House, 2010.
A memoir of growing up in Tehran with a domineering and difficult mother; nuanced and full of life and insight.

Ohanesian, Aline. *Orhan's Inheritance.* Chapel Hill, NC: Algonquin, 2015.
A novel about the Armenian genocide, describing Armenian village life before the genocide and a survivor's memories afterward.

Pezeshkzad, Iraj. *My Uncle Napoleon.* Trans. by Dick Davis. New York: Modern Library, 2006.
A translation, first published in 1996, of a well-known Persian comic novel published in Persian in Iran in 1973 and still in print. The story is set in the 1940s in a family compound in Tehran.

Polk, William R. *Understanding Iran.* New York: Palgrave Macmillan, 2009.
A good basic introduction to the history, geography, and practical aspects of life in Iran.

Roden, Claudia. *The Book of Jewish Food: An Odyssey from Samarkand to New York.* New York: Knopf, 1996.
Recipes and stories from the Jewish kitchens of Iran and Georgia, among many other places; a masterpiece.

Russell, Gerard. *Heirs to Forgotten Kingdoms: Journeys into the Disappearing Religions of the Middle East.* London: Simon & Schuster, 2014.
The author of this book is as fascinated as I am by the survival of a variety of peoples and cultures in the region. The book looks at a number of "smaller" religions in the area, including the Yezidis and Chaldeans.

Said, Kurban. *Ali and Nino.* London: Vintage, 2000.
A classic novel first published in German in 1937, this is a cross-cultural romance (between a Georgian Christian and an Azeri Muslim) set in Baku. The identity of the pseudonymous author is still a question.

Sarshar, Houman, ed. *Esther's Children: A Portrait of Iranian Jews.* Beverly Hills, CA: Center for Iranian-Jewish History, 2002.
With many archival photos, this gives a sense of the history of the Jewish community in Iran, especially in the last two hundred years.

Satrapi, Marjane. *The Complete Persepolis.* New York: Pantheon, 2007.
A memoir in graphic form by an Iranian artist, this is probably the easiest way to understand the outlines of the twentieth-century history of Iran, from the British and American interference that assisted the Shah by deposing the elected government of Mossadegh in 1952 to the background of the Islamic Revolution of 1979, the Iran-Iraq War, and beyond.

Scott, James C. *The Art of Not Being Governed.* Singapore: NUS, 2010.
An interesting analysis of people on the margins; Southeast Asia is the main area he talks about, but it applies to the peoples of the Caucasus too, caught between empires.

Shaida, Margaret. *The Legendary Cuisine of Persia.* London: Penguin, 1992.
A reliable, award-winning book of recipes by an Englishwoman who married a Persian and lived in Iran for a long time.

Skinner, Peter F. *Georgia: The Land Below the Caucasus.* New York: Narikala, 2014.
Sets out the history of Georgia over the centuries, making clear the complexities.

Slavs and Tatars, eds. *Slavs and Tatars Present Molla Nasreddin: The Magazine That Would've Could've Should've.* Zurich: JRP/Ringier, Christopher Keller Editions, 2011.
A compendium of many of the best articles and cartoons from a magazine published in the Caucasus between 1920 and 1933, remarkable in its openness and satirical content. (A new edition is forthcoming.)

Uvezian, Sonia. *The Cuisine of Armenia.* Rev. ed. New York: Hippocrene, 1996.
Recipes that are primarily western Armenian—that is, from the Armenian traditions that flourished in Turkey until the genocide, as well as in Syria and Lebanon. Originally published in 1974.

Vaughan, John, and Catherine Geissler. *The New Oxford Book of Food Plants.* 2nd ed. Oxford: Oxford University Press, 2009.
An indispensable illustrated book of fruits and vegetables; beautiful as well as informative.

Von Bremzen, Anya, and John Welchman. *Please to the Table: The Russian Cookbook.* New York: Workman, 1990.
A Russian perspective on the cuisines of the USSR; the book includes Azeri, Armenian, and Georgian recipes.

Ward, Terence. *Searching for Hassan: A Journey to the Heart of Iran.* New York: Anchor, 2002.
A memoir of childhood in Iran and of a return to Iran after the revolution; tender and appreciative.

Wearing, Alison. *Honeymoon in Purdah: An Iranian Journey.* Toronto: Knopf, 2000.
Travels in Iran by a young single Canadian woman who passed as married to the young man she traveled with.

Wynne, Antony. *Persia in the Great Game.* London: John Murray, 2003.
The story of Sir Percy Sykes, a British soldier who lived in Iran as consul and spy from 1906 to 1918.

Zubaida, Sami, and Richard Tapper, eds. *A Taste of Thyme: Culinary Cultures of the Middle East.* London: Tauris Parke, 2000.
Many excellent essays relating to the food history and culture of the Persian culinary region, as well as neighboring areas.

ARTICLES

Anonymous. "Weeping in Tehran; Scenes from the Uprising." *Harper's Magazine,* vol. 319, no. 1912 (September 2009): 70–76.

August, Oliver, et al. "Special Report on Iran." *The Economist,* vol. 14, no. 8911 (November 2014): special insert.

Cockburn, Andrew. "A Very Perfect Instrument: The Ferocity and Failure of America's Sanctions Apparatus." *Harper's Magazine,* vol. 327, no. 1960 (September 2013): 50–57.

Oborne, Peter, and David Morrison. "Changing Partners: Can Hassan Rouhani End the Iranian Impasse?" *Harper's Magazine,* vol. 327, no. 1961 (October 2013): 73–74.

Philliou, Christine: "The Armenian Genocide and the Politics of Knowledge," http://www.publicbooks.org/nonfiction/the-armenian-genocide-and-the-politics-of-knowledge.
A lengthy discussion of Ronald Grigor Suny's *History of the Armenian Genocide* (Princeton, NJ: Princeton University Press, 2015).

http://darragoldstein.com/files/2012/12/Darra_Goldstein_Georgia.pdf
Darra Goldstein's book on Georgia in a different form.

http://foodperestroika.com/2013/12/05/imeretian-cheese-the-gateway-cheese-from-georgia/
A story about Georgian cheese from Emereti.

http://georgianwine.gov.ge/eng/text/126/
Georgian government wine info: clear and complete.

http://www.ifrj.upm.edu.my/21%20(01)%202014/52%20IFRJ%2021%20(01)%202014%20Aliakbarku%20494.pdf
An interesting paper from Iran on the health benefits of *doshab* (grape syrup), which has antioxidant properties.

http://www.kvevri.org/the-wine-making-method/
Kvevri and the history of Georgian wine, by Dr. David Chichua, lecturer at Telavi State University, Georgia.

http://www.smithsonianmag.com/travel/the-great-georgian-fruit-hunt-68708316/?all&no-ist
A story about fruit diversity in the Caucasus.

http://www.thefreshloaf.com/node/36357
/persianiranian-barbari-bread
Persian breads: Omri at The Fresh Loaf
writes in detail about *barbari* bread.

https://www.youtube.com/watch?feature=player
_embedded&v=i3Kq-9CFIuQ
A video of an olive oil grower near Meghri in
southern Armenia.

GENERAL ONLINE RESOURCES
ON FOOD, TRAVEL, AND CULTURE

http://www.armeniapedia.org/wiki/Main_Page
Loads of history and info about Armenian
culture.

http://cookedearthblog.com/2011/05/23
/republic-of-azerbaijan/
Various food-related explorations in
Azerbaijan.

http://www.georgianjournal.ge/
Updated news on Georgia.

http://gernot-katzers-spice-pages.com/engl
/Trig_cae.html and general opener page:
http://gernot-katzers-spice-pages.com/engl/
An indispensable online spice resource, with
information on blue fenugreek and Georgian
spice blends.

http://www.indexmundi.com/agriculture
/?country=az&commodity= apples&graph
=production
For agricultural statistics and information.

http://www.iranicaonline.org/
Encyclopedia Iranica, a wonderful resource
on many aspects of Persian history and culture,
including food plants.

http://www.kaukaz.pl/caucasus-news.php
Recent news updates on the Caucasus.

http://www.news.az/
Azeri news.

WEBSITES AND BLOGS ABOUT
PERSIAN FOOD

http://www.aashpaz.com/newwordpress
/persian-cuisine-culinary-history/

http://www.mypersianfeast.com/

http://www.mypersiankitchen.com/

http://www.thespicespoon.com/

http://turmericsaffron.blogspot.ca/

In general, have a look at www.roadsand
kingdoms.com, for there are often articles, with
photographs, on out-of-the-way places and
people, including a number on the Caucasus,
Iran, and Kurdistan. And, to help contextualize
the Persian culinary region, look for culinary
writing about neighboring Turkey. One of the
best sources will be *Istanbul and Beyond* by
Robyn Eckhardt and David Hagerman, to be
published in 2017 by Rux Martin/Houghton-
Mifflin Books

FILMS

Iran has a wonderfully sophisticated film
culture. Recent films I have found illuminating
include:

A Separation, directed by Asghar Farhadi
(2012)
A portrait of a marriage coming apart in an
ordinary family in Tehran.

Red Rose, directed by Sepideh Farsi (2014)
A romantic thriller set in the middle of the
2009 failed revolution.

Tales, directed by Rakhshan Bani-E'temad
(2014)
A set of short stories about ordinary people.

Jafar Panahi's Taxi, directed by Jafar Panahi
(2015)
A lovely film in which the director acts
himself, driving a taxi in Tehran and having
conversations with the people he picks up.

ACKNOWLEDGMENTS

THE WORLD OF PERSIAN-INFLUENCED CUISINE IS A HUGE ONE, STRETCHING over vast distances in time and space. And so perhaps it's no wonder that the list of people to whom I owe thanks for help and inspiration with this book is a long one.

First, though, a word about the origins of the book. I firmly believe that through sharing food and food wisdom we can connect imaginatively and politically with people in other countries and situations. In the summer of 2012, I was thinking about the way in which the mainstream media causes people to demonize countries ruled by totalitarian regimes. I realized that it was time I wrote about Persian culinary tradition, to try to put a human face on the people of Iran, and to show the connection and contribution of Persian food culture to other cuisines and peoples in the region.

When I first proposed this book in a phone call to my editor, Ann Bramson, she was enthusiastic and took the idea to Peter Workman, the founder of Artisan's parent company. I am so grateful to him for having the confidence to sign the book, despite the rocky relationship that then existed between the United States and Iran.

Starting in spring 2013, I made trips to Georgia, Iran, Armenia, Azerbaijan, and Iraqi Kurdistan. And everywhere I had interesting conversations about food and politics and agriculture, past and present. I don't know the names of many of the people whom I met and learned from; I am indebted to a host of market vendors, farmers, travelers, and others with whom I had casual but valuable encounters.

In Georgia, Tamar Babuadze, who introduced herself to me on Facebook long ago, has become a great friend. She's helped me understand food words, plant names, and home-cooking traditions, and through her I have met a wonderful circle of like-minded friends in Tbilisi and beyond. I thank her and her family, including her mother-in-law, Dali, and Dali's sister Chuka, for their generous hospitality. Big thanks also to Elene Asatiani for introductions and miles of driving, and to her mother and grandmother in Kutaisi. Thanks to Paul Rimple and Justyna Melnikiewicz; Ana Mikadze-Chikvaidze the cheesemaker; and Gulnazi "Ana" Khutsishvili in Stepandsminda.

I thank Chamala and Matanet, and Chamala's husband, Ilgar, in Sheki, Azerbaijan, for recipe talk and patient teaching. Big thanks also to Jairan and her husband, Dadash, with whom I stayed in Lahich, for kitchen talk, cooking instruction, and more. Thanks to Ajdar and the other men I met in the apple orchard above Lahich, who plied me with food and drink both there and in the mountains; to Elvin, who drove me around for a couple of days out of Baku; and to the many strangers of all kinds who engaged with me while I was in Azerbaijan.

In Armenia, Sonia Tashjian shared wisdom and recipes from her years of research into Armenian culinary traditions. I bow to her in gratitude. I thank Anahit Stepanian, with whom I stayed in Yerevan; Ana Arshakyan of Tatev; many of the older villagers of Tatev who invited me in for shots of *tutovka*; Gayane Simonyan and her family in Yerevan; Armin for several days of driving; Gozeh and her son Georgi Tamoyan in the Yazidi village of Raya Taza; and Tsayhlik and her family in the village of Melikgyugh, who taught me about Armenian *gata*, bread, and a lot more.

In Kurdistan, I owe thanks to all in Ayub Nuri's extended family, and in particular to his mother, Hoshida; his sisters Dila the bread maker and Asti, and their families; and his brothers Mokhtar and Starr, all in Halabja. Much gratitude to Ayub's older brother Yusef; Yusef's wife, Cheeman; and their children, with whom I stayed in Sulaymaniyah, and to their Hawrami friend Hillal. Thanks also to Najad and his family, to Lidia and her sister-in-law Shler and family, and to Wazira Jala. Thank you to Shwan, who took me to meet Kurdish Syrian refugees at a camp outside Sulaymaniyah.

Before going to Iran, I had enormous help from Hamid and Anoosheh of IranTours, with getting my visa and making arrangements. That help continued while I was traveling in Iran, and included long conversations and a drive to look for saffron. Many other people in Iran offered assistance, some of them sharing frank views of politics and other issues in the country, others generous with food advice and instruction. They include Farahnoz and her sons; Fereshteh; the train compartment women whose names I never learned; Afsar and her husband, Abbas, and family on the farm northwest of Shiraz; Abbas's second wife, Leila; Leila's remarkable parents, Heshmat and Hajji Hos and the large nomad families in the mountains; and Vahid and his family in Shiraz, where we talked about food and I learned the Iranian way to grill eggplant.

Along the way I met other foreigners who were traveling or working in the place I was visiting and who shared not just meals but also transportation and information with me. I thank them all. They include Debby Corper, Nicholas Law, and his niece Kati Balázs; Brian John; Karen Stigant; French psychiatrists Marc

Vartabedian and Frédérique Netter, with whom I had memorable conversations in Tatev, Armenia; Todd Fabacher, CEO of Digital Pomegranate in Gyumri, Armenia; and Sepideh of the World Food Programme in Kurdistan.

Friends in Toronto and elsewhere have been of invaluable practical help: Karen (Kaz) Connelly, who went to Kurdistan a year before I did, introduced me to journalist Ayub Nuri in Toronto and to a number of her contacts in Sulaymaniyah. In turn, Ayub Nuri introduced me to his family in Kurdistan, who enfolded me with their hospitality, warmth, and protection, and taught me a great deal about Kurdish food and family. Haig Petrus, whose Armenian roots are deep and strong, found a contact in Yerevan who he thought might be of help, and indeed she was: the marvelous Sonia Tashjian (see above). Lily Tarba, a family friend who is Georgian-Abkhazian and lives in Toronto, passed along her grandmother's recipe for green *ajika*. Jennifer Klinec sent along cookie recipes from her mother-in-law in Yazd. I've had helpful advice and conversations with many others, including Georgian winemaker Irakli Nikolashvili, Fabi Jahanbin, Afi Mardukhi, Shayma Sadat (@SpiceSpoon), and professors Mohamad Tavakoli-Targhi and Jennifer Jenkins at the University of Toronto. Thank you, everyone.

I rely on food sellers in Toronto for advice as well as for meat, fruits and vegetables, cheese, and more. Thanks to Hiyam Samara and to all at Sanagan's Meat Locker, Hooked, Akram's Shoppe, and 4-Life, all in Kensington Market. Thanks too to farmers and vendors at Wychwood and Sick Kids markets.

Special thanks to Dawn Woodward of Evelyn's Cracker and Dina Fayerman, dear friends who are my go-to consultants for all food- and recipe-related puzzles and issues, and for book advice generally.

Thanks to the rest of my dear longtime friends in Toronto and environs for all your help, advice, and support, including occasional recipe tastings: Jennifer McLagan, Trisha Jackson, Carol Off, Xiaolan Zhao, Anne Collins, Sharon Klein, Ethan Poskanzer, Hilary Buttrich, Anne MacKenzie, Kathy Wazana, Lillian Burgess, and Ramsay Derry. And thanks to supportive friends in Chiang Mai and elsewhere, including Fern Somraks, Deb Olson, Trish and Gary Snell, Bob and Coleen Scott, and John Fu.

Freelance life has a great deal to recommend it, especially its diversity. I am grateful for various assignments that have challenged and enriched me. Huge thanks to Steve Jones, Wendy Hebb, Hannelore Suderman, and all who work at the Bread Lab in Mount Vernon, Washington, for creating a forum (the Grain Gathering) where grain, agriculture, and survival are discussed and explored each year, and for inviting me to contribute. Thanks to TIFF (the Toronto International Film Festival) for inviting me to host the Food on Film series, and to Ruba Kanaan for the invitation to speak about Persian art and food at the Aga Khan Museum in Toronto. I thank Rick Halpern and the Culinaria program at the University of Toronto for the invitation to be Culinaria's first Writer in Residence, and Peter Meehan, Rachel Khong, and others at *Lucky Peach* for inviting me to contribute pieces on Iran and other topics to their lively magazine.

Thanks to good friends in the food world Tina Ujlaki, Nathan Thornburgh, Martha Holmberg, Serge Madikians, Cameron Stauch, and Jeff Koehler, for your encouragement and for far-ranging conversations about food, culture, and politics. Thanks, too, to many at the Oxford Symposium on Food, including Elisabeth Luard and Ursula Heinzelmann.

Once I figure out the recipes and write them down, they are taken for a test-drive by others. I am so grateful to everyone who offered to retest recipes, for it takes work, not just the testing but also writing down comments. Big thanks to Deanna Welborn in Washington State, who did a lot of heavy lifting, and thanks also to Shalini Roy, Cassandra Kobayashi, Lisa Dahl, Cameron Stauch, Charles Hays, Linda Elvira Piedra, Anne MacKenzie, and Dina Fayerman.

Ann Bramson is a dream editor not only because of her wonderful aesthetic sense and good editorial judgment but also because she trusts me, and thus includes me in decisions about design, studio photography, and more. The rest of the team at Artisan is also a dream: Big thanks to publisher Lia Ronnen for her confidence in me; to book designer Jan Derevjanik, art director Michelle Ishay-Cohen, design manager Renata Di Biase, and artful mapmaker Rodica Prato for their lovely work; to production editor Sibylle Kazeroid, who kept me and everyone else on track; to Judith Sutton, who copyedited the rough manuscript with meticulous care, as she has done with all my books; to production director Nancy Murray for her meticulous attention to printing and photo quality; and to the wonderful Allison McGeehon, who takes on publicity early and with energy and imagination, and always follows through.

It was a real pleasure to work with Gentl & Hyers again (they created the photos for *Flatbreads & Flavors* in 1994), because they are still very collaborative and intuitive in the way they work. Big thanks to the food styling team, headed by Rebecca Jurkevich and assisted by Su Li and Linda Mancini, for all that wonderful prep and cooking. Everything turned out so beautifully.

Finally, on the home front, I've had the luxury of rich discussions and loving appreciation, always, from Dominic and Tashi; from my daughter-in-law, Fatema; and from dear Paul. Thank you.

INDEX

CONVERSION CHARTS

Here are rounded-off equivalents between the metric system and the traditional systems that are used in the United States to measure weight and volume.

WEIGHTS

US/UK	METRIC
1 oz	30 g
2 oz	55 g
3 oz	85 g
4 oz (¼ lb)	115 g
5 oz	140 g
6 oz	170 g
7 oz	200 g
8 oz (½ lb)	225 g
9 oz	255 g
10 oz	285 g
11 oz	310 g
12 oz	340 g
13 oz	370 g
14 oz	395 g
15 oz	425 g
16 oz (1 lb)	455 g

VOLUME

AMERICAN	IMPERIAL	METRIC
¼ tsp		1.25 ml
½ tsp		2.5 ml
1 tsp		5 ml
½ Tbsp (1½ tsp)		7.5 ml
1 Tbsp (3 tsp)		15 ml
¼ cup (4 Tbsp)	2 fl oz	60 ml
⅓ cup (5 Tbsp)	2½ fl oz	75 ml
½ cup (8 Tbsp)	4 fl oz	125 ml
⅔ cup (10 Tbsp)	5 fl oz	150 ml
¾ cup (12 Tbsp)	6 fl oz	175 ml
1 cup (16 Tbsp)	8 fl oz	250 ml
1¼ cups	10 fl oz	300 ml
1½ cups	12 fl oz	350 ml
2 cups (1 pint)	16 fl oz	500 ml
2½ cups	20 fl oz (1 pint)	625 ml
5 cups	40 fl oz (1 qt)	1.25 l

OVEN TEMPERATURES

	°F	°C	GAS MARK
very cool	250–275	130–140	½–1
cool	300	148	2
warm	325	163	3
moderate	350	177	4
moderately hot	375–400	190–204	5–6
hot	425	218	7
very hot	450–475	232–245	8–9